Reconstructing Professionalism in University Teaching

Teachers and Learners in Action

Edited by
Melanie Walker

The Society for Research into Higher Education
& Open University Press

To Ian

Published by SRHE and
Open University Press
Celtic Court
22 Ballmoor
Buckingham
MK18 1XW

email: enquiries@openup.co.uk
world wide web: www.openup.co.uk

and 325 Chestnut Street
Philadelphia, PA 19106, USA

First published 2001

A catalogue record of this book is available from the British Library

ISBN   0 335 20816 9 (pb)   0 335 20817 7 (hb)

Library of Congress Cataloging-in-Publication Data
Reconstructing professionalism in university teaching : teachers and learners in action / Melanie Walker (editor).
    p. cm.
  Includes bibliographical references and index.
  ISBN 0-335-20817-7 – ISBN 0-335-20816-9 (pbk.)
    1. College teachers–Professional relationships–Great Britain.   2. College teaching–Great Britain.   I. Walker, Melanie.

LB1775.4.G7 R43 2001
378.1′25′0941–dc21   00-050172

Typeset by Graphicraft Limited, Hong Kong
Printed in Great Britain by St Edmundsbury Press, Bury St Edmunds, Suffolk

Reconstructing Professionalism in University Teaching

Contents

Part 3: Endings and Beginnings   189

Notes on Contributors

Quintin Cutts has been a lecturer in the Department of Computer Science at the University of Glasgow since 1995. He gained his PhD from the University of St Andrews in 1992 in the area of programming languages and database systems.

Mike Gonzalez is a senior lecturer in the Department of Hispanic Studies at the University of Glasgow. He is joint editor of the *Encyclopaedia of Contemporary Latin American Culture* (2000) and a regular broadcaster for BBC Radios 3 and 4.

Alison Phipps is Senior Lecturer in the Department of German at the University of Glasgow. She studied for her PhD at the University of Sheffield in the Department of Germanic Studies and at the Universität Tübingen, Germany, in the Institute for Empirical Cultural Studies from 1991 to 1995. She is Chair of the International Association for Languages and Intercultural Communication, and author of *Acting Identities: An Investigation into South West German Naturtheater.*

Melanie Walker is Professor in the Faculty of Education at the University of the West of England, where she teaches graduate courses on social justice, qualitative research methodology and higher education studies, the last for new lecturers. Her research interests include social justice and higher education, the production of citizen identities in universities, and action research and narrative methodology. She is widely published in academic journals and has contributed to a number of books on education as editor and author.

Chris Warhurst is Senior Lecturer in the Department of Human Resource Management at the University of Strathclyde. Aside from the work published here, his main teaching, research and publication interests focus on labour, management and work organization issues. Current work focuses on economic policy development in Scotland, knowledge work and aesthetic labour in service sector industries. He has authored and edited a number of books, including *The New Scottish Politics* (2000), *Between Market, State and Kibbutz* (1999) and *Workplaces of the Future* (1998).

Judy Wilkinson has taught in the Department of Electronics and Electrical Engineering at the University of Glasgow for the past 30 years. She has been instrumental in the design and implementation of new courses, in particular the European MEng and the BTech Ed. She introduced and developed a mentoring scheme between postgraduate students and research assistants, and first year students in the department. For many years she has been concerned with the teaching of mathematics to engineers.

Preface

This book is the story of a higher education project, told from the points of view of the various academic participants. It is set within a changing context of higher education in which the question of what higher education is for is answered either increasingly mutedly or apologetically, or stridently in terms solely of its contribution to the national economy. It is primarily in the context of the 'bottom line', and its associated practices of 'standards', 'accountability' and 'quality control', that teaching in higher education has gained increasing prominence in public debate. Arguably it was always important, if not always as well done as it might be, to the vast majority of academics in British universities. It is the national pressure, taken up institutionally in different ways, which has opened up the possibility for this kind of project in the spaces between discourses of managerialism and older ideas of the 'liberal' civic university.

Ours is emphatically not a project which seeks simply to endorse a technicist understanding of teaching and learning in higher education, or to offer a text on 'innovative methods' for university teaching. Unlike many current 'staff development' approaches, this book seeks not to iron out complexity but to celebrate it. Nor does it offer a simplistic model of action research as a form of educational enquiry, but one that aspires to be evidence-informed and challenging. Unlike in the dominant literature on teaching and learning, the curriculum work explored in this book is overtly values-based and located in broader policy contexts and discourses, which it both challenges and seeks to shift and influence. It addresses Ron Barnett's work (notably *Higher Education: A Critical Business*) but tries to take his work further by relating it to the world of communities of pedagogic practice. Framed by the context of higher education, we thus explore a discourse of 'critical professionalism' and, in particular, an emergent 'new professionalism' in university teaching, through action in classrooms and a reflexive professional dialogue, within the space of an integrated education project.

Thus we have aspired to an 'alternative story' about teaching and pedagogy in higher education. While improving practice and enhancing student learning were vitally important to our project goals, equally so have been the questions of what kind of professionals in higher education we would want to be, and how we might realize the educational values which flow from this in our classroom teaching. We have tried to tell stories about teaching and learning in which we problematize what counts as 'good' teaching and learning, and how we might work for a fairer society through education. At issue are how we struggled over these issues in our daily educational lives and practices, and how successfully we generated micro-instances or moments of 'criticality', of 'equity' and of 'justice'.

We did not set out to explore what 'effective' teaching is and then pass on a checklist of findings to others. Instead we set out to establish a community (albeit a small one) of six academics concerned to work collaboratively in researching their own teaching, and in supporting and challenging each other through a shared critical dialogue about higher education. Central to this has been our 'live' engagement with our students and with each other, and the excitement that comes with forging what we regard as 'teaching' and 'learning' relationships in pursuit of subject knowledge and knowledge about education. Equally evident in our work are the contradictions and complexities of trying to do things differently under constrained circumstances. What then counts as critical thinking for transformation, and what as critical skills for normalization, can only be addressed through the particulars of each case, and even then not definitively. As Hannah Arendt (1959) reminds us, we cannot know with certainty what the outcomes of our actions will be.

We have used action research as our approach to educational enquiry and professional development. The book as a whole seeks to represent the multiple voices in this research process, both of all the academic participants and of students. Even where one person has taken responsibility for writing a particular chapter, in one way or another the voices of others will be threaded through or heard murmuring in the background.

Part 1 of the book presents the changing and changed context of higher education and debates on critical professionalism within which the project was initiated and unfolded. The second chapter sets out to explain why we chose action research as a methodology to explore teaching and learning in higher education, and how we find it to be consistent with our concerns around 'fairness'. The third chapter explores and theorizes the process and content of the collaboration which was central to our construction in practice of a new form of professional agreement-making.

Part 2 presents case studies written by each of the subject lecturers. Each lecturer identified his or her own issue of concern and chose the learning site where he or she wished to explore this. In my educational researcher role, I assisted with refining the questions, with the feasibility of each project, with data collection and with analysis in all the projects. We all read all the draft chapters and made comments on them at two group meetings. The chapters are not uniform in their style or their deployment of action research methods; each is influenced by the disciplinary location and language of the lecturer and the particular nature of the project. It is, however, interesting that the two scientists in the group were probably more influenced by the writing styles of the two arts and two social scientists writers in adapting their own approaches. Differences remain, however, and we hope readers of the whole text will find these productive and challenging.

Judy Wilkinson contributes two chapters (Chapters 4 and 8). The first deals with the establishment of a mentoring programme which set out to support first year students in adapting to university life in an engineering department. At the same time, she traces the significant development opportunities for the graduate students who acted as mentors. Her second contribution takes up her long-established concern with issues and practices around teaching first year mathematics to engineering students, where students complain about learning mathematics, lecturers worry about 'declining' standards in schools and differences occur about how mathematics is best taught to engineering students. Chris Warhurst (Chapter 5) was intrigued by the possibility of peer assessment and critical thinking in his honours course in international management. His case study is slightly different, in that we worked together on this question in the academic year before the group was formed; the data collection and much of the analysis took place before the group was established and we jointly published a version of his project in a higher education journal. Chris brought this experience to the group, which offered him a space to revisit and review what had happened in that particular course, this time focusing his account through the lens of critical thinking and the current context of higher education, society and economic development. Quintin Cutts (Chapter 6) chose to look at the teaching of computer programming to a large first year class, generated by his concern about a particular view which claims that programming ability is 'innate' and cannot be 'taught'. He set out to explain the 'autobiography' of his concern, the content constraints of programming and how he and students responded to a course which set out to teach programming skills. Alison Phipps's chapter (Chapter 7) reflects on the situatedness of the teacher and a value-based, reflexive practice which seeks to create certain conditions of learning through the relations between students, the teacher and a body of difficult knowledge. She employs the metaphor of 'dancing' to understand the difference between sets of performance indicators: between those that tend to produce students who are merely compliant, and those that encourage critical engagement with difficult subjects and consequently lead to a critical enjoyment of 'dancing'. She is strongly influenced by the language of her own subject, a cultural studies approach to the teaching of German studies, and the influence of this language is clear in the structure and style of her case study. Mike Gonzalez (Chapter 9) had long taught a self-directed study module on history which required the production of a group project. It appeared to work 'well', with students working hard to produce sensitive and insightful work each year. He therefore wanted to find out from the students themselves how they came to know what they did by the end of the course: what their understandings and expectations of history were and are, as well as their experiences of working collectively in this way. His own philosophy of history – that if history can be understood as the result of conflicting human agencies, then we can all participate as actors rather than passive observers – informs how he understands teaching and learning on this course and shapes the values he brings to his own evaluation of its successes.

Part 3 of the book does not attempt anything as definite or final as a 'conclusion'; nor does it offer 'findings'. Instead it prefers to leave some of this work to readers. The final chapter returns instead to the issues around critical professionalism, offers some reflections on what has been learnt and tries to orient both the project and readers to new beginnings and 'future' work which might prise open the often rather numbing contemporary discourses which dominate higher education.

Melanie Walker

Reference

Arendt, H. (1959) *The Human Condition*. Chicago: University of Chicago Press.

Acknowledgements

Above all, all the authors in this book wish to thank their students for participating in the various action research projects, and for their sensitive and insightful discussions on how they experience teaching and learning in higher education. If this were a single authored text by any one of us, there would be appreciation for the support and contributions by all members in the group. As it is, we cannot emphasize strongly enough that this text is much more than a collection of single authored chapters. We owe to each other both an intellectual debt and an experience of practising a different way of being in higher education. In different ways we are all contributors to each other's work for this book.

As editor, and director of the project, I particularly wish to thank a number of people at the University of Glasgow. The Principal, Professor Sir Graeme Davies, not only provided the funding which made the project possible, but also consistently encouraged and supported this work. His very 'light' touch regarding our attempts at innovation allowed us to take the project in whatever direction we saw fit. Dr Ron Emanuel, Vice-Principal Learning and Teaching, also provided exemplary institutional support and encouragement. Academic colleagues in the Teaching and Learning Service, especially Vicky Gunn, Sarah Mann and Bob Matthew, assisted project participants in various ways, as did Linda Mackay-Rolfe during her period as a part-time research assistant. Over three years, administrative staff at the Teaching and Learning Service, namely Tricia Cloherty, Lynn Costa and Pam Luthwood, were consistently helpful with various administrative arrangements.

On a personal note, my own work on this project has benefited greatly from conversations during its unfolding and afterwards with academic colleagues. In particular, Jon Nixon has consistently and generously both challenged and enriched my own thinking about higher education. I would also like to thank Ron Barnett, Jean Barr, Carolyn Brina, Stella Clark, Morwenna Griffiths, David James, Forbes Munro, Stephen Rowland, Judyth Sachs,

Richard Smith, Miriam Zukas and Rob Walker for stimulating exchanges of ideas.

Finally, I should like to express my appreciation to John Skelton at Open University Press for his encouragement and assistance, from my initial idea to this completed book.

Part 1

Towards a New Professionalism in University Teaching

1

Mapping Our Higher Education Project

Melanie Walker

We must speak for hope, as long as it doesn't mean suppressing the nature of danger.

(Raymond Williams, 1989)

How it all started

By way of a very brief overview, the University of Glasgow is a large, urban, 'ancient' Scottish University established by Papal Bull in 1451. The University is funded by the Scottish Higher Education Funding Council (SHEFC), and has the largest number of 'excellent' ratings from SHEFC for teaching of any Scottish university. It currently has around 17,000 students, 45 per cent of the undergraduates being recruited from homes within 30 miles of the city. As one of the 'Russell Group' of elite universities, it is also a strongly research-led institution, with significant research grants and contracts, and faces pressure, both financial and reputational, to perform well in the research assessment exercises. There are eight faculties, each led by a dean with devolved planning and budgetary powers, with departments having their own heads. Unlike in English universities, students are admitted after completing Scottish Highers (12 years of schooling) and, except in professional schools, most complete a four-year honours degree with a mix of general and specialist subjects. The University is led by the Principal and a team of appointed Vice-Principals, as well as by the Clerk of Senate, elected by Senate, to act as a check on executive power. In 1998 the first Vice-Principal for Learning and Teaching was appointed. In short, the University, despite some regional and local peculiarities, faces external funding and policy pressures and internal tensions not dissimilar from those of other 'old' universities in the UK.

At the end of 1996 I left South Africa to take up the post of Director of the University's Teaching and Learning Service (TLS) in the following January. TLS had been established in 1994 as a free-standing academic unit reporting to the Clerk of Senate, and later to the Vice-Principal, Learning and Teaching. It had responsibility for supporting 'innovation' in methods of teaching, learning and assessment, for working with new lecturers, and by invitation with academic departments. With my arrival, and after a certain amount of lobbying and struggle, the encouragement of higher education pedagogic research was added to this brief.

I was particularly keen to facilitate and support educational action research as a form of research-led professional development. Although it took time as I familiarized myself with the University and raised funding, as part of my academic staff development and educational research work I finally began working in September 1998 with a group of five academic staff at the University. They had been invited by myself to participate in a collaborative teaching and learning project, and comprised lecturers from Electrical Engineering (Judy Wilkinson), Computer Science (Quintin Cutts), Management Studies (Chris Warhurst), Hispanic Studies (Mike Gonzalez) and German (Alison Phipps). I had encountered all five lecturers over the previous 18 months of working at TLS at workshops and seminars, or by being invited to work with them. As a group we were not entirely alike. We included people from across very different academic disciplines; we were of different ages, ranging from early thirties to late fifties; and different status, with three lecturers and three senior lecturers in the group. Our length of service at the University ranged from 30 years to 18 months. We included men and women. We were similar in all being white and middle class (although one of us had a working-class background). Five of the six of us were English, and two were fully bilingual speakers.

All five members of staff, with the agreement of their heads of department, were offered a 10 per cent secondment with TLS to provide time and space to research an aspect of student learning that intrigued them in their own classrooms in 1998/9. They were also required to meet at least twice a term with others in the group. Funding came from my successful bid to the Principal's Strategic Development Fund and additionally included small sums to fund the research, with a further 10 per cent secondment envisaged in year two (1999/2000) to enable staff to write up their projects for publication. One of the group meetings each term was always held on campus in my office; the other happened socially over a meal in one of our homes. In May 1999 we also spent a day together at Ross Priory on the banks of Loch Lomond, and in between circulated emails, texts and thoughts, met individually, met others in the group and so on. In June 1999 I left TLS to take up a Chair in Education at the University of the West of England, but we maintained sporadic email contact. We were able to meet as a group again in Glasgow in January 2000 to discuss our draft chapters, and finally in June of the same year.

We playfully named ourselves the 'Barcelona Group' after reading a newspaper article on the city of Barcelona. We decided that 'Barcelona' could serve as a metaphor for the processes and practices of the group, which were mirrored in the architecture, aesthetics, and regeneration of Barcelona itself. We had fun with metaphors of dance, jokingly at one level, but also seriously, for dance seemed a good example of an exclusion engendered by what counts as 'proper' intellectual activity in the academy. A concern with the scholarship of teaching seemed equally to lie in this excluded zone. We were intrigued by the new imaginative possibilities that opened up if we thought of education and our collaboration as a dance and dancing. We generated a range of different types of evidence, shared and circulated in the group, including email conversations, poems, story fragments, reflective conversations, transcriptions of group meetings and academic texts, to construct a collage of the process of building ourselves as an educative community. We were deeply serious and we had great fun! The processes of our collaboration are explored in depth in Chapter 3; suffice to note Judy Wilkinson's words here when she wrote to us in November 1998 that all of us were 'learning, challenging and changing'.

Not only were the group members all active researchers in their disciplines (and myself in education), they also had in common their commitment to teaching and to their students, critical views about increasingly dominant managerial trends in higher education and concerns about broader political and social inequities. This last issue mattered to me. The dominant paradigm in academic staff development seemed to me, as a newcomer to the field in Britain after working in educational development in South Africa, too often to emphasize the practice and perfection only of methods and techniques. Academic staff development in the UK, as I came to understand, had its roots not in issues of access, critiques of academic discourse or the purposes of university education, as had been the case in South Africa, but in a 'training' tradition and a language of skills, objectives, outcomes, prediction and control of what is to be learnt and how (Malcolm and Zukas, 1999). As Malcolm and Zukas (1999) argue, teaching has become a focus of attention in higher education, but much of this attention has been marked by a technicist discourse and a 'surface learning' about teaching (Rowland, 1999). I wanted instead to engage with people who certainly wanted to improve their practice, but it also seemed important to acknowledge power and its educational effects. I guessed that it might be worthwhile to establish a group who were interested in constituting themselves as, on the one hand, a cross-disciplinary pedagogic community of practice (Lave and Wenger, 1999), while at the same time exploring student learning from their particular disciplinary sites. The idea was to explore generic questions about learning, but also questions about how these students learnt *this* subject knowledge under *these* institutional conditions, suffused with relations of power.

This in turn raised the issue of our professional identities: what kind of academics and teachers were we, or could we be? What were our educational purposes and values as teachers in higher education? How might we 'do' critical forms of professionalism and reconstruct professional identities under changing conditions of higher education (see Nixon, 1996)? Underpinning the project, at least in my view (and I assumed in that of this group from what I already knew of them), was a concern with how we might take a stand over 'social justice', 'fairness' and 'equity' when nothing seems certain, including academic knowledge or the sites of its production. Under such circumstances I personally worried over where the intellectually and politically defensible place to stand might be. How does each of us individually and collectively respond to a 'crisis of positionality' (Goodson, 1999)? Where is the activist academic identity now in a changing world shaped by the aridity of a marketized civil society (that is, a market society, not only a market economy)? What might educational possibilities and oppositional politics within and against postmodern markets in education actually look like in practice? Do new 'learner-centred pedagogies' and a teaching discourse of 'facilitation' necessarily have effects of equality? What new forms of professional association and agreement (Nixon and Ranson, 1997) might take us forward? What were the stories we told about our practices, and the professional identity work we did in telling one set of narratives, rather than another? Moreover, our professional identities were inescapably political identities: in education it matters, in my view, who and what we care about; these are always questions to be asking ourselves. While our focus on students' learning should not be lost in a definition of the 'political', which sees relevant action in terms of public, social movements, it must also not lose sight of them. The professional and political (writ large and small) articulate in complicated and ambiguous ways.

Added to this is a general shift in education away from nuanced and subtle languages of possibility. As Fielding (1999) passionately explains, languages of education are increasingly 'deeply disfiguring', 'metallic' and 'dull', the language of markets, quality assurance, effective performance management and so on. Why, asks Fielding (1999: 287), do we have so little confidence in 'the much more subtle, ethically nuanced language of education to express what is important to us as teachers and learners.' He argues for the need for different languages (more intellectual and emotional) which might enable us to think differently about our lives and our work. The dominant 'psychologized' discourse (see Malcolm and Zukas, 1999) used to discuss teaching and learning in higher education is dull and predictable; it simply fails to connect with notions of the public good, of worthwhileness and purposes. In this project we wanted to talk about teaching and learning differently.

Our 'critical professionalism' project

We wanted to occupy a space from which to 'talk back' to the marketization of higher education, to assert critical agency for ourselves and our students, and to reclaim the wisdom of our own professional judgements in the face of the 'moral ascendancy' of managerialism (Inglis, 1989). Thus we set out to do educational work individually and together, which, despite the uncertainties and rapidly changing globalizing world in which we live, took education still to be a worthwhile site of struggle over resources, meanings and identities, a struggle for better knowledge and a fairer society. In higher education this is a time of increasing emphasis on 'standards', benchmarks, measurable and comparable outcomes, a hard-edged accountability and the 'bottom' line'. Yet we believe the purposes of higher education go beyond increasingly narrow concerns with higher education's contribution to economic growth. Our concern is also with the kind of society we might build through building a higher education which educates for the democratic life. If we are to do this then we ought to be concerned about nurturing what A. N. Whitehead called 'knowledge and the zest of life' (quoted by Richard Smith, *Times Higher Educational Supplement*, 18 August 2000), enabling students to find and develop something of value on which to build a life, while learning to value what others offer as well.

Initiated, then, by myself, we set out to explore our professional activity in education framed by an overlapping, interwoven patchwork of layers of discourse and practices:

- a framing context of higher education policy and discourses;
- collaborative and reflective professional dialogue in an interdisciplinary group of lecturers;
- action in classrooms;
- action research processes which sought to understand and improve curriculum practice;
- the development of a reflexive 'model' of continuing professional development in higher education.

This project assumed the importance of our professional work to our identities and self-worth. As Ozga (1999: 69) remarks, '[our] freedom to exercise informed judgement in work is a vital part of being human.' While the meanings, interpretations and definitions of ourselves as agents creatively shaping our responses and processes is central, in the early stages of this project the notion of 'critical professionalism' was kept deliberately broad. Other than my circulating Ron Barnett's (1997) ideas about 'critical being' as involving engaging with action, with self and with knowledge, this was not an initial focus for discussion. Instead, the early and continuing emphasis was on practical action to improve life in classrooms and a reflective and collaborative exchange about such classroom action. The common purpose was about 'teaching and learning' and *doing* critical professionalism. As Mike Gonzalez said, 'This collaboration would be less valuable for me if it didn't lead to changed practice, to a different way of engaging with the world' (Group discussion, November 1998). And Quintin Cutts added, 'Yes, it's not just about sharing ideas, it's the fact that as you put yours out, somebody else takes it in and augments it and improves their practice, and vice versa' (Group discussion, November 1998).

Crucially, while we discussed practice, it was practice informed by particular values of what counted as 'worthwhile'. Taking action thoughtfully and reflectively in our teaching worlds was different but not apart from our wider equity concerns. Alison Phipps, in an email to me after our first meal together as a group, an occasion at which we had had often heated exchanges about life and the world, wrote, 'I loved last night because for the first time since working here I suddenly realised I was surrounded by people with ... mutual concerns and a complete commitment to engagement ... [who] are actively working to fulfil a vision they have of a just world' (email, September 1998). Judy Wilkinson commented, 'I haven't had such a good discussion for ages, great fun' (email, September 1998).

At this early stage, the dialogue was allowed to unfold around the learning issues and the politics embedded in such issues (notions of 'resistance', 'courage', 'struggle', 'daring', 'knowledge about knowledge' and so on), which were then excavated from time to time for overt debate. For example, this comment in March 1999 by Mike Gonzalez is a discussion on teacher authority and pedagogical practices which raised issues about teaching 'methods' but located them in a wider context of practice:

> Sometimes it is right to step back to let the students tell me what they want. But this is not a general truth. It's all right in a period when people are active, engaged, committed, struggling, then you assume that in such an active environment, the kinds of questions that ought to be asked will eventually be asked. But if we live in an environment where the opposite is true, where the common sense is passive, consumerist, individualizing, then actually you don't go with the flow ... and that might be the most ethical and democratic position you could adopt.
>
> (Group discussion, March 1999)

He then related this position to notions of professionalism: 'I mean to me that's quite important, in the professionalism thing, somebody refusing to go with the flow'. In response, Alison suggested:

> It seems to me that it's not about converting students or each other to our own points of view, however much we may wish to attempt to harness the power of language to that effect, but engaging with ideas and issues, about widening the definition of 'political' to life itself. Our professionality informs our lives outside the learning and teaching contexts, it disturbs our lifestyles (perhaps), our choices to engage (or not) in public social movements.
>
> (Group discussion, March 1999)

As I came to understand as a relative stranger in this new landscape, British higher education, no less than schooling, is located within current (postmodern) conditions of (im)possibility, looking increasingly corporate rather than collegial, as politically and socially regulated as other institutions. Academics in what has been described as the postmodern world face dilemmas of fragmentation, consumerism, individualism, efficiency, regulation, the erosion of community and collegiality in the face of the 'new managerialism' (see Smith and Sachs, 1995). As Morley (1997) points out, universities by the early 1980s in the UK were increasingly being perceived as being too remote from the world of industry and commerce, and too dependent on government largesse. The concept and practice of a technicist 'new managerialism' has penetrated the academy as a means to encourage efficiency, productivity, value for money and so on. Of less concern have been issues of equality, given that such values are seen as irrelevant to management based on marketization, so that we now have individualism rather than community, efficiency rather than justice, competition rather than cooperation.

Nixon (1996) has argued that under present conditions of higher education there has been a crisis of professional identity among academics because there is no serious public debate regarding the values and purposes of higher education – at least outside constant calls for higher education to prepare people for the workplace. In the context of marketization, quality assessment, research assessment and reduced public funding, the current dominant ethic of professionalism in teaching, and arguably higher education, is that of efficiency and effectiveness. In short, universities are to cost the public purse less, and deliver more in market terms, academic staff are to do more work as researchers, teachers and administrators, to be appraised, monitored, made accountable upwards to management and outwards to government (although not downwards to students). Rifts have appeared between 'management' and 'academics', between permanent staff and casual contract workers. Increasingly, business and industry are seen as a source of funding, income generation becomes a key activity in its own right and entrepreneurial skills are valued and rewarded. The difficulty was expressed by Mike Gonzalez in a short paper he circulated to the group in November 1998:

> In professional terms our role has shifted to become one of consistently and successfully fulfilling targets and objectives that arise not from an ethical set of imperatives but instrumental needs and ends. Insofar as we are organic to the institution we are obliged to fulfil institutional targets and objectives – and increasingly external tests and assessment designed to measure that. Insofar as we are educators, we have ethical obligations which generate different logics which are not measured or assessed, and indeed are probably impossible to quantify in that way. The big question is whether they can be reconciled.

Traditionally, as Nixon *et al.* (1997) suggest, claims to professional status have involved a strong service value orientation. They trace shifts in professional discourses from the post-war model oriented to public service, autonomy, self-regulation and expert knowledge. The ethic was that of public service, with professional legitimacy grounded in public acknowledgement of a disinterested exercise of specialist knowledge and expertise. The interests of the community were placed above those of narrow self-interest. They argue that this public service ethic 'remains a powerful residual element in the construction of professionalism, particularly within the public sphere' (Nixon *et al.*, 1997: 7). As an occupational group, professionals were then distinguished by their altruism. However, as Nixon and his colleagues note, more recent theorizing of professionalism turns on asking whose interests professionals control and who has power over their exercise of that control. Professionalism can no longer be unproblematically grounded in a service ethic with the rise of marketization and discourses of efficiency and markets. Nixon (1996) elsewhere points to shifts in the automatic assumption of autonomy and status for university academics and the accompanying crisis of professional identity that follows, while new conditions of managerialism are reworking the status advantage of academics. The views of academics have arguably been displaced (or are contested as being appropriately authoritative) and authority invested instead in consumers (students) and employers (institutions, government, business).

Barnett (1997: 132) further notes that professions are 'socially sanctioned sites of power' (and some professions are more powerful than others) based in their deployment of their expertise in society. Yet this, he suggests, requires them to speak out, to 'profess-in-action', intervening purposefully in society and working an expanded notion of professionalism which embraces not just professional work but professional life. Barnett (1997: 155) is blunt in his explication of the academic role: 'Endorsers is too polite a term for these modern academics . . . Academics now have their livings in the world and simply fall in with dominant frameworks . . . [offering] solutions to the problems as defined by the state and its dominant powers.' Alongside the cramped languages which seek to bound professional life, Barnett (1997) further argues that the professionalization of academic life through the capture of the production and dissemination of knowledge in the modern age has 'extinguished' the category of intellectual.

This separation of 'academic' and 'intellectual' generated heated discussion at one point, with Mike articulating a compelling argument at some length. He begins by saying, 'The word academic makes me nervous because it assumes this is kind of social action as opposed to function' (Ross Priory, May 1999). Later, he elaborates:

> The job that we do is both knowledge diffusion and knowledge generation. But you see that doesn't really tell me what I need to know because I want to know what the knowledge is for, what kind of knowledge I'm diffusing. The fact that I am generating knowledge doesn't actually tell me how I function in the world until I ask a further question which is to what end. Now the academic in the professional jargon in which we operate tells me I am professionally employed to diffuse and generate knowledge. But it doesn't actually tell me anything about my relationship with the knowledge. I don't think the word academic can be infused with ethical content and values. I think the word teacher is wholly different . . . It's also very easy to imagine the word intellectual being used in a whole range of quite different contexts with a similar power whereas it isn't possible to imagine the word academic being used outside higher education.

Nonetheless, Barnett (1997) suggests that academics might recast their role and reshape their identities against the grain by working with critical frames of reference. He distinguishes between the academic who looks inward, to the peer community and its internal norms and culture, and the intellectual whose gaze is outwards to wider society, although also conceding that there is nothing inherently radical in this outward gaze. Gramsci's (1971) conceptualization of traditional and organic intellectuals stands as a clear reminder of historic collusion between academics and state power. (My own home country of South Africa offers a compelling example of 'traditional' academic justifications bolstering grievous oppression, and, equally, of 'organic' intellectuals challenging and resisting such views.)

The broader, more 'public' notion of 'intellectual' work, as opposed to narrowly functioning as an 'academic', might conceivably be enabled in a third form of professionalism posited by Nixon and Ranson (1997), which they characterize as 'emergent professionalism'. They draw on Raymond William's conceptualization of 'dominant', 'residual' and 'emergent' cultural elements, where residual elements might be incorporated into the dominant culture and where the emergent is substantially oppositional in meaning and values, rather than merely novel or innovative. The dominant culture (or discourses) and emergent cultural formations are involved in a complex and ambiguous relationship which is never static but involves dialectical struggles over incorporation. This ambiguity and complexity then require precision in understanding which discourse is 'residual incorporated and residual not incorporated' and which 'emergent incorporated and emergent not incorporated' (quoted in Nixon and Ransom, 1997: 204–5). Williams's conceptualization then provides analytical tools to examine professional discourses, purposes and values. In what ways might our practices in higher education be characterized as having the potential to challenge and oppose dominant discourses (an emergent professionalism)? In what ways are our practices amenable to incorporation into dominant discourses and practices? In other words, while we might lay claim to an 'emergent professionalism' in our work in higher education, how and when is our practice 'emergent incorporated' and 'emergent not incorporated'?

Such a view of professionalism as oppositional maps on to Yeatman's (1994) notion of 'subaltern' intellectuals, whom she describes as 'hybrid' professionals positioned between professionals as experts and non-professionals as passive consumers of that expertise (in our case students as non-professional consumers of academic knowledge). The point is not to flatten or spuriously to equalize differences between lecturer and student, or to obscure the power relations inherent in relations of expertise. Instead, while acknowledging this differentiation, we ought to require both dialogue and accountability across it. Subaltern professionals would have or would develop the capacity to migrate trangressively across boundaries, audiences and hierarchies, from below as well as above (Yeatman, 1994).

In setting up and developing the project, I had also been particularly attracted to the idea of 'professionality', with its robust action implications. Nixon *et al.* (1997: 12) explicate professionality as focusing on 'the quality of practice in contexts that require radically altered relations of power and control'; 'professionality' further includes 'a renewed commitment to building a learning profession'. Such a learning profession for Nixon and his colleagues is defined in terms of its 'commitment to the internal goods of learning, and the maintenance of a critical distance between the practice and the external goods of schooling' (Nixon *et al.*, 1997: 13). Indeed, they argue that teachers (and, we would argue, also lecturers in universities) 'might be seen as having a *professional* duty to adopt an explicitly oppositional stance to policies that prioritise the external goods of the institution or militate against the internal goods of learning' (*ibid.*, authors' emphasis). Commitments to equal opportunities or fairness and social justice, must, in this view be intrinsic to professional practice, not stand outside of it. This stands counter to the current emphasis on performativity, diminished professional autonomy, increased paperwork and more stress (see Smyth, 1995).

At issue in all this is that discourses are never closed fields; there are always many ways of seeing and understanding, some of which accord with dominant, hegemonic discourses which then appear 'natural' and appeal to 'common sense'. Other discourses challenge the common-sense view in attempts to construct 'good sense' (Gramsci, 1971), to understand differently and oppositionally. Crucially, hegemonic and subordinate discourses are relational, so that the construction of professional identities will be both with and against the grain of dominant and subordinate possibilities in the struggle over which discourses retain or surrender their hegemonic truth effects. As Kenway (1995) points out, social institutions are made up of many different, often competing, discourses and discursive fields. Universities are then 'fragile settlements' between and within competing discourses, 'subordinate, dominant, co-existing and competing but always open to challenge and change to re-work meaning and "truth"' (Kenway, 1995: 141). We sought, optimistically, to work the spaces in between and the contradictions, as Mike explained:

> There isn't a way, there is just a commitment to doing it where the opportunity presents itself, there's no guaranteed method which will enable us to shine blinding light in the midnight of the century and suddenly people will wake up ... [but] it is not possible for a system to impose uniformity ... there will always be spaces ... one of the extraordinary things is the way in which ideas which in one moment seem incredibly isolated can also for unexpected reasons, kind of, break through.
>
> (Group discussion, March 1999)

We were further influenced by Barnett's (1997: 1) notion of 'criticality', which is more than critical thinking and requires critical persons able 'to engage with the world, with themselves as well as with knowledge'. Thus criticality 'requires that one be moved to do something' (Burbules and Berk, 1999: 51). The practice of criticality leads one to interrogate practice and its contexts, to ask what are the conditions that give rise to critical thinking, to rethinking and to thinking in new ways (Burbules and Berk, 1999). What daily everyday work might build community and criticality, for ourselves and our students, along the intersecting axes of the self, of knowledge and of action in the world? What we were concerned to do was to build on the work of Barnett and others to demonstrate what such professional practices and 'criticality' might look like in practice at local sites of higher education classrooms. By 'doing criticality' we hoped to open up the fragile settlements that obtain between different discourses, subordinate and dominant, coexisting and competing.

Central, then, to our collaborative process were our educational action research projects and the reflective cycles of improvement which constituted the 'content' of our collaboration, and realized practically our commitments to being learners ourselves. The case studies show us coming to terms with a radically altered higher education landscape, yet also redrawing our own maps of commitment and practice within changed conditions. This in turn articulated with a view of professionalism that acknowledges and celebrates the complexity of professional judgements in which outcomes may, but cannot always, be determined in advance, and where reflection and improvement are integral to professional work. Uncertainty is part of the job, not a troublesome process to be expunged: 'Teacherly judgements, in so far as they may be said to be professional judgements, acknowledge the intrinsic complexity of the teaching and learning processes. Emergent professionalism involves a commitment to living with that uncertainty and to learning to live with it' (Nixon *et al.*, 1997: 15).

Finally, through processes of collaboration and action research we thrashed out our understandings of teaching and learning consistent with our values and a view of critical professionalism to which we could subscribe both theoretically and practically. This fragment of dialogue at Ross Priory in May 1999 suggests some of this, while also suggesting some of the flavour of our exchanges:

Chris: So critical professionalism would be about not accepting the mainstream in terms of higher education, both in terms of content and process. It's not simply about teaching students theories, didactically, but about getting them to engage and engage other ideas?

Mike: But our challenge isn't to that [the mainstream] necessarily, it isn't necessarily contesting one prevailing set of ideas with another set, except insofar as what we contest with is an idea of the multiplicity of knowledge. What we set against the mainstream is not an opposing dominant set, but the idea that knowledge is diverse, conflictual, contradictory.

[...]

Judy: But Barnett says that the university has a responsibility to develop the capacity of its students to take up critical stances *in* the world and not just *towards* the world.

Mike: Good. That's brilliant! Did he say that?
Judy: Page 112.
Mike: Bloody good that is!

Alison chimes in to add the importance of reworking notions of profession-alism through conversations across fragmented disciplinary communities and symbolic boundaries:

It's not about being territorial, you know, totally allowing yourself to be enclosed within the disciplines that have produced some of the passions about what it is that we do. Barnett talks about interdisciplinarity and says that's an appropriate way of working in today's society . . . But the ways the University is organised do not allow me that freedom and this [group] has been one of the spaces for that and I think that's absolutely key to being critically professional.

Somewhat later we roll these comments together:

Chris: We're critical of subject content which is what our students want but we're also critical of subject delivery.
Mike: OK.
Chris: Would that be fair?
Mike: And indeed of the world more widely.
Alison: And of the way knowledge is divided.
Mike: And of the education system itself.
Alison: Yes and it's about a stance.
Quintin: It's about going back and saying 'Well what do I want to be doing here?' and actually standing up and being counted and saying, 'I believe in this and I want you to listen.'

We had a clear practical agenda, then, as a group of lecturers, engaged together in educational research and professional dialogue. The action took place in our own classrooms, and also in the constitution of a collaborative and dialogic group, reconstructing professional identities and professional-ism under particular relations of power and control in one institutional setting. We sought to be co-authors of higher education's cultural narratives, and this, together with our focus on change and improvement, made for a 'patchily' optimistic project, despite our recognition of the problems and constraints. One position was articulated by Chris Warhurst:

The problem with [micro level change] is it's about being critical within the world rather than of the world; you would have to make a huge leap of faith to suggest that people can tinker with the system through education. It's like critical thinking in management studies where it's not about changing the nature of business from capitalism to socialism, it's about making the system work better or at least more fairly.

This was modified in turn by Alison: 'But it's also about having the courage to put forward alternatives.' Chris then responded with greater optimism:

'Having the courage to offer alternatives I think is right, but to do that you have to have alternatives, and that's the research we've been doing here.'

Thus, while not ignoring problems, or saying that we were able to construct victory narratives and act out heroic interventions, our concern was to act practically in reworking our professional identities, collaboratively, recognizing that discourses of professionalism are historically located in local, material settings of time and space. These 'regimes of truth' govern what can be said and who may speak, so that truth is discursively constructed and always imbricated in relations of power. Dominant discourses determine what counts as true, important or relevant:

> [Truth] induces regular effects of power. Each society has its regime of truth, its 'general politics' of truth: that is, the types of discourse which it accepts and makes function as true; the mechanisms and instances which enable one to distinguish true and false statements, the means by which each is sanctioned; the techniques and procedures accorded value in the acquisition of truth; the status of those who are charged with saying what counts as true.
>
> (Foucault, 1980: 131)

Yet there was/is room for optimism insofar as a number of discourses, muted and strident, hegemonic and subordinate, circulate in and around higher education, and in and around concepts of professionalism. The sphere of higher education is still an important public space for contestation and struggle. It produces and reproduces particular storylines of how to live ethically and politically, it constructs and reconstructs what it means to be a 'teacher' and a 'student', and through its teaching practices and institutional relations of power it confirms what knowledge is of most worth and what counts as knowing. What we aspired to was a practice of professionalism exemplified in Edward Said's (1993) notion of 'amateurism', which he offers as an alternative to a dominant professionalism which seeks 'not to rock the boat'. While we did not want to replace professionalism by amateurism – we preferred to contest and rework what it means to be a professional in higher education – Said usefully describes what kind of professional we were trying to be. Such a person would be motivated by 'care' and 'affection', someone 'who considers that to be a thinking and concerned member of a society one is entitled to raise moral issues at the heart of even the most technical and professionalized activity as it involves one's country, its power, its mode of interacting with its citizens, as well as with other societies' (Said, 1993: 61).

Marginality or 'mind the gap'

While there is room for optimism, we believe, regarding the possibilities of improvement in universities, there is equally a need for a kind of 'reflexive vigilance' (Bourdieu and Wacquant, 1992) in analysing the power relations in which we work, including our own self-interests. In particular we often returned to discussing our own marginality, recognizing that we contested the dominant discourse but were also complicit in the system we were struggling against. In the end we are within education, even if we stand on the margins. Thus, responding both to Alison's and Mike's descriptions of the group as an 'alternative space', Chris said: 'Can I say that what worries me is marginalisation, because we're also saying that this place [group] is a refuge from the mainstream and really what we're doing should *be* the mainstream' (Ross Priory, May 1999). The conversation continues:

Alison: Yeah.

Mike: Quite right!

Quintin: Maybe it should be but that's not the reality at the moment.

Judy: It's a reflection space where you can get space and share.

Mike: . . . this collaboration . . . its purpose is not to, and you're quite right, the purpose is not to create a space where we can talk about things we couldn't elsewhere, it is a place if you like in which to address issues but the purpose is outside the group, not inside . . .

[. . .]

Alison: The positive side of being able to say this is a refuge is the spin-off of bringing us together, rather than it being the purpose, and what it actually leads me to do is actually create spaces in other places for people to work more like this because I've seen the value of it.

[. . .]

Mike: I see it as a kind of armoury where I come back and get weapons!

Chris: So, this is the sort of place where you pick something up and carry it out.

A few cautionary words seem in order, nonetheless. We agreed that marginality is not easy and not always of our own choosing (although sometimes it may well be) in that, as one of us said, 'it's safer for the institution not to have these dissenting people going "Wait a minute this isn't very human, is it? What you're doing is reducing people to products."' Group members said things like: 'I just feel like it's ripping me apart and I'm going to end up in lots of little fragmented bits'; and, 'Sometimes marginality is incredibly painful and at times like that if I don't have the support of something else then there's nowhere I can fit'; or 'I need to have the resources to cope with being marginalised and the kind of attack on, you know, "But you're a teacher and that's pathetic" kind of thing.' Thus, while the margin might at times offer a safe place to be different, it operates its own exclusions, which run the risk of sedimenting over time into impermeable borders that might leave us stranded without the papers to cross backwards and forwards. Then too, Nixon and Ranson (1997) alert us to the power that institutional arrangements have over what cannot be said or done in order to protect institutional agendas and boundaries. In this context, reworking institutional discourses can be 'severe'. At the very least the rewards of promotion might not be forthcoming. Barnett (1997: 155–6) reminds us of the need to work strategically by finding a voice that 'both resonates to some degree with those occupying the sites of power and yet does justice to the new insights being offered'. *Strategic* critique must be the art of the possible! Unless we attempt this, he argues, we risk marginalization at best, and self-indulgent dilettantism at worst.

Strategically, we sought to disseminate the work of the group through a one-day University Learning and Teaching conference in May 1999, to which we invited the Vice-Principal, Learning and Teaching, and at which we sought to speak in ways which would resonate with our colleagues. That the day was 'successful' and that the work of the project has been favourably received by university management is both an indicator of a certain kind of institutional success which 'buys' space for continuing the work, and indicative of a kind of radical failure. Yet on the other hand we cannot know the effects of what we do with any certainty. It may yet be that, as Judy says, a few of us 'flapping our wings in Glasgow' might yet have an unexpected influence, insofar as we can never predict with certainty what the outcomes will be of our actions.

Landscapes of possibility

With all its limitations, the classroom remains for us a location of possibility for education as 'the practice of freedom' (hooks, 1994). The language that emerged in our practice and dialogue was one of risk, adventure, openness, community, collaboration, dialogue, carnival, sensory enhancement, embodied learning, struggle and confusion, trust and respect, participation in learning communities, running against the grain, civic awareness, teacher presence and absence, enjoyment and fun, gifts and exchanges, responsibility and ownership, personal identity and reflective learning. All these languages are taken up and threaded through the action research case studies.

Briefly, an example of what Alison and I would describe as 'communitas' illustrates what we are trying to grasp. We do not mean 'group work' as a 'technique' or some kind of legitimating ritual of 'participation' (Anderson, 1999), although these third and fourth year honours students do indeed work in groups and participate. More than this, they also over time construct learning communities which are hard work, collaborative, critical and participatory, and which enable their access to esoteric knowledge and to academic success. They learn together:

> *Jen*: I think we didn't realise, we hadn't a clue until, even though it
>   [the theories] kind of clicked we still didn't realise that until much
>   later on by which stage it had clicked with everyone.
> *Jane*: I think sometimes somebody would understand something then if
>   you didn't understand it they can explain it to you. If different people
>   are learning different things at different times you can kind of explain,
>   share what you've learned with other people and they tell you what

they think and you can kind of build up something from that. We had so many different books that we could read as well. Everyone was reading different books and different theories and because you'd found out different things in your own interviews you would use different theories. So each person would be using a different theory maybe something you didn't know much about because it wasn't applicable to your data, they could explain it to you and so you could share.

Helen: But do you not think as well it was the fact that we were in the same groups all the way through and we started off just discussing things that nobody knew anything about so we were all in the same boat? And as we got more information and knowledgeable about different things, we kind of worked through a lot of things and helped each other, and you never once think 'Well I know it and I'm not going to tell anyone.'

(Student interview, November 1998)

In the next extract, one of Mike's level two students, who work with a small group of their peers on an independent history project in which the product is a group video and group text on their chosen topic, speaks. He trangressively inverts taken-for-granted language about learning by saying:

One thing I'd like to say to other teachers that are thinking about this type of approach is that we are all cheats you know. We cheated because we saw each other's work. We cheated because we set our own questions and we cheated because we actually really enjoyed ourselves when we were meant to be doing some serious work. I think cheating is very educational, you know. I would say to them, you should give it try.

(Student interview, April 1999)

As Nixon *et al.* (1996: 49) explain, in a way more adequate for our moves to understand student learning than only using a limited and limiting language of aims and objectives and deep and surface learning, 'the deeper significance of learning lies through its forming of our powers and capacities, in our unfolding agency.' They acknowledge the role of skills and the development of particular 'competences', but add that 'the central purpose of learning is to enable such skills to develop our distinctive agency as a human being.' Thus, Alison talks about 'enhancement', explaining: 'There's a sense that these students are more fully aware of their potential than maybe they were when they first went into the classroom and more fully aware of what being alive means, more alive to themselves' (Group discussion, May 1999).

At the same time, we struggled to articulate what Smith (1998: 8) reminds us are 'feelings which seem to call out for expression. We sense that there are things to be said in languages which we cannot find.' He cites Lyotard's notion of the 'differand', which is 'the unstable state and instant of language in which something which ought to be able to be phrased cannot yet be phrased' (quoted in Smith, 1998: 7). As Smith argues, the dominant cognitive, performative and economic genres currently work very effectively to drive out or silence other ways of understanding and acting and speaking in society. But, suggests Smith, Lyotard's idea of 'little stories' (*petits recits*) and dissensus rather than consensus might take us forward. Such little stories would both offer new forms and different statements about learning and education. The issue then would be to explore, writes Smith, how such *petits recits*, say of critical communities in universities and the university as a critical community, might establish their own claims to be heard, to be listened to and to be taken seriously against dominant and grander narratives of universities as 'corporations'.

At our Ross Priory meeting in May 1999, Mike rehearsed our past, present and future hopes:

> I think part of what brings us here in the first place is to ask a question which could be framed in exactly the same way in two different contexts. One is what is 'effective' teaching, which might be answered by saying it more efficiently produces the functional ends to which the institution is dedicated and therefore renders it more efficient, more effective, more cost beneficial. The other might be an altogether less tangible purpose which is to more effectively encourage a critical response to the world by individuals and groups of people, whose outcome is not easily quantifiable or measurable or functional, except in a broader sense of making people richer, fuller in their engagement with the world . . . The real benefit, the most profound benefit, for the students is discovering how to discover the world, how to ask and answer questions about the world and how to do it with other people in a context which they define. They create their own educational milieu. I think that's in a sense what we're doing.

How we set about enabling students to question and construct meaning and knowledge, to persist, to engage with excitement and interest in encountering new ideas and to work for participation and sustained involvement in academic learning in different disciplinary contexts is explored in and through the case studies which follow. Through our action research projects (our version, if you like, of *petits recits*), we trace student learning and our own reflexive and collaborative development as teachers and critical professionals in higher education.

References

Anderson, G. L. (1998) Towards authentic participation: deconstructing the discourses of participatory reforms in education, *American Educational Research*, 35 (4), 571–603.

Barnett, R. (1997) *Higher Education: A Critical Business*. Buckingham: SRHE/Open University Press.

Bourdieu, P. and Wacquant, L. (1992) *An Invitation to Reflexive Sociology*. Oxford: Polity Press.

Burbules, N. C. and Berk, R. (1999) Critical thinking and critical pedagogy: relations, differences and limits, in T. S. Popkewitz and L. Fendler (eds) *Critical Theories in Education: Changing Terrains of Knowledge and Politics*. New York: Routledge.

Fielding, M. (1999) Target setting, policy pathology and student perspectives: learning to labour in new times, *Cambridge Journal of Education*, 29(2), 277–89.

Foucault, M. (1980) *Power/Knowledge: Selected Interviews and Other Writings by Michel Foucault, 1972–1977*. New York: Pantheon.

Goodson, I. (1999) The educational researcher as a public intellectual, *British Educational Research Journal*, 25 (3), 277–98.

Gramsci, A. (1971) *Selections from the Prison Notebooks*. London: Lawrence and Wishart.

hooks, b. (1994) *Education as the Practice of Freedom*. New York: Routledge.

Inglis, F. (1989) Managerialism and morality, in W. Carr (ed.) *Quality in Teaching: Arguments for a Reflective Profession*. Lewes: Falmer Press.

Kenway, J. (1995) Having a postmodernist turn or postmodernist angst: a disorder experienced by an author who is not yet dead or even close to it, in R. Smith and P. Wexler (eds) *After Postmodernism: Education, Politics and Identity*. London: Falmer Press.

Lave, J. and Wenger, E. (1999) Learning and pedagogy in communities of practice, in J. Leach and B. Moon (eds) *Learners and Pedagogy*. London: Paul Chapman/The Open University.

Malcolm, J. and Zukas, M. (1999) Models of the educator in higher education: perspectives and problems. Paper presented at the Annual Conference of the Society for Teaching and Learning in Higher Education, University of Calgary, 16–19 June.

Morley, L. (1997) Change and equity in higher education, *British Journal of Sociology of Education*, 18 (2), 231–42.

Nixon, J. (1996) Professional identity and the restructuring of higher education, *Studies in Higher Education*, 21 (1), 5–16.

Nixon, J., Martin, J., McKeown, P. and Ranson, S. (1996) *Encouraging Learning: towards a Theory of the Learning School*. Buckingham: Open University Press.

Nixon, J., Martin, J., McKeown, P. and Ranson, S. (1997) Towards a learning profession: changing codes of occupational practice within the new management of education, *British Journal of Sociology of Education*, 18 (1), 5–28.

Nixon, J. and Ranson, S. (1997) Theorising 'agreement': the moral bases of the emergent professionalism within the 'new' management of education. *Discourse*, 18 (2), 197–214.

Ozga, J. (1999) *Policy Research in Educational Settings*. Buckingham: Open University Press.

Rowland, S. (1999) The role of theory in a pedagogical model for lecturers in higher education, *Studies in Higher Education*, 24 (3), 303–14.

Said, E. (1993) *Representations of the Intellectual: The 1993 Reith Lectures*. London: Vintage.

Smith, R. (1998) The justice of the differend. Paper presented at World Conference on Philosophy of Education, Boston, April.

Smith, R. and Sachs, J. (1995) Academic work intensification: beyond postmodernism, in R. Smith and P. Wexler (eds) *After Post-modernism: Education, Politics and Identity*. London: Falmer.

Smyth, J. (ed.) (1995) *Academic Work: The Changing Labour Process in Higher Education*. Buckingham: SRHE/Open University Press.

Williams, R. (1989) *Resources of Hope*. London: Verso.

Yeatman, A. (1994) *Postmodern Revisionings of the Political*. New York: Routledge.

2

Action Research for Equity in Teaching and Learning

Melanie Walker

We ask you to make society's problems your laboratory. We ask you to translate data into direction – direction for action.

(Martin Luther King, 1966)

Introducing (educational) action research

As Chapter 1 explains, a concern with a form of critical professionalism, enacted in our own teaching practices, underpinned our higher education teaching and learning project and the educational action research projects which constituted the core of this work. This chapter focuses on action research as our method for change and a means for taking up our own particular concerns with doing critical professionalism in order to improve the educational experiences of our students and ourselves. Each member of the group undertook a study of student learning in his or her own classroom. My own role was slightly different. I wanted to collect data and reflect critically on our collaboration and the higher education context. But in addition I formed a 'partnership' with each lecturer to talk through his or her research questions, helped in all cases with collecting data, with analysing and interpreting these data and with editing the draft case studies. I made available texts on learning, some to all group members, others in response to a particular concern of a group member. What, then, does educational action research have to do with democratic practices of education, or with making the lives of students and the people (ourselves in this case) who teach them any better?

The history of action research is now well documented (see, for example, Kemmis and McTaggart, 1988; Elliott, 1991; Noffke, 1997). Only a brief review is offered here. The term 'action research' is credited to the work of John Collier, a United States Commissioner of Indian Affairs, and/or Kurt Lewin (see Noffke, 1997), a North American social psychologist. Collier had concerns with education and community, and his work focused on collaboration, grassroots interests and direct links to social action. For his part, Lewin wanted to develop a form of research which not only investigated social problems but also influenced social action. Action research turns on the method proposed by Lewin of a cycle spiralling into further cycles of action and involving planning, action, reflection and further (new) action. This spiral of activities is a method to create change and then study that change and its effects. In practice, the cyclical process is less neat and more ragged and fluid, and might involve a number of smaller cycles rolling along inside a bigger cycle, as well as problems spinning off into new cycles. More important is that these are stages in the research process, with recurring reflection leading one to modify the action throughout the study in an iterative rather than a linear research process. The influence of this work is to be seen in the educational theories of Kolb (1984) and his model of experiential learning as turning on concrete experience, reflective observation, abstract conceptualization and active experimentation.

Lewin's ideas were taken up in education by Stephen Corey at Teachers College Columbia (see Corey, 1949); he saw action research by teachers as a means to better action and better decisions. He had a view of teachers' work as in need of constant renewal and rethinking. Action research fell out of favour in the late 1950s, however, not helped by critiques of its 'rigour', exemplified in a particularly ascerbic article by Hodgkinson (1957), who mocked action research as 'easy hobby games for little engineers'. For reasons which are not entirely clear (see Noffke, 1997), it came to be seen as a process limited to individual development. However, in the late 1960s and 1970s, Lawrence Stenhouse (1975) in the UK began to highlight the role of teachers in curriculum development and the production of knowledge about education. His work, and that of key associates like John Elliott (1991), developed a concept of curriculum grounded in teachers' own theorizing, fuelled by their changing practice at a time of the comprehensive reorganization of schooling. In this way action research was reconnected to larger questions about knowledge claims, and the individual and situational aspects of educational practice restored. This seems especially relevant today in the face of moves which seek to entrench a view of teaching as the imparting of neatly packaged answers to limited questions, a sort of back to common sense movement. This shift celebrates the notion that we can have fairly direct access to knowledge ('you can see what is there'), and that knowledge is produced elsewhere and then distilled by staff developers into generic 'teaching tips' for lecturers. This is best exemplified in teacher training in England and Wales, which requires lengthy lists of competences to be met, and in some of the worryingly technicist features of recent moves in the professional accreditation of university lecturers.

Thus, as a methodology, action research in higher education raises questions about knowledge production, for whom and by whom, and potentially reconnects questions of professional development and pedagogy to academic disciplines and research. It potentially embraces personal development, professional development and the assumption that 'all educational works are political works' (Noffke, 1997: 308). Action research offers teachers working in higher education the possibility of developing an evidence-informed, critical view on their own educational action. It involves researching practice in order to change or improve practice, and at the same time critically reviewing practice. Teachers in higher education might on the one hand create and advance knowledge through situated case studies, and at the same time improve practice and their understanding of practice in a creative process of professional learning. As Somekh (1995) explains, the findings of action research are fed back directly into practice in an iterative process to bring about change. Thus action research is not research *for* social change, or research *on* social change, but research *as* social change (Schratz and Walker, 1995). We investigate reality in order to change it; we change reality in order to investigate it (Kemmis and Wilkinson, 1998).

Why did we undertake action research?

While action research was new to others in the group, it had been the basis of my funding bid (which had preceded the group's formation) to the Principal's Strategic Development Fund in 1997. My own earlier involvement in action research in teacher education and higher education in South Africa, and my commitments to research-based academic staff development, led me to think that there ought to be exciting possibilities in encouraging interested lecturers in researching learning and teaching. My idea was to start with a small pilot group and then see what developed.

My own action research (see, for example, Walker, 1996), conducted under volatile and contested conditions in South Africa, had led me to understand that, in exploring my practice through action research, I might as an educator make more explicit the lines of power, develop improved understanding of my own working life and so become more critical of the power relations in which I and others are embedded. Thus might I act as wisely as possible, with others, in my own particular social circumstances, to construct 'really useful knowledge', and build democratic education, persistently, step by step. The attraction of action research for me was then, and still is, in the never ending spiral of action, reflection, inquiry, theorizing and scrutiny into what one is doing, and who one can become. Through systematic action research I came to know that my responsibility was to change myself, to search and struggle for collective social spaces in which I might develop greater self-knowledge, publicly shared. Through a disciplined research process, the quality of reflection on my practice was deepened, enriched, made more subtle, establishing patterns of thoughtful interpretation which continued long after my action research had been concluded, thereby enabling a continuous revisiting and reworking of my professional experiences and ideas.

While my own action research in South Africa had recognized the limits of a research process or product to effect structural changes in people's lives, I began work with the Barcelona Group, aspiring still to action research as critical, committed and collective work in the interests of fairer education for a fairer society. It involves reflective practice, but should not be reduced to this. Nor do I take it for granted that reflective practice is necessarily 'good practice', outside of the values and moral purposes which inform it, and the institutional and disciplinary contexts within which it takes place, with effects for both the practitioner and the learners. In short, action research for me was exemplified in the notion of 'praxis' as a dialectical and interactive shaping of theory and practice, research and action, underpinned by an explicit commitment to social justice (Lather, 1986). It seemed a good way to research our *doing* of critical professionalism. Put simply, action research was a research vehicle for me to address and take up the 'so what do we do (about injustice)?' question in educational practice and research.

Action research and social justice

My work with the Barcelona Group, and their work in turn in their own classrooms, sought to locate itself within a tradition of educational research for social justice (see Griffiths, 1998). 'Social justice' is understood here as not only a distributive issue, but one that is also relational, encompassing attempts to address how the structures of inequality manifest in educational lives as processes of domination, oppression and marginalization (Young, 1990). At issue is to understand social justice (and critical professionalism) less as an abstract definition and instead to focus on actual instances of injustice and how we might oppose their reproduction through education; for example, teaching processes in which students are not constructed as active meaning-makers. Not surprisingly, the process can be fraught with contradiction, surprise, institutional and departmental politics, challenge and frustration. As Marion Dadds (1995: 8) comments, 'courage, tenacity, collaborative prowess, and interpersonal saintliness are but a few of the qualities which usually help.' Social justice as a principle is to be explored, negotiated and tested for meaning in concrete circumstances and educational practices. Our research seeks to find those moments when progress towards more equitable relations are present in higher education classrooms, but also to explore the ambiguities that occur when people try to change power relations and question forms of privilege and domination.

There are many ways to do action research, not all of which seek to challenge dominant practices in education and society in this way. The tension is mainly between those who argue for a social justice perspective, and those more concerned with professional development (see Weiner, 1989). But the action research case studies presented in this book are stories about both of these aspects: stories about professional learning, and stories about the ability of action research to pose questions and struggle over equity in our daily lives in higher education. Action research for us has been a powerful way for us to understand how we and our students make and re-make the curriculum, raising questions about what counts as knowledge and ways of knowing, and how these work to construct symbolic boundaries which include some learners (and teachers) and exclude others, and make our identities as teachers. In this the personal and professional selves are also political selves (Noffke and Brennan, 1997). Thus our action research explicitly locates itself within a tradition of critical social research:

> [which] does not take the apparent social structure, social processes, or accepted history for granted. It tries to dig beneath the surface of appearances. It asks how social systems really work, how ideology or history conceals the processes which oppress and control people. Critical social research is *intrinsically* critical. It assumes that a critical process informs knowledge.
>
> (Harvey, 1990: 6; author's emphasis)

We assume that our experiences in education are open to reflection, re-working and critique within a 'democratic knowledge-making project' (Barr, 1999). Knowledge about practice and the self in educational change is, as Jean Barr (1999) so clearly explains, a cultural and intellectual project and a set of material and cultural practices which embody a particular way of knowing the world.

What we take action research to involve

Our intention has not been to develop or offer a new, improved definition or version of action research, but instead 'a recognition of the partiality, the need for attention to circumstances, the specifics of history, without getting lost in globalized concerns that are constructed as separated from the local' (Noffke and Brennan, 1997: 67). There are numerous (and competing) 'definitions' of action research. We do not wish to add to these, nor do we see producing definitions as central to our action research. Nonetheless, we have found it helpful to bear the following two explanations in mind:

> [Action research] emphasises small-scale action, which is planned and evaluated by the people *within* the situation, rather than by those researching *on* it, or trying to change it from the outside . . . it focuses on the rigorous examination of a single situation, using knowledge drawn from experience and research findings to illuminate it, in order to improve it. The purpose is always to improve practice on the ground, rather than to find the exact truth about a particular situation, let alone about education in general.
>
> (Griffiths and Davies, 1995: 195)

Carr and Kemmis (1986: 165–6) assert that:

It can be argued that three conditions are individually necessary and jointly sufficient for action research to be said to exist: firstly, a project takes as its subject matter a social practice, regarding it as a form of strategic action susceptible of improvement; secondly, the project proceeds through a spiral of cycles of planning, acting, observing and reflecting, with each of these activities being systematically and self-critically implemented and interrelated; thirdly, the project involves those responsible for the practice in each of the moments of activity, widening participation in the project gradually to include others affected by the practice, and maintaining collaborative control of the process.

While the shifts that result may be only small accretions of local change, the broader purpose is still for equity in learning and society. The process involves action, participation, improvement, collaboration, inclusion and critical self-reflection. The practitioner is also the researcher, and research and practice unfold simultaneously, the one does not follow or precede the other. Reflecting on this, Quintin commented:

> If I do traditional computer science research, the fact that I'm doing it is not really particularly important in my reporting of it. I mean, it's the mechanisms that have happened in the machine and what goes on and I report on that and I relate it to other work. But in action research, I am part of the research and I'm prepared to be reflexive upon myself and I may change. I mean the whole research project involves me in a way that it doesn't always. It's actually that I'm in it. It's not just that my beliefs go into it, or my viewpoint on the world, it's about us writing about us doing our own teaching.
>
> (Group meeting, January 2000)

Central to the process were our attempts to find clarity about the practical implications of our critical stance towards higher education, what Noffke (1995) describes as 'becoming practically critical'. This involved us in a dialectical exploration of our theories about learning and our practices. The data generated through our research were used to clarify and reconstruct or challenge our theories and assumptions. At the same time, the efficacy of those theories was subjected to interrogation by the themes that emerged from the data. But these changes in practice must take seriously who we are – ourselves and our capacity to reflect on what we see, including trying to tease out our peripheral vision where we might see less and where we are most likely to be unreflective strangers to ourselves. As Alison put it, 'I have eyes that I might see you; you have eyes that I might see myself', with Quintin adding, 'That's what we get from being together' (Group discussion, January 2000).

The focus of our stories is thus on: (a) teaching the subject; (b) students' perceptions and experiences of learning; (c) power relations in specific subject classroom contexts; and (d) voices for action and change. They are set within the context of our collaborative relationship in the Barcelona Group, which offered a space in which we discussed our educational practice, theorizing and research methodology.

Self, identity and educational change

Our accounts are all written in the first person. To do otherwise would be odd indeed when the tales told are of our own teaching, professional learning and relationships with each other and our students. We set out to do action research in order to understand the complexities of our own work in learning sites, and to implement and evaluate changes in our practice. Thus changing what we do involved changing ourselves. How we come to see and understand ourselves in a particular way (and not in others) must then be central in action research and its processes of social relationships, discourses and practices. Whitehead (1993), for example, has developed a philosophy of action research grounded in the concept of the 'living contradiction of the I'. The self is part of the change process; as the study unfolds the self changes so that action research involves acquiring new identities or reworking existing ones. The self who began the project is not quite the same as the self who finishes. For example, in the final months of writing up their action research projects, group members in response to my question 'How are you different or changed?' said things like:

> *Quintin*: I feel more confident to stand up for things I believe in.
> *Mike*: I felt like a coming in from the cold after years of isolation pedagogically, and the separation of my pedagogical and political responsibilities. I have developed a vocabulary of understanding to talk about teaching and learning.
> *Judy*: I've been freed up to laugh with my students. I have a more holistic and 'political' view of what I am doing; I'm not frightened of education as political work.
>
> (Group discussion, June 2000)

It also follows that to understand change in action research we need to theorize the self in the change process. Griffiths (1993) argues that theorizing the self in action research is important because as we act to change our situation, so we ourselves change – the self that ends the project is not entirely the same as the one who began. Thus processes of deep self-knowledge are critical in research as/for social change. Indeed, Griffiths goes as far as to argue:

> Reflective practice/action research models are a necessity not an option for anyone trying to introduce a change. They are the only models with a hope of working because any change must be part of a rolling programme. [My] theory is a theory of the self as embedded in circumstances, which are partly of its own making. The result is that change

can never be introduced once and for all, because the selves who implement it are themselves always in a state of re-making themselves. This
re-making alters the situation and contributes to further change.

(Griffiths, 1993: 157)

Of course this is even further complicated, in that the process of education
involves many other selves who will also be changing, so that we become
and be who we are with and from others, and in relations with and to
others (Castells, 1997). Hence the importance of accessing and including
other epistemic communities and voices in our own processes of development and reflection. Reflexivity is a moving goal: it can never be achieved
once and for all because the 'self' in self-knowledge is dynamic and changes
with the change being studied through action research. The key question
then becomes 'Am I being true to myself', and what this might mean when
the self itself is changing over time and space. Authenticity of self is then
not unchanging. According to Griffiths (1993), only the reflective practice/
action research model can cope with the instability of implementing change,
which then carries within it the seed of further changes because it incorpor-
ates them within itself.

One way to understand the self in the process of educational change is
also to employ the theoretical lens of identity and processes of identification and identity construction. As Cockburn (1998: 10) forcefully points
out, identity processes are 'second only to force as the means by which
power is effected in oppressive and exploitative systems'. Where processes of
identification articulate with dominant professional identities, for example,
'compliance has been won' through these very same processes. Such compliance holds existing lines of power in place. What, then, are the discursive
'storylines' through which our practice and we ourselves speak and are
spoken and concretely taken up and lived? What is it possible to be? Castells
(1997) describes three forms of identity. 'Legitimizing' identities are introduced and sustained by the dominant institutions in society to secure control. Such selves would identify with dominant forms of professionalism, for
example. 'Resistance' identities are generated on the margins, in opposition,
by the excluded. They would dis-identify with such dominant processes and
seek to create alternative, but not necessarily oppositional, professional selves.
'Project' identities involve building new identities that redefine subjectivities
and by so doing seek transformation of the overall social structure. Thus there
exist possibilities of compliance with dominant identities, or resistance to
these without necessarily seeking to transform them, or new forms of identity which go beyond compliance and resistance to build new transformative
forms of subjectivity. This resonates with a question posed by Noffke (1995)
and which can only be answered by looking at the action research accounts
that follow. She asks whether action research might enable practitioners to
seek alternatives to current practice. This would involve constructing a resistant identity, and possibly even a project identity. On the other hand, she
also asks whether action research might help practitioners to reproduce

what currently exists. In other words, does action research contain within its own processes the potential for more just educational practices and, at the same time, the problematic that such research may be used to create a new authority of practice, so that it involves both transformation *and* reproduction? This is a question not dissimilar from considering how 'emergent professionalism', discussed in Chapter 1, might take a form in which it might be incorporated or not-incorporated.

Importantly, the self (or selves, or identity if you will) is not fixed, absolute or pre-given 'but rather a product of historically specific practices of social regulation' (Henriques *et al.*, 1984: 12), in continual construction and reconstruction. Identities shift and fragment across 'discourses, practices and positions' (Hall, 1990: 4) and are 'constantly in the process of change and transformation', always in process, never entirely complete. We are all located in myriad power relations at the micro level of society, and in a complex web of discourses which offer many ways of seeing and being. Thus processes of identification, Hall argues, mark symbolic boundaries and produce 'frontier effects', working to exclude as well as include. It follows that subject positions are neither static nor homogeneous, not smooth and seamless; we are neither always victim or always hero. Identity construction is a dynamic process grounded in biography and history, subjected to description and reflection, and constantly presented to and negotiated with other people. Again, Griffiths's (1995: 191) theorizing of the self (identity) is particularly useful. She develops the idea of a 'patchwork self', embedded in circumstances which are only partly of its own making:

> My argument about the construction of self shows it is like a patchwork, making a self is relatively easy, though it always takes time and attention. However, again, like patchwork, making a good one is very hard indeed. Understanding which pieces of old cloth will fit into the whole is a difficult and painstaking matter. Like patchwork, the construction of an authentic, autonomous self depends on the context of each fragment, and where it fits within the overall design.

In this view, and the conceptualizations of identity presented above, there is no unchanging core self or identity. For Griffiths (1995: 185), 'being true to oneself' does not require a unitary self: 'It means undertaking the difficult business of assessment and transformation within a changing context of self. Authenticity requires re-assessing the changing self, not preserving a sameness.'

The narratives of self that we construct are agentic but they are also constrained by the circumstances within which we find ourselves. This is evident in the ways in which we each struggled to construct and be an authentic professional self. The crisis of positionality mentioned in Chapter 1 is not simply a political crisis, but a crisis of professional and personal selves and the narratives we construct to make meaning of our lives in education and in the world. For example, Quintin expressed the importance for himself of connecting his practice and values:

It seems like something happens when you start performing your teaching or when I start performing my teaching from my deepest convictions; I mean I can only get to my deepest convictions by a bit of reflection to see what's there in relation to the subject matter I'm trying to present. So I can look in a text book or whatever and teach according to somebody else's beliefs and view on it, but I'm only going to start really teaching in any kind of passionate way when I start connecting that with what matters to me.

(Group discussion, January 2000)

Importantly, through the kind of action research advocated by Carr and Kemmis (1986), that reconnects the individual and the social, we can develop our situational understanding, which might enable us to take better strategic action to transform aspects of that situation.

Chapter 1 touches on experiences of marginality which were also experiences of exclusion from the self one wants to be. As this chapter argues, the costs of inauthenticity in terms of our feeling and being can be high, attacking our very sense of self:

- 'It's ripping me apart . . .'
- 'Marginality is incredibly painful . . . there's nowhere I can fit.'
- 'You're a teacher and that's pathetic.'
- 'I do generally find it very hard "to roll out my maps" in this university . . . I have experienced a serious loss of personal identity at times while working here, in that I believe myself forced to fit into some mould.'

As Anderson (1998: 596) reminds us, constituting ourselves as authentic selves is not simply a kind of private indulgence, but central to what we do and how we do it, individually and collectively, and spinning out from this the kind of society we end up by shaping. It is crucial, he says, that we better understand 'not only how authentic forms of participation can constitute more authentic private selves and public citizens but also how they lead to the constitution of a more democratic and socially just society.' Or, as Alison said, 'It strikes me that in this space we're getting two of the things that we really crave. One of them is the ability to exchange who we are and what we believe in with other people who will put that in a good place' (group discussion, January 2000). To feel as if one is playing false to oneself, or being forced to play out the part of one kind of lecturer in higher education – for example, not so much the inspiring teacher as the efficient bureaucrat, or the teacher as technocrat who must not raise questions about the moral purposes of his or her educational work, or the woman who must 'pass' as one of the boys to gain acceptance in her department – has implications for how one is to be authentic. Reflective practice thus cannot be a technical process.

At the same time there is a sense in which we are always strangers to ourselves, struggling to see what lies at the periphery of our vision, in contexts which can never be fully known to us. Nor can we know with certainty the effects of what we do when we do it. None of this is an argument against doing action research. It is a reminder of what one of our working 'definitions' of action research has to say: 'The purpose is always to improve practice on the ground, rather than to find the exact truth about a particular situation, let alone about education in general' (Griffiths and Davies, 1995: 195). The purpose is to work optimistically with the possible, for all its limits, rather than only pessimistically reiterating the hopeless.

What kind of identities are constructed in and through action research would turn partly on circumstances or conditions of possibility, but also on the strategic and professional choices we make in our bid for authenticity of the self. Certainly action research assumes some form of human agency in relation to structures and social processes. Authenticity 'requires acting at one's own behest both at a feeling level and an intellectual, reflective one' (Griffiths, 1995: 179). But, says Griffiths, because our action and that of others changes the context, 'authenticity has to be achieved and re-achieved'. The notion of the researcher's voice is understandably both central and significant in action research – the researcher is a key research 'instrument'. But what is being sought is not just any old voice, but a voice which can be identified as belonging to oneself.

A dialectic of theory and action

In our action research we used our academic and our everyday knowledges (life, experience) as a resource and a source for our knowing. Our personal experiences of practice are significant in our action research stories, even though the academy still demonstrates a limited tolerance for the personal, the popular and the passionate – which seems strange when education is so embedded in our personal lives and the subtle messy details of the everyday. At the same time as we argue for the significance of experience, we acknowledge its limits as a way of knowing. Myles Horton, the radical adult educator, put this clearly and simply when he said 'There is a point when experience runs out.' At issue is how we avoid recycling common sense, or victoriously celebrating practice without facing up to the fact that experience is never unmediated but structured by particular cultures and settings (racist, sexist, classist and so on). It may be that when we think we are producing our most 'true' selves we are simply ad libbing our way, playing the parts in someone else's script or living out someone else's storyline. Michael Schratz and Rob Walker explain how theory might help:

> theory is not just a back-up that can be turned to when all else fails, rather it is what makes it possible to see the world differently and so be able to act in different ways . . . theory is concerned with giving meaning and intent to action, and with reading meaning and intent in the actions of others. Theory extends our capacity to see alternatives, reminding us of the lost opportunities we create with every action we take and

every word we speak. Its concern is not simply to say why the world is as it is but to provide us with the space *to think how it could be different.*
(Schratz and Walker, 1995: 125; emphasis added)

Thus improving our theoretical understanding and developing our practical action are not isolated one from the other, but intimately connected, related and enmeshed one within the other. Academic theories (about the structure of the discipline, about learning, about epistemology, about educational change and so on) provide, then, a source of ideas, but not a warrant for them (Schratz and Walker, 1995). Instead, theory and theorizing push us beyond common sense to construct 'good sense' (Gramsci, 1971).

Not one but many voices

Crucially, our studies involved other epistemological communities: our students, and their thoughts and concerns. If ours is to be a dialogue, as claimed earlier, then a 'banking' process between full vessels and empty receivers (Freire, 1970) is as inappropriate in our research as our teaching. Readings (1996: 155) cites Bahktin's observation that 'it is not a mute, wordless creature that receives such an utterance but a human being full of inner words.' Student experiences and their voices count in the creation and legitimation of knowledge about education and learning. But for us, action research is also consistent with the kind of pedagogical principles that we had been articulating – where students are agents of their own knowing, and agents in the construction of knowledge about curriculum, about teaching and learning. Our discussion on this issue unfolded in this way, with Mike first explaining how he saw the processes:

Well the first thing is that in the act of engaging in the research, you are making active that which is passive, aren't you? I mean you're taking what is characteristic of higher education learning in this country, which is what we're talking about, which is that it is really passive, it is consumption. Part of the starting point, both the purpose and the consequence and the result of doing my course, both in the doing and as a result of concluding things from it, both you and the learners are drawn into an active relationship with the subject matter, the material. That is good in the sense that it enriches, makes more profound, makes more complex and more critical, the business of learning at that time. But the other effect of it is that it brings about a re-encounter between the business of learning and those other aspects of people's lives in which they are continually evolving. This idea that you, especially here, where you learn for four years and having reached the end point, you have learned. It's a process with an end, it closes off, it's locked up, you know, you've then done it. I mean the moment you draw people into a debate and a discussion about the nature of the process, then you make it open-ended, you project it back into the past beyond the beginning and forward into the future beyond this notional ending which comes simply because of the end of an administrative process, of career-making exams at the end of it. That would be, you know, a concrete, palpable and extraordinary positive outcome of this kind of research would be that it would generate lifelong learning both among us and among our students.

(Group discussion, January 2000)

Alison continued:

> I think there's more than that though. I think what this sort of research sets off, is a chain reaction, not just in ourselves and in each other, but also in the students that we've been involving, and I think, for me, that was one of the most unpredictable bits of doing this. I thought at first, here is another opportunity for me to go and milk the students for all the data I can get, and write another text which is one of the things which is always a problem for me in any kind of research that involves human subjects. And yet what seems to have happened for me is that, suddenly, I've seen that these focus groups, these opportunities for the students that we have given them because we want to reflect on our practice, actually gives them an opportunity to reflect on their practice. They get very excited by discovering that other people feel the same way about learning as they do and other people feel that what they are experiencing with us in certain ways is different and unusual and is part of what they think they're at university for. What we're doing is releasing it through the method of looking at our practice.

Our education and research processes can only be 'liberating' if everyone has a stake in developing knowledge. What Alison highlights is not just that it creates another layer of reflective spaces for students, but they have the opportunity to be in some way co-constructors of public knowledge about teaching and learning; they have an expertise about their own learning which we need to 'hear' and take seriously.

On the other hand, involving students is not uncomplicated; it may work patchily in practice. As Judy pointed out, she had found it hard to get maths students to come to interviews with her (although this had been much less a problem with mentees and mentors on the Mentoring Project). She had asked the small group who did volunteer to speak to her about why they thought other students were reluctant to participate. The students' view was that they 'weren't sure what they were going into'. In her view this reluctance may have been shaped by the pedagogical relationship with different maths tutors. Not surprisingly, this affects the research process and what we might come to know about learning, while it also serves to remind us that educational research is a cultural system permeated by relations of power. When power 'speaks' in particular ways in higher education pedagogy, it is not surprising that students were unsure. Was this to be a kind of hidden assessment? Was it really about their best interests? It also throws up quite clearly that there needs to be a consistency and authenticity in our pedagogical work and our research work, although in Judy's case the issue was not her own tutorial group but those taught by colleagues.

'Insider' work

Of course this kind of research process generates particular kinds of responsibility and challenges which are rather different in this kind of 'insider' research (Elliott, 1989). Our discussion continued:

> *Mike*: There's a further element, which is that when you start this process, you participate in it and you draw us into it, you're also creating a kind of alternative possibility; a critical university in miniature and there is a subsequent responsibility which we have to address. I mean you can't if you are an action researcher in any kind of serious way, you must take responsibility for the changes that will result from your work. And in doing that you can't do what an [outsider] researcher does which is announce that the two year grant is over and leave the world as you found it, 'cos if you leave the world as you found it as an action researcher, you've failed. But if you haven't left the world as you found it, then consequences flow and one of the consequences of the participatory research process is really problematic – you create a group of dissatisfied students where previously there had been a group of satisfied students.
>
> *Alison*: Compliant students.
>
> *Mike*: And I think you have to take that on board and say actually that is a positive outcome but it has consequences. Consequences in that it creates conflicts and paradoxes where there may not have been any before, not that we have created them, but allowed them to find expression. Maybe in the last analysis it's also the kind of research you can't walk away from and what you've done. You have to be part of whatever consequential activity flows from it at whatever level, you know, you then have a responsibility and maybe this is what you were saying before about the way you go from there, which is to try and draw these things to the attention of a bigger audience, to create a bigger space, to draw more people into this alternative space we've created, 'cos if you don't, you rest, you leave it there, then in a sense, the octopus will come back and swallow it all.
>
> *Alison*: The process is also empowering us to give students back some of the insights that we're gaining . . . they're seeing us embodying that praxis and they're learning from, you know, the fact that we're working this out inside us and on our bodies and in those spaces, that it's not some kind of theoretical abstract idea that they have to somehow acquire. They're seeing it in action, seeing it lived out in front of them.
>
> (Group discussion, January 2000)

Arguably, being responsible for the effects of what one does makes for a more ethical practice. It is also more ethical in that the people who are at the heart of the change process are then also in control, admittedly to different degrees, of a research process which is looking at the change which affects them all.

At the same time, there is no equality of power in the research relationship between teacher and students (or between myself as 'expert' educationalist/action researcher and lecturers in the Barcelona Group), and it would be patronizing to pretend otherwise. As action researchers we occupy a different space in which we get to ask most of the questions, interpret the answers and write about the research to share with each other and other colleagues (and, less often, with students). As Joan Didion (1968: 2) sharply observes, 'Writers are always selling someone out.' But we do not live in a perfect world, and our dilemmas around participation and the ownership of knowledge about pedagogy are not simply personal problems but 'genuine ethical dilemmas that the broader society, built on inequalities, strategically induces us to disregard' (Patai, 1991: 145). As Patai argues, we have to decide whether our research is worth doing, and in the doing of it, try to serve our democratic values.

Final thoughts, by way of introduction to the action research studies which follow

We live in uncertain times, even in a time of 'supercomplexity' (Barnett, 2000). This has implications for the certainty and predictability of our claims to know our students, to know what and how we teach, and the effects of what we do. It is ironic that the drive in higher education teaching and learning is towards prediction, control and certainties. Action research is one way to prise open these claims to certainty about the way the (educational) world is, in pursuit of better educational practices for ourselves and our students. It means recognizing that our own stories about practice are partial and situated, and hold their own potential for repression as much as empowerment. It means welcoming complexity and resisting the smoothing out of unevenness. It means resisting resolution, as far as we can, and action research's own preferred moral journey of 'triumph over adversity and contradiction' (Maclure, 1996: 283). Without wanting to turn notions of 'messiness' into a new kind of dogma, it is the case that our action in classrooms has elements of instability and complexity, which are not easily resolved. Nor would we want to resolve them. What we can do is construct 'patterns' and talk about them. It does mean that we can make knowledge claims about our own practice, as the case studies which follow demonstrate, and that we can speak about the ways in which we seek ethically and pedagogically to realize our professional values. It means finding the diverse languages to speak about what we do, of which the language of practicalities and common sense is only one among many, with no claim to a privileged position; even though, as Smith (1998) warned, to speak a different language is difficult. Still, through our reflective conversations and pedagogic research we might struggle against and away from performance indicators, outcomes and efficiency, towards a language we do not yet have. Smith (1999) suggests it is the difference between the language of 'university life' and the language of 'human resource development in the higher education context'! At issue is that action research is not simply a set of methods or techniques to investigate and report on practice. It is a methodology that raises questions about what counts as knowledge about educational practice, about how we come to know, about who counts as knowers and about how we write about higher education and our lives within it.

We think action research does have the potential to build more democratic ways of working with our students insofar as it enables us to investigate the ways in which we do our educational values, and the ways in which we fall short of these aspirations. Through evaluating our successes and failures, we can engage in continuous action for democratic change. We think action research has had something to do with making the lives of our students better by engaging them in reflection on their own learning, and, we hope, through us improving our practice. It has certainly offered a holistic and fulfilling professional experience to us as teachers in higher education. The practical implications of our critical professionalism are taken up in the action research studies, together with the unevenness of action and its effects under our particular circumstances. Action research, then, has offered a space and way for us to speak out to the potent discourses and practices of 'new managerialism', even, and perhaps especially, when we are not spoken to.

This chapter has not said much about the methods and techniques used to generate data. These can be found in the case studies. Instead the focus here has been on methodology. Nonetheless, it is important to note the importance of the empirical evidence generated in such projects, whether in the form of interviews, diaries and journals, observations, reflections and so on. Altricher *et al.* (1993) offer a particularly comprehensive account of the range of possible methods available to action researchers. In our view, this empirical material, jammed up against personal knowledge, academic theory and collaborative discussion and critique, offers a particular kind of rigour grounded in a dialectic of practice and theory.

From all this emerges a kind of agenda of principles for the conduct of our action research:

1. Improvement of our educational practice.
2. Constructing authentic selves in and through the process of educational change.
3. Making and getting knowledge with others, and learning from it professionally.
4. Developing reflexivity (self-knowledge) about our assumptions, interests and values.

5. Paying careful attention to the empirical data, and to the dialectic of theory and action/data.
6. Acknowledging and understanding the connections between individual and context, between education and society, between the personal, professional and political.
7. Acting ethically even while recognizing that society is not perfect.
8. Making our knowledge available to those for whom it might be useful.

It is a loss in our view that action research as a form of pedagogic research, even social justice, remain subjugated discourses in higher education, placed outside the parameters of dominant constructions of research and legitimate knowledge in the academy. Perhaps this ought to be the occasion for us all to reflect critically on our taken-for-granted assumptions about what counts as 'research' and why. As Michael Apple (1994: xi) suggests, 'if you want to understand how power works, look at the knowledge, self-understandings, and struggles of those whom powerful groups in society have cast off as "the other". Whose knowledge and which knowers are at the margins, and which at the centre?'

References

Altricher, H., Posch, P. and Somekh, B. (1993) *Teachers Investigate Their Work*. London: Routledge.

Anderson, G. L. (1998) Towards authentic participation: deconstructing the discourses of participatory reforms in education, *American Educational Research Journal*, 35 (4), 571–603.

Apple, M. (1994) Introduction, in A. Gitlin (ed.) *Power and Method: Political Activism and Educational Research*. New York: Routledge.

Barnett, R. (2000) *Realizing the University in an age of supercomplexity*. Buckingham: SRHE/Open University Press.

Barr, J. (1999) *Liberating Knowledge: Research, Feminism and Adult Education*. Leicester: NIACE.

Carr, W. and Kemmis, S. (1986) *Becoming Critical: Education, Knowledge and Action Research*. Lewes: Falmer Press.

Castells, M. (1997) *The Power of Identity*. Oxford: Blackwell.

Cockburn, C. (1998) *The Space between Us – Negotiating Gender and National Identities in Conflict*. London: Zed Books.

Corey, S. M. (1949) Action research, fundamental research and educational practices. Reprinted in S. Kemmis and R. McTaggart (eds, 1988) *The Action Research Reader*, 3rd edn. Geelong: Deakin University Press.

Dadds, M. (1995) *Passionate Enquiry and School Development*. London: Falmer Press.

Didion, J. (1968) *Travelling to Bethlehem*. London: Andre Deutsch.

Elliott, J. (1991) *Action Research for Educational Change*. Buckingham: Open University Press.

Freire, P. (1970) *The Pedagogy of the Oppressed*. London: Penguin.

Gramsci, A. (1971) *Selections from the Prison Notebooks*. London: Lawrence and Wishart.

Griffiths, M. (1993) The self and educational change, *British Journal of Educational Studies*, 41 (2), 150–63.

Griffiths, M. (1995) *Feminisms and the Self: The Web of Identity*. London: Routledge.

Griffiths, M. (1998) *Educational Research for Social Justice.* Buckingham: Open University Press.
Griffiths, M. and Davies, C. (1995) *In Fairness to Children.* London: Longman.
Hall, S. (1990) Introduction: who needs identity?, in S. Hall and P. Du Gay (eds) *Questions of Culture and Identity.* London: Sage.
Henriques, J., Hollway, W., Urwin, C., Venn, C. and Walkerdine, V. (1984) *Changing the Subject.* London: Methuen.
Hodgkinson, H. L. (1957) Action research – a critique, *Journal of Educational Sociology*, 31, 137–53.
Kemmis, S. and McTaggart, R. (eds) (1988) *The Action Research Reader*, 3rd edn. Geelong: Deakin University Press.
Kemmis, S. and Wilkinson, M. (1998) Participatory action research and the study of practice, in B. Atweh, S. Kemmis and P. Weeks (eds) *Action Research in Practice: Partnerships for Social Justice in Education.* London: Routledge.
Kolb, D. A. (1984) *Experiential Learning: Experience as the Source of Learning and Development.* Englewood Cliffs, NJ: Prentice Hall.
Lather, P. (1986) Research as praxis, *Harvard Educational Review*, 56 (3), 257–77.
Maclure, M. (1996) Telling transitions: boundary work in narratives of becoming an action researcher, *British Educational Research Journal*, 22 (3), 273–86.
Noffke, S. (1995) Action research and democratic schooling: problematics and potential, in S. Noffke and R. Stevenson (eds) *Educational Action Research: Becoming Practically Critical.* New York: Teachers College Press.
Noffke, S. (1997) Professional, personal and political dimensions of action research, *Review of Research in Education*, 22, 251–304.
Noffke, S. and Brennan, M. (1997) Reconstructing the politics of action in action research, in S. Hollinsgworth (ed.) *International Action Research: A Casebook for Educational Reform.* London: Falmer Press.
Patai, D. (1991) US academics and Third World women: is ethical research possible?, in S. B. Gluck and D. Patai (eds) *Women's Words: The Feminist Practice of Oral History.* New York: Routledge.
Readings, B. (1996) *The University in Ruins.* Cambridge, MA: Harvard University Press.
Schratz, M. and Walker, R. (1995) *Research as Social Change.* London: Routledge.
Smith, R. (1998) The justice of the differend. Paper presented at the World Conference on Philosophy of Education, Boston, April.
Smith, R. (1999) Higher education: reading the words. Paper presented at the British Educational Research Association Annual Conference, Brighton, September.
Somekh, B. (1995) The contribution of action research in social endeavours: a position paper on action research methodology, *British Educational Research Journal*, 21 (3), 339–55.
Stenhouse, L. (1975) *An Introduction to Curriculum Research and Development.* London: Heinemann Educational Books.
Walker, M. (1996) *Images of Professional Development: Teachers, Learning and Action Research.* Pretoria: Human Sciences Research Council.
Weiner, G. (1989) Professional self-knowledge versus social justice: a critical analysis of the teacher-researcher movement, *British Educational Research Journal*, 15 (1), 41–51.
Whitehead, J. (1993) *The Growth of Educational Knowledge: Creating Your Own Living Theories.* Bournemouth: Hyde Publications.
Young, I. M. (1990) *Justice and the Politics of Difference.* Princeton, NJ: Princeton University Press.

3

Collaboration with/in a Critical Community of Practice

Melanie Walker

Marco Polo describes a bridge stone by stone. 'But which is the stone that supports the bridge?' asks Kublai Khan. 'The bridge is not supported by one stone or another', Marco answers, 'but by the line of the arch that they form.' Kublai Khan remains silent, reflecting. Then adds: 'Why do you speak to me of stones? It is only the arch that matters to me.' Polo answers: 'Without stones there is no arch.'

(From *Invisible Cities* by Italo Calvino)

A kind of textual collage

Chapter 1 explains how our group came into being and how as an interdisciplinary group of five lecturers and an educationalist we set out to explore a discourse of 'critical professionalism'. Through overlapping layers of practices framed by the context of higher education, and employing action research as a methodology, we involved ourselves in a collaborative, interdisciplinary and reflective professional dialogue focused on improving learning in our classrooms. Our concerns were always located in our classrooms within an integrated range of activities where the outcome would be learning; but we were all also insisting in different ways that the effect should be to draw in other areas of experience and send students, actually and metaphorically, out into the world beyond the classroom. The problem that had brought us together was a sense that the classroom was seen by many as an autonomous site of learning. So our action was not simply to improve life in classrooms, but to improve life.

I explain in Chapter 1 that after struggling for a while to find a name that might capture what we felt ourselves to be and to be doing, we hit upon the name of the 'Barcelona Group'. We saw this as a metaphor for the processes and practices of the group and for our universities, mirrored in the architecture, aesthetics and regeneration of the city of Barcelona itself. An article in the *Guardian* (22 March 1999) suggested that 'Barcelona's multi-layered quality is evident at every turn', rather like our complicated collaboration we thought. 'Here [in the UK]', the writer continued, 'we treat our cities as some sort of low-rent department store to be cut up deregulated, privatised and trashed at will' – this sounded all too much like the marketized changes wrought in higher education. But, says the *Guardian* writer, 'the men and women who have raised Barcelona to new international heights over the past 24 years see their city as an organism to be nurtured and treated as a whole, not a book of bits.' In the face of a contemporary remapping of higher education, dominated by a discourse and practices of 'new managerialism', we sought not to be a 'book of bits'.

This chapter tries to capture something of the unruly excess of the exchange and interchanges that constituted our work as a collaborative group over two academic years, and my attempt to theorize this collaboration. While I try to work the spaces between what Ellsworth (1997: 193) describes as the 'the uppercase of academic realism' and the 'lowercase of subsurface drama', it remains rather difficult to represent a dynamic process in textual form. I shift from 'uppercase' to 'lowercase' for a loosely braided, rather than a tightly woven, text, which attempts to demonstrate in its own construction that our collaboration was many voiced, multilayered, had its uncertainties and could be interpreted in more than one way. Our communications were of various kinds – audio-taped group discussions, email conversations, an electronic webboard, the circulation of news clippings, poems and academic texts, and meetings with each other, only a small selection of which case record can be shared here. We were by turns playful, argumentative, sad, angry, comforted and inspired.

We played with metaphors of dance, marking our steps, marking time, having fun in our emails, delightedly sharing a piece from the *Times Higher Education Supplement* (26 February 1999), which used Gene Kelly's and Fred Astaire's styles of dance to compare different approaches to essay writing. In 'An Astaire and Kelly model of argument', Alan Dignam characterizes essays as being either technically brilliant (Astaire) or more natural and graceful (Kelly). At the time we discussed this in terms of the precision Judy liked in developing her engineering courses, and the more free-flowing style of teaching cultural studies preferred by Alison. We even watched the Australian film *Strictly Ballroom* together one night after a meal for its central theme of 'doing one's own steps' and its storylines of diversity, love, friendship, conflict and integrity. Maxine Greene (1995) reminds us all of the importance of happiness and laughter, as much as clarity and logic, in our collective work. She also argues powerfully for 'releasing the imagination' and the role of metaphor in this. I was fascinated by her evocation of dance, of laughter, of release in this respect. She discusses at one point the importance and place of 'criticism from within' a shared context or human community. The richness of her writing necessitates a lengthy quote:

> Recalling Henri Matisse's wonderful depiction of human solidarity and abandonment in the painting he called 'dance', I call the action of

critiquing within a shared context 'the dance of life'. Not only does Matisse's work present an authentic human involvement with others and the natural world; it somehow draws us into the dancers' movements and suggests the vital networks in which we live or ought to live our lives. Nietzsche wrote that the value of what we read or hear depends a great deal on whether the writer or composer can walk or dance, because if he or she cannot, he or she more than likely composes under closeted conditions. We ought to dance even if we move ponderously.

(Greene, 1995: 62)

Importantly, says Greene (1995: 72), we develop our social vision as subjects present in a public space, 'where at odd times and spontaneously, people feel themselves part of the dance of life'.

Probably ponderously, but also enthusiastically, energetically and, at moments, gracefully, this chapter represents our 'dance of life', presented publicly. A more adventurous telling of our stories, ourselves, our teaching worlds, our pleasures and our pain seemed necessary, even if this chapter does not, in the end, dance too far off the stage of academic conventions.

Process, methodology and ethics

There are also complicated and sensitive ethical issues in the presenting and representing of our intimate collaborative processes to a public gaze. Our collaboration was and is private in many ways. From a methodological point of view, this private space is akin to John Berger's explication of the meaning of a private photograph:

the photographs one has of the people one loves, one's friends, the class one was in at school, etc. In private use a photograph is read in a context which is still continuous with that from which it was taken . . . private photographs are nearly always of something which you have known . . . The private context creates a continuity which is parallel to the continuity from which the photograph was originally taken.

(Berger, quoted in Goodson and Walker, 1995: 187)

An account such as this chapter wrenches the private 'snapshots' of our group from their context, and displays them before the public gaze, at which point they are 'severed from life when it was taken' (Berger, quoted in Goodson and Walker, 1995: 188). Yet we wanted to find a way to make public the work which underpinned our action research studies and, indeed, provided the glue that held them together, without producing an invasive 'public photograph' which did no more than voyeuristically shout 'Look!'

While finding ways to represent and theorize practical collaborative processes is extraordinarily difficult, as tricky are the sensitive ethical issues that surround the substantive story. In one of the few extended considerations of collaboration which attempts to hold theoretical insights and practical action within the frame of understanding, Griffiths (1998) explores telling stories about collaboration as a process of 'secrets and lies'. The difficulty, as she notes, is that collaborative projects might be exceptionally reward-ing and productive, but they are also 'ethical minefields' and may well unravel destructively. It is, writes Griffiths (1998: 5), 'a worthwhile but chancy business'.

In our case one person had the major responsibility for authoring this chapter, and the main interest in theorizing collaboration. Even though we would agree that this collaboration has been immensely rewarding for all of us, it has nonetheless been important that all members of the group read and commented and discussed how data were used in the construction of the account. Clearly, anonymizing data has not been an option here. In areas of sensitivity, therefore, data have not been ascribed to a particular speaker, or have been slightly fictionalized. We remain aware of the riski-ness of this chapter. Moreover, feelings and ideas, the affective and the cognitive, are at play in any learning encounter, so that is it not surprising that the 'ethical, political and epistemological problems of publicly discuss-ing a failed – or even a successful – collaboration are enormous' (Griffiths, 1998: 7). On the other hand, learning and working together was so central to the work we did that it seems odd not to write about it and to try to convey at least some of what it meant to us, and how we tried to work together. Besides, the idea of 'ethical minefields' ought itself to be open to critique. If by ethics we mean a kind of traditional professional ethics, then much of what this group had to say about education, collaboration, experi-ence and freedom rejects any notion of a protective moral regulation which keeps professional processes 'secret', in favour of a different ethics of agree-ment based on social justice, openness and collectivism.

Dialogue, shared work and community

We met twice a term as a group over one academic year, and maintained contact electronically and through two one-day group meetings in the second year. At one of these termly meetings (in the first year), we focused on the unfolding of each of the learning development projects. Importantly, each action research project was determined by the lecturer concerned, who identified the issue, the class and the course he or she wished to investigate. At times discussion was more structured, so that at one meeting we each chose readings from the materials circulated which 'spoke' to us in some way about learning or collaboration or critical professionalism. The away day at Ross Priory in May 1999 attempted to pull some of our sprawling discussions together as we developed principles for 'engaged' learning and collaboration and produced statements of our own on 'critical professional-ism'. We also spoke of the way forward in terms of how we might continue our work together after I left Glasgow at the end of June 1999 to take up my job in Bristol. This book is one of the projects I initiated to focus our continuing conversations.

At the second meeting each term, always over a meal, our talk ranged widely over our individual hopes and passions. In addition, members of the group met others in between. Judy and Quintin developed a strong collaboration; Quintin and Alison met to discuss shared interests; Mike and Chris met to talk politics; Mike and Alison met to discuss modern language teaching; and I met everyone to discuss their projects, to help to refine the questions and to assist with data collection and analysis. We generated a range of different types of evidence which were shared and circulated in the group, including email conversations, poems, story fragments, clippings from newspapers on social class, on academic life, on language teaching and on university teaching, and academic texts, in order to construct a kind of collage of the process of building ourselves as an educative community. Our early and continuing emphasis was on practical action to improve life in classrooms and a reflective and collaborative exchange about such classroom action. Our collaboration (like the learning communities we simultaneously were trying to establish with our students) thus had both content and process (John-Steiner *et al.*, 1998). For all of us, both process – dialogue and understanding each other's work in the forum where we came together as a group and through our action research projects – and content – the construction of knowledge about learning – were central to our collaboration. Dialogue and a range of activities around our common purpose of 'teaching and learning' underpinned our work.

Quite early on in our work together (October 1998), I circulated via email this extract from Barry Lopez's (1986: 270) *Arctic Dream*. It exemplified for me, at the time, the kind of community I hoped we might become. Lopez writes:

> I thought about the great desire among friends and colleagues and travellers who meet on the road to share what they know, what they have seen and imagined. Not to have a shared understanding but to share what one has come to understand. In such an atmosphere of mutual regard, in which each can roll out his or her maps with no fear of contradiction, suspicion or theft, it is possible to imagine the long graceful strides of human history.

The next day Alison responded: 'It is equally possible, and ultimately more fruitful, to see the limping, halting, painful progress of human history and to use the atmosphere of mutual regard to discover again and again that it no sin to limp' (email, October 1998).

Thus we did not aspire to all be the same, or to all agree all the time, or to build an artificial consensus. Our values in terms of shared commitments to students, to developing critical persons (Barnett, 1997) and to equity for all the students we teach is captured compellingly in the poem by Laurel Richardson, herself an academic writer 'at play', and circulated by myself early in the life of the group:

Educational Birds
(found poem, Raptor Barn, Felix Neck Wildlife Sanctuary)

The Raptor Barn Houses
Various Birds of Prey
They are being Rehabilitated
for release. Those that
cannot be released
successfully
are kept
as Educational Birds

(Richardson, 1994: 206)

The poem cleverly catches us by surprise – the educational birds are not the magnificent raptors flying free, but trained birds, confined and cramped. It was not such 'educational birds' we were hoping to encourage in our classes or ourselves. Instead, we wanted to construct a space in which we might build some kind of community with a shared commitment to teaching well in the world and to learning (our own as much as the students') as the development of personhood and agency (Nixon *et al.*, 1996). We limped, haltingly, but also danced our way together; we sought to establish which possibilities existed for us as human actors in concrete settings in which we might rework 'dominant', 'residual' and 'emergent' cultural narratives. Crucially, we tried to construct a provisional space or 'home' in our academic travels which was positive, supportive, collective, even utopian at times, in which we might articulate our values yet also strengthen and sustain our wholeness and integration.

In a text written by Mike and circulated to us all in November 1998, he offers a set of opening, almost poetic statements, as part of a longer paper in which he sets out the parameters of his argument:

Education is responsive to the market
The market is governed by interests not ethics
Therefore education will respond to argument from interest not ethics

Education is concerned with ethics
The market rejects ethical criteria
Therefore education and the market are in conflict

The market is governed by pragmatism
Education is governed by humanism
Therefore the market and education are in opposition

The market is based on the concept of competing individuals
Education is based on the concept of cooperating collectives
Therefore education and the market are in opposition

The circulation of these various and different texts was important in the development of our thinking; different people took different things away and not all of us read or wanted to read the same pieces we gathered in our project 'archive'. Mike's text pushed us to think about the changing conditions of higher education under which we worked; the Richardson poem led us to focus on educational processes and their effects. We shifted backwards and forwards between a focus on micro processes and discussion of the bigger picture, and how both shaped our professional work. Our dialogue served as a way to make explicit the shared values and concerns we held.

Practising collaboration

There was something about authentic participation, not understood in any essentialist way, which was important in the building of our collaboration. We understand participation to have been authentic 'if it includes relevant stakeholders and creates relatively safe structured spaces for multiple voices to be heard' (Anderson, 1998: 575). We did not want participation to operate simply as some kind of 'legitimating ritual' (Anderson, 1998) for us or for our students. At our Ross Priory meeting in May 1999 (our third term of working together) we used the space to reflect on the process of collaboration and tried to generate, individually first, and then collectively, a set of shared principles and practices. We played with notions of trust, reciprocity, cooperation, common values and purposes, diversity and complementarity, interdisciplinarity, exchange and the dilemmas around being and feeling 'marginal' and what at times seemed like our 'connivance' with the system.

Part of a wide-ranging discussion, the following piece of dialogue suggests a developing theory of collaboration, important in which is the idea of an exchange of 'use values', rather than competitive and individualized approaches to academic work. The extract also works to capture some of the ebb and flow of our dialogue:

Melanie: Shall we start with trust? We all wrote trust as a principle of collaboration. Trust in what?

Chris: In the authenticity of the relationship and of the partners.

Alison: In the process.

Mike: And that means authenticity in the sense that there's no bad faith, that there's no hidden agenda. There are certain things that infect relationships elsewhere which are abandoned, principally probably competitiveness, probably the exploitation of one another in a career context. I mean that's what I understand the authenticity to be about.

[...]

Chris: The other phrase I wrote down was 'exchange in dialogue' because we're exchanging ideas and benefits.

Mike: If there's a core of reciprocity, you could call it exchange.

Chris: But exchange can also be a one-way opportunity.

Mike: No it can't. By definition it can't. It's not just a donation. It's an *exchange*.

Melanie: I think it also has to be about shared values.

Chris: Isn't the key then a common purpose?

Alison: A common cause, a sort of sense of struggle, a stance, a responsibility for justice.

Chris: Collaboration ought to have a common purpose for it to be collaboration.

Alison: You need to collaborate around something.

Chris: If you take our group, our common purpose is about teaching and learning, but we actually might get different benefits out of the group.

Quintin: The purpose is something about improving our understanding of teaching and learning, and kind of sharing ideas and fertilising.

Alison: And there are quite deep purposes underneath about what it is we think is going to be good for each other. And beyond that. Other human beings.

Quintin: Yeah.

Mike: But there's also a practice that flows from it. Otherwise this collaboration for me would be less valuable if it didn't lead to improved practice, the ideas and collaboration lead to different ways of engaging with the world.

Quintin: Yes, it's not just about sharing ideas, it's the fact that as you put yours out, somebody else takes it in and augments it and improves theirs, and vice versa.

Mike: It takes us beyond this context into dealing with the world in a different way.

Alison: Yeah, and that's what Melanie's been saying about she's been able to learn more quickly than she would have done on her own. It's about the whole being much bigger.

Chris: I don't know about diversity but you only collaborate with people if they're bringing something to the relationship that you don't have.

Mike: Absolutely.

Melanie: Different experiences, different perspectives.

Mike: That's right, because the idea of collaboration doesn't fit with two people with identical experiences and identical views coming together. It comes back to this idea of exchange. You put one set of experiences on the table which have relevance to and in some ways correspond to other experiences but they're not the same and the product of the meeting is a third thing.

Chris: People have to bring something which bolts on to what you are doing which is different.

Alison: Or which doesn't and precisely because it doesn't, it's useful.

Quintin: It helps you sharpen your ideas.

Alison: Or sharpen up where you want to stand.

Chris: You can be different though and not be able to work together, but surely for collaboration you've got to be different *and* be able to work together.

Mike: Mmmm.

Chris: Which is this notion of complementarity.

Mike: That's right and it's difference in complementarity because a hostile difference doesn't allow collaboration. The question is on what basis are they complementary. I think somewhere along the lines it's about values, it's about ethics.

[...]

Mike: You can't even talk about these things except in a space like this group.

Alison: Work differently, think differently, be different actually. It's an alternative space to be authentic.

Our practice of collaboration thus turned on trust and the reciprocity of exchanging ideas in ways where both the 'giver' and the listeners gained from the exchange, focused by action research projects. We also pushed our own development forward through engaging different experiences and different perspectives in a social and cumulative process of professional learning. The 'space' of collaboration provided the safe space for dialogue and development, and our shared commitments to student learning held it all together.

Talking across subject boundaries

The comparative and complementary aspects and our shared work across disciplines were important as comments elsewhere in this and other chapters, and in these remarks made in my report to the Principal in May 1999, suggest:

- I have gained considerable insight into pedagogical practices both generally and across a range of subject areas, and better understand how such ideas might be incorporated into my own discipline. (Quintin)
- The comparative and critical context shed new light on my own concerns; it has been a stimulating experience. (Mike)
- The collegial support and constructive criticism from other seconded staff with their different disciplinary backgrounds has been invaluable. (Alison)
- The interdisciplinary composition of the group offered frequent and mutually beneficial peer review and critique and productive cross-fertilization of ideas about teaching and learning. (Chris)
- The collaboration has not only widened my academic perspective through cross-disciplinary discussions and joint projects, but also honed my teaching skills. (Judy)
  Importantly, this conversation across disciplines was not intended to generate a prescriptive set of generalizable generic principles. Rather, the encounters with ideas about teaching other subjects were always grounded in each person's own subject context.

It was not always the case that people were able to find any connections. Thus, in one of our conversations, Quintin remarks on the difficulty he has in trying to see how the ideas being generated by Alison for teaching cultural studies and language to small groups can be of any use in his teaching of a large (360–400 students) first year computing science course where the basic ('factual') rules of programming must be learnt. Nor did everyone want to read the same kinds of texts on learning. Alison was drawn more to the writing on academic literacy, Bahktinian notions of 'carnival' and ethnography as performance, all of which were grounded in her own subject teaching of German popular culture. Judy was drawn more to particular reports and papers which explored the teaching of mathematics for engineers. Mike had a particular philosophy of history which informed how he constructed his second level history course. These individual approaches by a group of practitioners in different disciplines were as important and valuable as the common conversations, and they are detailed in the separate action research stories about learning which follow.

Rowland (1999) problematizes making any special case for educational theory in the process of academics learning about teaching. In his view such theory can be a useful resource or source of insights but it should not occupy a privileged position. Moreover, as Rowland (1999: 306) emphasizes, the close relationship between theory and practice is of more concern; we use theory 'to reflect on our own practice of teaching with the aim of developing theories which may then go on to inform future practice.' This is not unlike the argument constructed by Judy as she considered the interdisciplinary and disciplinary bases of our work brought to bear in different action research projects. Thus she wrote in an email (February 2000) to all of us:

> It seems to me to be central to the whole business of communication that we appreciate the allusions and the metaphors of people engaged in other disciplines. It is this web we form in our meetings and for me the nub of our work. Interwoven with this is, of course, using action research and applying that to improve our educational practice.

This approaches Barnett's (1997) idea of 'critical interdisciplinarity', in which the different assumptions and values underlying disciplines are explored. However, for Rowland the question of value must also spin out from disciplinary frameworks of understanding into discussions of the values and purposes of *education*. Referring to lecturers sharing their ideas about learning, he adds: 'a significant question for them to go on to consider is how their understanding of the nature of learning (from their disciplinary standpoint) relates to their practice as teachers and learners' (Rowland, 1999: 312). When this happens in a shared context, a community might be established for critical debate and continuous professional learning:

> Reflection upon practice within the context of the available theoretical resources from the different disciplinary frameworks may lead to new

insights. However, unless one tests out such insights within the shared context itself, one is inevitably thrown back upon one's own personal resources as interpreter of one's practice. Opportunities for critique are then no longer available.

(Rowland, 1999: 312)

At issue, as Malcolm and Zukas (2000: 4) point out, is the current oddity of separating teaching from other forms of disciplinary activity (in a way which would be unimaginable for research). They claim that this separation of pedagogy from the disciplines and research 'has serious implications for the status of teaching in higher education, the prospects of "connective specialization", and the process of knowledge production itself.' They argue strongly for 'the return of pedagogic practice to the site of knowledge production' (p. 12). What counts as 'learning' will be shaped epistemologically by whether this is learning of chemistry, philosophy, mathematics, history and so on. Arguably, then, an effective collaboration in higher education must include participants' disciplines and their discourses or languages, a shared conversation about teaching and practical efforts to improve learning. Any professional identity is then multi-layered, and includes both pedagogic and disciplinary identities. In more or less a similar vein, Rowland (1999) argues for three contexts of knowledge-building about learning in higher education: public (con)texts which may or may not be from within each person's disciplinary field but which draw their validity from canons established within a discipline; personal contexts in the form of the stories we construct to give meaning to our experience; and a shared context of the process of a group's work. Arguably, all three contexts were present in the collaboration of the Barcelona Group: disciplinary languages and ways of thinking and writing, individual experiences of teaching and a shared professional dialogue.

Coming unstuck

Building this community was never smooth or straightforward. How we travelled and what was in our baggage was always an issue – we were similar in many ways, different in others. Alison had commented on the Lopez text: 'There is something about locality here too – and therefore about community. Not the nice cosy, woolly, New Labour version but the difficulty of living with different modes of travel, different speeds, different vantage points on the route' (email, October 1998).

We certainly came unstuck from our different vantage points from time to time during heated political debates (mostly over dinner), which then simmered and resurfaced in odd ways in the meetings that followed. Gender proved a sticking point, in that the group included two very vocal men with well worked out political positions. They were used to making regular and confident interventions in any discussion and enjoyed sparring with each other, leaving the rest of us (two women and one younger man) watching at times bemused or irritated from the sidelines, even as we learnt! Different styles of interacting which might be broadly described as 'masculine' and 'feminine' (see Tannen, 1995) generated somewhat painful tensions from time to time. As women in the group, we could be silenced, or talk ever more loudly in order to win a space in the conversation. Related to this issue of communicative approach, and central to our interactions and hence our professional learning, was emotion. We had to work a precarious boundary (or at any rate I tried as facilitator at our meetings) between what Kenway *et al.* (1997) describe as 'therapeutic' and 'authoritarian' orientations to practice. We were not an 'encounter group', but feelings were implicated in what we did and how others responded. Writing about their own research on gender reform in Australian schools, Kenway *et al.* (1997) identify a therapeutic approach as one which makes emotional worlds and personal lives central. On the other hand, an authoritarian approach ignores emotional life. This is further complicated in our case by the ways in which 'toxic emotions' (Goleman, 1996) generated elsewhere in our teaching lives spilled into our collaborative space. Because our group comprised men and women, the differences not only in communicative approaches but also, arguably, in emotionality further added to the complexity. For example, Carol Gilligan (1982) has argued that women and girls are more likely to prefer inclusiveness, connection and attachment in social settings, while men and boys are more likely to perform emotional neutrality and competitiveness. However, this risks reinscribing essentialized gender stereotypes, and while it helps us to understand some of the processes in our group, it did not map precisely over our gender identities. But there is certainly evidence that men and women in the group told their stories differently. As Kenway *et al.* (1997: 139) explain, 'Girls more readily talk the language of interior whereas the boys more readily talk surfaces', with girls attending more carefully to others' feelings and doing the 'emotional housework' required to hold the fabric of the interaction together.

However, as Cameron (2000) has recently pointed out, the egalitarian, non-judgemental and cooperative approaches of women in the group are not calculated to empower speakers in confrontations with authority or contexts of persuasion. Of course, this group was not meant to operate as a debating club, or to persuade all members to one point of view. While we did raise this issue of communication directly from time to time, we failed perhaps to explore it as systematically as we ought to have. Nonetheless, at least one group member moved from a denial of gender as an interactive and communicative issue, to recognising his need to listen more, and sometimes to speak less. We were less successful in reflecting at the time on our different rhetorical skills and what we might learn from each other that would stand us in good stead in making strategic 'communicative choices' (Cameron, 2000) – both feminine and masculine – in our institutional encounters. With hindsight, the danger in such collaborations lies in our constructing 'defensive identities that function as refuge and solidarity to protect against a hostile, outside world' (Castells, 1997: 65). As Castells (1997: 66) points out, we develop codes of self-identification as a community of 'believers' trying to stabilize 'new patterns of meaningful communication', which might work to reinscribe identities (and hence dominant discourses). This can be limiting in the cut and thrust of university politics, which we sought to influence pedagogically. On the other hand, we would also want to argue that emotions as much as intellectual processes are central to more holistic professional learning and to collaborative commitments.

Still, we did not necessarily seek to resolve all tensions, nor would we want this account to gloss over our differences as if all was agreed and open. Friction kept us open to the challenges posed to our own thinking, rather than dissipating them, even though the rasp of disagreement and difference was hard and difficult in practice. For example, in a meeting one of us says 'I don't want to chuck big buckets of cold water at you and sound like a miserable old pessimist', and another of us tartly retorts 'It's OK, you have done!' Yet this kept our conversation moving on rather than allowing it to subside into a cosy comfort of consensual thinking. This fragment captures the mood:

Mike: I think that what this group is is a kind of recreation or an attempt to create an atmosphere where people argue and talk and laugh and read and get excited, not necessarily in agreement.
Melanie: But it's not about agreement.
Alison: It's not about agreement, it's definitely not about agreement.

Furthermore, individuals need the support of groups that reinforce their own values and aspirations. Through participation in collaborative groups we work to resist the 'individualization of identity attached to life in the global networks of power and wealth' (Castells, 1997: 65) and our own identification with dominant trends in higher education. Thus, working together is part of our attempt to construct a resistant practice of professionalism, of our doing of criticality. The risk is, as Castells notes, that these same collaborative spaces might work defensively so that we sediment resistant identities which privilege solidarity over difference and consensus over critique, so that we risk confirming rather than challenging each other's assumptions. Alternatively, of course, we might shift from a protective solidarity in the early part of a collaboration, to a more confident critical approach as relationships take root. At issue is that interactive spaces are always risky and emotional, saturated with feelings as well as ideas, and that the effects of collaboration might not always be as we would wish and hope. Collaboration is not inherently liberatory; much turns on the context and practices that give it form and there is no one trajectory that defines all collaborations. These spaces are unpredictable and complex, as the 'ideas and actions of one person interact with the ideas and actions of another to produce a co-construction' (Griffiths, 1998: 13). Yet therein also lies their richness and possibility.

Samara and Luce-Kapler (1993) emphasize in their exploration of collaboration the idea of 'labour' not as cosy cooperative work; instead they trace the roots of 'collaborate' back to the Latin *laborare*, which in turn orginates from *laborem*. *Laborem*, as they point out, means 'toil, distress, trouble, exertions of the faculties of the body or mind especially when painful or compulsory'. Thus collaboration is *work* in the sense of (hard) labour, leading them to conclude that 'collaborating within a community should be understood as an activity which is at times likely to be uncomfortable rather than comfortable' (Samara and Luce-Kapler, 1993: 283). They suggest that it is at the knotty points and moments of disagreement and unpredictability that we gain insights into each other and ourselves and generate the spaces and intersections which are simultaneously uncomfortable, yet satisfying and productive. The issue for collaboration is whether a group seeks merely to engage in dialogue, or whether it faces up to difference and its discomforts through careful and respectful work. The Barcelona Group certainly attempted the latter.

'A network of replenishment' (Alison)

While we did not ignore problems, or proclaim that we heroically triumphed over all adversity, our concern was with what Raymond Williams (1977: 212) called 'creative practice':

> [an] active struggle for new consciousness through new relationships . . .
> a process often described as development but in practice a struggle at
> the roots of the mind – not casting off an ideology, or learning phrases
> about it, but confronting a hegemony in the fibres of the self and in
> the hard practical substance of effective and continuing relationships.

At least some of this process and struggle is exemplified in Judy's email in November 1998:

> I am still excited, happy and full of ideas after yesterday's session . . .
> Academia needs a vital, exciting, committed dialogue about what it
> means to be an academic, what our values are, what we are trying to do
> and how we achieve this . . . I started thinking that Mike, Alison, Quintin
> and Chris were all charismatic lecturers but then realised that their
> strengths were that they are all trying to engage the intellect of stu-
> dents; when the students are really thinking then we feel that we are
> achieving something . . . Then, Melanie we need your voice, almost as
> an overarching circle that reflects our experiences with students in
> your experience with us, how you encourage us to debate, question
> and learn, and then out of this spins Quintin convincing his colleagues
> and me enthusing my tutors. All of us learning, challenging and chang-
> ing. Finally, we should remember the poems and quotes they prompt,
> question, move us into new dialogues, really exciting, very positive.

While speaking passionately towards the close of one of our meetings, Alison said:

> It strikes me that in this space we're getting two of the things that we really crave and one of them is the ability to exchange who we are and what we believe in with other people who will put that in a good place. And we need narrative, which is the way we exchange, we crave the chance to say 'Look this is how it is, this is how I feel and this is how I've experienced it'.

> (Group discussion, March 1999)

Besides, the costs of inauthenticity in terms of our feeling and being can be high, attacking our very sense of self, as Quintin suggested in an early email (October 1998):

> For whatever reason, whether it is reality or in my head, I do generally find it very hard 'to roll out my maps' in this university. The support gained from talking to you, Judy and Alison has allowed me to take a much firmer stand on this. The support is about losing the fear to stand up and be counted for my beliefs. I have experienced a serious loss of personal identity at times while working here, in that I believe myself forced to fit into some mould. This rather goes against the point of working in a university for me. The work we are carrying out is allowing me a bit of space to rebuild that identity and with that in place to choose clearly the particular form I take. It is an exciting moment.

On another occasion, he said: 'It's about going back and saying "Well what do I want to be doing here?" and actually standing up and being counted and saying "I believe in this and I want you to listen"' (Group discussion, Ross Priory, May 1999). Quintin highlights here what Anderson (1998: 596) reminds us of: that in the face of a growing consumerist and market-oriented hegemony, and divisions along race, class and gender:

> the constitution of an authentic self through participation in democratic community may become increasingly rare . . . it is crucial that we better understand not only how authentic forms of participation can constitute more authentic private selves and public citizens but also how they lead to the constitution of a more democratic and socially just society.

Of course, the meetings of the whole group constituted only one public space, albeit a key one in building our sense of critical community. There were many other spaces and times when group members sought each other out to discuss work, or to work through tensions.

Our educational action research projects and the reflective cycles of improvement constituted the 'content' of our collaboration, and realized practically our commitment to being learners ourselves. Such collaboration is also consistent with a view of professionalism as dialectical rather than consensual, where 'constrained disagreement' might be a productive basis for action, critique and collaboration (Lomax, 1999). We sought to explore the building of 'educative relationships' in which learning was mutual, generated through self-reflection on what we did and how we did it, but also inter-subjectively, where we communicated our understandings to others who challenged and questioned. Lomax (1999: 14) describes this as a 'double dialectic of learning' of both personal development and critical community. It affirmed the social, the intersubjective and the collective, not in order simply narcissistically to glorify our 'voices', but to understand and theorize our experiences as part of a broader politics of (educational) engagement.

Different voices, different perspectives and better knowledge

We had set out to 'do criticality', shifting from what we actually did, the real concrete images and detailed everyday moments of student learning, struggle and achievement, to wider issues of intellectual, social and economic possibility. Such moves, embedded in our collaboration, involved reflecting on our own views and assumptions in particular cultures of power, and holding these perspectives open to challenge. Being able to do this with others was crucial for all of us; indeed reflecting alone on the silences and contradictions in ones' own thinking and practice is arguably rather more difficult. As Burbules and Beck (1999: 61) remind us, 'we are enabled to do it through our conversations with others, especially others not like us.' They go on to emphasize the importance of the conditions under which such conversation is possible, 'conditions of plurality, tolerance, and respect', as well, they write, as our own personal and interpersonal willingness to engage in such exchanges. Of course, criticality always had a double loop of meaning – we sought to enable our students' development as critical persons, yet we were also working to realize a critical professionality for ourselves.

There are important epistemological aspects to collaboration as well, as Griffiths (1998) emphasizes. If hegemony works to perpetuate the status quo and maintain control, then keeping open different ways of seeing and voicing different experiences seems significant if we are to avoid consensual relations (or a search for them) hardening into their own hegemonic regime of truth within a group. Obliterating disagreements and eliminating frictions may well simply mask the power relations which are anyway present in any interactive encounter. Thus consensus and agreement may well be more rather than less problematic. As Lukes (1974: 23) warns, 'the most effective and insidious use of power is to prevent conflict arising in the first place.' At issue is that working with many different voices and different perspectives in a framework of mutual support and knowledge generates more responsible and inclusive knowledge. This is very unlike dominant modes of knowledge production in the academy, which are competitive and adversarial (even where working in teams is part of the process). Perhaps, then, rather than coming unstuck through our differences we were building participation and acknowledging the power circulating in our group.

Collaboration, for all the 'secrets and lies' it demands in the telling, is ethically desirable, as Griffiths (1998) explains. Learning together through educational research is better done with, rather than on, others. From a methodological point of view, working together enabled the serious exploration of different insights across disciplines and experiences. Lather (1986) describes this as 'construct validity', in that the inquiry process draws upon the perceived truths of all participants (in the case of our research projects, including those of our students). This facilitates the emergence, Lather writes, of 'counter patterns' which help to push at our own thinking.

Patricia Williams tells a story about herself and her younger sister driving one summer along the highway to Maine and arguing about the colour of the road. Her sister insisted the road was purple; Williams countered by insisting it was black:

> After I had harangued her into admitting it was black, my father gently pointed out that my sister still saw it as purple . . . My sister and I will probably argue about the hue of life's road forever. But the lesson I learned from listening to her wild perceptions is that it really is possible to see things – even the most concrete things – simultaneously yet differently; and that seeing simultaneously yet differently is more easily done by two people than one, but that one person can get the hang of it with time and effort.

> (Williams, 1993: 149–50)

In the end, travelling the highway together, the conditions needed to establish our collective work involved resources of time and shared commitments to doing justice to the tricky business of teaching and student learning. Shared dialogue and shared work nurtured our collaboration, while our mutual regard framed a supportive space. The conversations across our disciplines were important; and our differences offered points of challenge and growth. As importantly, we had fun! We enjoyed the work, we loved hearing about the different projects and our meetings over shared meals cemented friendships alongside professional relationships. Not only did we work to build a community, we recognized the need for respect and care for each other as individuals as well. We came away not quite the same people as when we began working together.

Nor should these processes be underestimated or dismissed under present conditions of (im)possibility in our universities. One of us captured the fragmentation and alienation that seems increasingly to pervade academic life with the following anecdote, which followed his comment that pressurized staff in his department no longer bothered to meet and chat over coffee:

We don't even have a room to meet for coffee. We finally, after several years of insistence, bought a coffee machine but had nowhere to put it. The secretary is allergic to the smell of coffee so we couldn't use her office. I offered to put it in my room but at least two members of the department wouldn't dream of having coffee with me. So the coffee machine sits in its pristine box in the office while we try to work out what to do with it!

(Group discussion, March 1999)

Nor do we experience much genuine collaboration through our research, where assessing our productivity requires knowing which bits of the research belong to whom. The basic idea turns on the assumption that all our understandings are entirely our own and no one else has any part in them.

With this seems to go a climate of suspicion and envy, where there are no spaces to share success. In Chapter 2 I discussed the feelings of acute, rather than productive, marginality that caught up with us from time to time. Alison, trying to capture something of how this felt to her, had sent me a piece from a poem by Elizabeth Jennings called 'Rather like a Peacock'. The extract explained how when a bird is seen by its fellows as too 'bright', this brightness (enthusiasm, say, for university teaching) is seen not as attractive or enticing or embracing, but as a threat, a danger to be driven off. The 'bright' bird who attempts to break set and to challenge the normalizing discourses of teaching and learning in his or her subject in higher education, might similarly provoke a backlash from colleagues.

In sending the poem, Alison was highlighting again that conditions, both local and institutional, might not always work in the interests of authentic participation or 'difference', where this difference is one in which teaching is talked about and practised in ways which might threaten more established (and comfortable) ways of working. Guerillas at the chalkface sounds bold, exciting and dramatic (the poem uses the language of threat, danger, attack) – the everyday reality may be far less welcome and, as the poem suggests, more hazardous. Practising new forms of professional agreement and different kinds of intellectual exchanges for wholly different learning communities generates both safety and threat. This is exemplified in these comments by Mike in response to an earlier draft of this chapter, which, at the same time, provide the connecting threads to the issues raised and discussed in the first chapter:

Somewhere along the line we are implying that this is a kind of rehearsal, an evidential base for a wholly different kind of learning community. It is that which provokes such extreme reactions from some of those around us. Of course people might be jealous that we talk, and debate, learn and so patently enjoy the encounter . . . But the hostility has to do with something else I feel – the suggestion that at every level, learning environments could be characterized by free exchange as opposed to trade and barter. And the implication of this is the end of the view of ideas and learning as commodities 'owned' by X or Y, and in turn the abandonment of the commerce in ideas, which is what so much academic life is actually about today. Isn't that the ultimate implication, albeit a fairly distant one at this stage?

For us, then, critical collaboration was a practice, 'a way of being as well as a way of thinking, a relation to others as well as an intellectual capacity' (Anderson, 1999: 62), a challenge to dominant discourses of professionalism and a market in higher education. In writing about learning and agency as social and collective, ours and that of our students, Nixon and his colleagues (1996: 135) capture the processes that I think occurred in the Barcelona Group, even given the qualifications about 'success' and 'victory' raised in this and previous chapters:

There is no solitary learning: we can only create our worlds together. The unfolding agency of the self always grows out of the interaction with others. It is inescapably a social creation. We can only develop as persons with and through others; the conception of the self presupposes an understanding of what we are to become and this always unfolds through our relationship with others . . . The self can only find its identity in and through others and membership of communities.

References

Anderson, G. L. (1998) Towards authentic participation: deconstructing the discourses of participatory reforms in education, *American Educational Research Journal*, 35 (4), 571–603.

Barnett, R. (1997) *Higher Education: A Critical Business*. Buckingham: SRHE/Open University Press.

Burbules, N. C. and Berk, R. (1999) Critical thinking and critical pedagogy: relations, differences and limits, in T. S. Popkewitz and L. Fendler (eds) *Critical Theories in Education: Changing Terrains of Knowledge and Politics*. New York: Routledge.

Cameron, D. (2000) *Good to Talk?* London: Sage.

Castells, M. (1997) *The Power of Identity*. Oxford: Blackwell.

Ellsworth, E. (1997) *Teaching Positions: Difference, Pedagogy and the Power of Address*. New York: Teachers College Press.

Gilligan, C. (1982) *In a Different Voice*. London: Harvard University Press.

Goleman, D. (1996) *Emotional Intelligence: Why It Can Matter More than IQ*. London: Bloomsbury Press.

Goodson, I. and Walker, R. (1995) Telling tales, in H. McEwan and K. Egan (eds) *Narrative in Teaching, Learning and Research*. New York: Teachers College Press.

Greene, M. (1995) *Releasing the Imagination: Essays on Education, the Arts and Social Change*. San Francisco: Jossey-Bass.

Griffiths, M. (1998) Telling stories about collaboration: secrets and lies? Paper presented at the annual conference of the British Educational Research Association, Belfast, August.

Jennings, E. (1986) 'Rather like a Peacock', *Collected Poems 1953–1985*. Manchester: Carcanet.

John-Steiner, V., Weber, R. J. and Minnis, M. (1998) The challenge of studying collaboration, *American Educational Research Journal*, 35 (4), 773–83.

Kenway, J. and Willis, S., with Blackmore, J. and Rennie, L. (1997) *Answering Back: Girls, Boys and Feminism in Schools*. London: Routledge.

Lather, P. (1986) Research as praxis, *Harvard Educational Review*, 56 (3), 257–77.

Lave, J. and Wenger, E. (1999) Learning and pedagogy in communities of practice, in J. Leach and B. Moon (eds) *Learners and Pedagogy*. London: Paul Chapman/ The Open University.

Lomax, P. (1999) Working together for educative community through research, *Research Intelligence*, 68, 11–16.

Lopez, B. (1986) *Arctic Dream*. New York: Bantam Books.

Lukes, S. (1974) *Power: A Radical View*. Basingstoke: Macmillan.

Malcolm, J. and Zukas, M. (2000) *Becoming an Educator: Communities of Practice in Higher Education*. Leeds: Department of Continuing Education, University of Leeds.

Nixon, J., Beattie, M., Challis, M. and Walker, M. (1998) What does it mean to be an academic? A colloquium, *Teaching in Higher Education*, 3 (3), 277–98.

Nixon, J., Martin, J., McKeown, P. and Ranson, S. (1996) *Encouraging Learning: towards a Theory of the Learning School*. Buckingham: Open University Press.

Nixon, J., Martin, J., McKeown, P. and Ranson, S. (1997) Towards a learning profession: changing codes of occupational practice within the new management of education, *British Journal of Sociology of Education*, 18 (1), 5–28

Richardson, L. (1994) *Fields of Play*. New Brunswick, NJ: Rutgers University Press.

Rowland, S. (1999) The role of theory in a pedagogical model for lecturers in higher education, *Studies in Higher Education*, 24 (3), 303–14.

Samara, D. J. and Luce-Kapler, R. (1993) Action research as a writerly text, *Educational Action Research*, 1 (3), 278–89.

Tannen D. (1995) *Talking 9 to 5*. London: Virago.

Williams, P. (1993) *The Alchemy of Race and Rights*. London: Virago.

Williams, R. (1977) *Marxism and Literature*. Oxford: Oxford University Press.

Part 2

Teachers and Learners in Action

4

Introducing a Mentoring Programme

Judy Wilkinson

The need for a mentoring programme: 'to chase the mental fogs away'

Reflections on my personal journey over the two years I spent on the mentoring project and with the Barcelona Group are exemplified by the quotes in the section headings, from Thomas Crichton (1990: 53–4) and Norman MacCaig (1993: 233). It was an experience that contained both joy and anguish, during which my attitude to learning and teaching was challenged and my perception of the role of an academic was radically changed.

After joining the Department of Electronics and Electrical Engineering as a lecturer in 1968, I became increasingly involved with issues of teaching and learning. At first I was concerned with questions like the following. Should engineering students be aware of the role of engineers in the community? Are they motivated by the social side of engineering or just the technical challenges? Should ideas of the responsibility of an engineer within society be fostered, or is it sufficient to teach them a high level of technical competence? I believed that, because engineering is a vocational subject, I should think about the personal as well as the technical skills required by a practising engineer. I accepted the importance of developing critical awareness and behaviour in engineering students, and after discussions in the Barcelona Group, I wondered whether the curriculum should be developed to fulfil Barnett's (1997: 104) dictat that 'understanding has to be reunited with performance so as to produce action. Critique in the domain of knowledge has to be brought into a relationship with critique in the domain of the world.' The tension in engineering education comes in balancing the overlapping domains of technical, social and industrial knowledge without overburdening the students. How do our students learn to be competent engineers, who are also socially aware and concerned with the problems facing the world today?

The content, teaching and assessment for these domains was the focus for a series of reports and consultation documents from the 1970s onwards – outlined, for example, in the Finneston Report (1980) and occasional papers from the Engineering Professors Conference (1991, 1993). In 1997 the Engineering Council produced a remit on Standards and Routes to Registration (SARTOR) for the accreditation of engineers. This document interweaves the social and industrial requirements with the technical ones. As well as technical knowledge and understanding, all engineering students are expected to 'develop skills in managing people, projects, resources and time and be aware of the financial, economic, social, ethical and environmental factors of significance to engineering' (Institution of Electrical Engineers, 1999: 4). In addition, masters of engineering (MEng) students will be 'provided with a wide educational foundation for leadership, social and business awareness and wider awareness of risk, environmental, health and safety and regulatory issues.'

Until the formation of the Barcelona Group and the inter-curricular discussions this forum engendered, my educational concerns were mainly based on analysing and considering ways of implementing the recommendations from these documents for the curriculum. The technical understanding and knowledge were well covered in the existing courses but I felt that the social and industrial domains required a different approach. Engineering as a subject is not taught at school. Students have been exposed to mathematical and physical concepts on which the discipline is based but have little idea what it means 'to be an engineer', what an engineer does or the ethos of the discipline.

During the 1980s and 1990s, I set up and organized the fifth year of the MEng degree course. As part of this I worked with industrialists both in Scotland and abroad, placing students for six months on technical research projects in companies outside the UK. While visiting the manufacturing plants and talking to personnel managers, I became aware that, very often, when people joined a company as new employees, they were given 'induction' training. They were introduced to the company, philosophy and culture, as well as specifically trained for the task in hand. The length of the course depended on the level of employment, but new employees were not usually placed straight on the production line. However, apart from one 'induction day' in the week before term began, new students in the department started on the first day with a lecture in mathematics. They were not told why they were taking mathematics, how they were expected to take in or use the information or, apart from a guide to course content and assessment, what the expectations of the department for their progress were. I had found that when the more mature fifth year students went abroad it took about three months for them to recover from the culture shock and settle into their project. New undergraduates also suffer a culture shock. Recently, Caroline Baillie (1999: 9) realized that the problem is widespread when she surveyed over seventy institutions in twelve countries and found that 'a whole range of approaches have been implemented from survival kits and study guidance or activity weeks to a complete revamping of first year to make it an induction to academic studies.'

Most of our students feel disorientated at the start of university. They are thrown into a strange environment with about a hundred people they have never met before, expected to absorb information from lectures where probably they have been used to worksheets and constant feedback, to manage their time without 'nagging' from parents and teachers and to behave sensibly. At the same time there is immense advertising and peer pressure to take part in a hectic social life.

In 1997, with these issues in mind, I wrote a proposal to set up a mentoring scheme for first year students in the department, in which a group of about eight or nine of them met once a week with a research associate or postgraduate student to act as facilitator. The programme was designed to identify actions and events which would help students to settle into the department, make friends, develop good patterns of working and begin to understand the philosophy of engineering. I believed that such a programme would help to overcome the initial culture shock and allow the students to start thinking holistically about their course. Rather than compartmentalizing their technical knowledge they would start to see the 'joined up thinking' between the technical, industrial and social domains of engineering. Until students are settled and confident it is very difficult for them to address the curriculum with more than a reflex action, responding only to assessment requirements. Mentoring would offer an opportunity to introduce an ethos of caring and debate into the first year that could be developed in subsequent years through a curriculum that addressed all three engineering domains – technical, social and industrial. The programme also sought to acknowledge the importance of the students as people and the importance of their development as confident learners.

This programme was supported and funded by the Head of Department, Professor Steve Beaumont, because he was concerned about the drop-out rate from engineering courses, which had been as high as 30 per cent of the initial intake. This issue is intertwined with trying to bridge the difference between school and university – it has been shown that students drop out because they do not see the relevance of the course work (Entwistle and Hounsell, 1989), or are not interested in the basic engineering skills, which are inculcated in first year. Either they have misconceptions about what an engineer does and hence about what an engineering course should contain, or they do not want a purely technical curriculum. Of course, there are many other reasons why students drop out or do not achieve their potential and some of these were identified and addressed in the mentoring programme. Steve hoped that a successful mentoring scheme would motivate and hence retain the first year students; a particular concern in engineering departments where recruitment remains an ongoing problem.

Structure of the degree: 'To teach the youth within his studious bower'

Most students take a four-year honours degree course, with 90 first year students entering in 1997 and 88 students in 1998. In common with many other engineering departments there is a significant drop-out rate in the first and second years, which, in Glasgow, is compensated for by a large cohort of foreign students entering in the third year. About 50 per cent of the graduating class are home students and between eight and 18 students take the fifth year MEng degree course. Most of the students come directly from school, having taken either Highers or Sixth Year Studies.[1] There are a small number of women (average between 10 and 15 per cent) and a few mature students.

The course is very technical, with 20 specialized options offered in the fourth year, based on the research interests of the staff, many of whom have international reputations in their fields. (The department is grade 5 in research.) The first year curriculum for most students consists of 40 credits in electronics and electrical engineering, 20 credits in engineering physics, 50 credits in engineering mathematics and 20 credits in computing. Students studying joint honours with music take 40 credits in music instead of physics and computing. Other joint courses in avionics, software engineering and physics have slightly different technical courses in place of physics and computing. Because of this technical bias, I wished to introduce some wider awareness of the role of the engineer in society, some help with communication skills and some leavening of the syllabus through the mentoring scheme that would tie in with the recommendations of SARTOR. I focused, in particular, on the development of skills in team working and communicating effectively. However, in order to engender these skills there must be an ethos of respect and cooperation, and students should realize the importance of sharing knowledge and gaining understanding by working together. I hoped that, through the mentoring scheme, the mentors would create a safe environment in which the students could begin to discuss, argue, reflect and grow.

Engaging with action research methodology: 'Designed to rouse the latent powers of man'

At the same time as the mentoring scheme was started, Melanie Walker became Director of the Teaching and Learning Service (TLS) in the university and we decided to evaluate the first two years of the programme together. This method of collecting data was a revelation to me. Trained as an applied physicist and working as an engineer, I was used to analysing experimental data and applying rigorous numerical analysis. At first I struggled with the relevance of focus group meetings, written reflections and recorded conversations. I wanted to follow the procedure of object, method, results and conclusions, and find results that were reproducible or at least statistically significant and measurable. In her funding proposal (1997) Melanie had described the principles of action research as 'collaborative, critical inquiry by the teachers/lecturers themselves into their own teaching practices (the practitioner is also the researcher, the research and practice occur simultaneously), into problems of student learning and curriculum problems. Importantly, personal knowledge is valued and integral to the

Figure 4.1 An adaptation of Kolb cycle

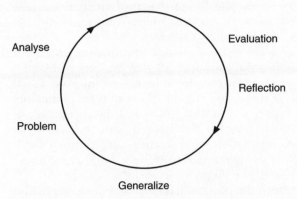

process of critique . . . it should be underpinned also by values of democratic participation and equity.'

I persevered with this rather different approach to research and finally
realized that personal knowledge was important and notes and diaries could
be used as evidence. This practice could be useful for student development as
well as for me. This was reinforced when John Cowan (1998) gave a seminar
at TLS on reflective practice and discussed the Kolb cycle of learning (see
Figure 4.1).

I think that the Kolb cycle appeals to engineers and scientists because we
can relate it to the procedure of scientific research. Scientists often get hung
up with problems of proof and reproducibility of data that they feel are
missing in action research methods. Using the Kolb cycle enables a structure
to be imposed on reflective practice, and even though the types of questions
posed are different, the procedure is familiar. Engineers are also meeting
this approach when talking to industrialists, and increasingly discussions of
strategy in a boardroom context are based on experience and analysis generated by reflection cycles and spirals. Therefore, I could relate the action
research methodology to experience from my engineering background.

Framework of the mentoring scheme and the evaluation: 'to spend, improv'd his idle vacant hour'

As the mentoring scheme started, I was gaining experience in action research and reflective practice. The framework for the scheme, the aims and
the objectives had been determined in the original proposals and were
consistent with current thinking from the Engineering Council. I had read
several books on peer mentoring and mentoring but I was not sure how the
scheme would work in practice. Others, with slightly different aims and
objectives, had failed (Maggie Pollock, personal communication) because

the students and mentors had not engaged together. Maggie had used final year students to mentor first years. She found that in their final year the students are concerned with the work for their degree and many did not have the time or inclination to mentor at this stage.

I wanted sessions in which the groups shared information on career possibilities, branches of engineering, summer jobs, electronics companies in Scotland, sponsorship etc. I envisaged the students finding out about how people think and learn: perhaps studying the different types of memory – visual, oral, learning through practical work etc. – and the psychology of communication – verbal and non-verbal. Interwoven with this would be help for the students in their adaptation to the learning environment, with discussions on time and stress management. Finally, they would argue about issues connected with the role of the engineer in society.

However, the first meeting with the postgraduate mentors made me realize that they did not have the background to facilitate many of these sessions. Research students in an engineering department come from diverse disciplines; they are often physics, chemistry or computing science graduates, so have not thought about engineering and the role of engineers. They have been brought up in technical disciplines and have not confronted the social issues. Therefore I decided that I should try to implement Paolo Freire's teacher/learner approach; Freire (1996: 73) writes that 'without dialogue there is no communication and without communication there can be no true education.' A general framework for the sessions would be agreed but we would meet each week for half an hour to discuss the previous session, share good practice and successful scenarios and try to identify material and training needs for the mentors and the students.

After the first year of the programme (1997/8), evaluation of both the design and the success of the scheme in meeting the objectives was explored through the following questions:

- In what ways is the mentoring/induction project effective (or not) in supporting the first year students in coming to terms with academic work, the departmental culture and expectations, and interpersonal life at the university?
- What ought the shape of such a programme to be in order to be effective in relation to student needs?
- What are these student needs in the first year?

At this stage it was not a research project. I, working with Melanie, just wanted to collect sufficient, reliable evidence to be able to evaluate the effectiveness of the project in terms of its own aims. If the data had sufficient quality and depth then a research-based paper on student experience in coping with the first year of study was possible. Melanie and I collected data from email and reflective conversations between us, my written reflections on meetings with the mentors and on the project as a whole, documents on the project, student attendance sheets, written reflections and audio-taped interviews with focus groups of mentors and students.

The first year of the programme: 'Prepare for action on life's bustling stage'

During the year, the format and content for the mentoring programme were developed from discussions, learning from the mentors' experience and building on their observations. This was not an easy approach, though the evaluation showed that it worked in part and that there were many unexpected benefits and no disasters. Melanie commented:

I was intrigued by what appeared to be, for most of the time, a high level of trust in you ... what they didn't do at any stage was say 'this approach is not working. We want more structure. We don't like the way you are doing this' ... they were then able to reflect on what was going on which was a very sort of facilitative, caring style on your part ... given that it was predominately a group of male students [two women and ten men were involved] they seemed to respond and cope with that in ways I found most intriguing.

(Discussion, May 1998)

I responded: 'I think it works in two ways, that I was respecting them and respecting what they were trying to do ... we were mutually exploring ... I was confident that this [programme] was right and, although there were mistakes, that this was necessary.'

Other engineering departments were also working on helping students to make friends, gain confidence and discuss the course content and requirements, so that symptoms of homesickness and lack of confidence would be alleviated and they would be better equipped to start developing as independent learners. Edward and Middleton (1997) reported a week-long induction course with a team-based contextual investigation. The most positive outcomes from the challenge were noted as integration of students into the school, interaction with their peers and experience of using the university facilities, but the students did not believe the exercise had improved their transferable or technical skills. However, I was attempting a more ambitious programme, wanting to develop independent learning and critical thinking.

In the written reflections from students at the end of the first year of the programme, Melanie and I asked the questions:

* What surprised you about this project?
* What did you enjoy most and why?
* What did you enjoy least and why?
* In general what do you feel you have gained?

And from the mentors we asked:

* What surprised you about this project and your participation in it?
* What did you gain?
* What do you think the students gained?
* What could be done differently next year?

Although the questions were simple, the transcripts and written reports were extremely rich, and that surprised me. The authentic voices of the students shifted my understanding of what was happening and why. The meetings with the mentors, which had taken place after each session during the year, together with their reflections, built a web of attitudes, thoughts and relationships that changed the organization and focus of the scheme.

At the beginning the mentors talked about facilitating a discussion of study skills, so helping the students to learn more effectively. However, neither mentors nor students favoured a didactic approach to this. It was felt that the students had enough formal lectures and mentoring should be more relaxed, focusing on the students' needs. As Mike, a mentor, explained:

> [it was expected] that we would give them talks about personal develop-
> ment, learning skills and so on. Now that is fine if they want it but my
> lot didn't . . . they seemed reasonably confident and they had a mind
> of their own about what they wanted to do . . . they have started to set
> up a non-classically orientated musical society. Now if they were con-
> strained to doing this personal development thing then I think that
> kind of creative input from them wouldn't work.
>
> (Discussion, April 1998)

Gordon, another mentor, introduced visits round the research labs and 'fun' activities because, he said:

> for the first couple of meetings we had a few handouts and I sat down
> and talked to them . . . and I actually got bored about half way through
> the second meeting. I thought that if I'm getting bored with this and
> I'm driving it then they [the students] must be really bored so I said
> 'Let's put the papers down and go to my lab'.

He showed them round his laboratory, got other mentors to show their research areas and also organized activities like petrifying fruit in liquid nitrogen and then breaking it with hammers, 'the sort of thing we have the materials available for in the university but not in high school.' In his written report Gordon amplified his idea:

> I think the mentors are in a unique position of almost authority, which
> allows them to organise an experiment, or activity that is high-tech or
> totally alternative to the students' experiences in the labs. Activities of
> this sort will be fun and informative for the students (and mentor).
>
> (Report, April 1998)

Mentors also changed the venues; some of the groups wished to meet in the union, which is more comfortable than departmental spaces. Food was important in cementing friendships and relaxing the students, and contrib-uting to a friendly, informal atmosphere.

Our evaluation at the end of the first session (Wilkinson *et al.*, 1998) suggested that the limitations of the programme were mainly organiza-tional. One problem was that the scheme was not compulsory, so several of the students dropped out when they had formal assessments due. However, the mentors recognized that, because the programme was not compulsory, they had to offer the students something that they valued. When the students turned up the mentors felt they had achieved something worthwhile. Not surprisingly, several mentors agonized about the attendance figures and felt guilty if students did not attend their sessions. A good suggestion from Craig was that we needed to have some policy on reaching students who were not attending. He explained that 'I was guilty of concentrating on the strong group members and not those who were not attending. We need to stay accessible to all the students – not just those who turn up' (Report, April 1998).

As explained above, there was a mismatch between my expectations, as convenor, and the level of development and experience of the mentors, so that some mentors felt there was a lack of structure in the programme. Background materials were produced as requested at the meetings but, as Chris said, 'A greater "bank" of material could be available on a variety of topics. This could be in the form of notes and key points for specific topics.' Another mentor suggested that:

> it would be a good idea in the future if the information that we wish to impart to the students should be collected well in advance of the start of the sessions so that any problem that we may have in knowing how to approach the subjects can be discussed. For example, I don't think I could confidently start up a discussion about psychology without having either a training session or a discussion with the rest of the mentors.

One of the strengths of the programme was that the mentors were not lecturers, but this also created problems because they were not sure of their function. As Craig said, 'We weren't sure whether we were mentors or kind of guidance teachers or just sort of, what do they call them, prefects I suppose all these different things.' Another comment was:

> it would be useful if the role of the mentor were more clearly defined. This definition may not be static but could reflect that roles do change with time, for instance at the beginning mentors are required to encourage group formation but later they act as facilitators to the demands of the group.

There was a dichotomy between the function of the programme being to ease the transition between school and university for the majority of students or to reduce the drop-out rate. Craig wrote:

> I believe the mentoring programme has been worthwhile with many students gaining something from it. However, I remain slightly sceptical about the overall drop-out rate being reduced as the students who did not attend regularly are the ones I would predict are most likely to drop out or fail. Those with regular attendance are more than likely to continue with the course.

The programme was not always supported openly by the staff in the department. One mentor commented that 'staff input and endorsement is needed to ensure students see the importance and relevance.' Another wrote that 'although the department initiated the sessions I feel there was little encouragement to attend . . . better department back-up may lead to better attendance at sessions and hence targeting people who really need help.'

The evaluation showed that in order for this programme to work well there had to be a level of trust not only between the mentors and the students, but also between the mentors and the academics. Although the mentor was neither friend nor lecturer, he or she had both 'friend-like' and 'teacher-like' characteristics. The students felt close enough to the mentors to be critical of some aspects of university life (in a way in which they never could with a lecturer), while, at the same time, they were confident enough of the mentors' expertise to be able to rely on their greater knowledge and experience for help and advice.

The end of first year: 'to place before the mind a world all new'

At the end of first year I felt that mentoring had helped the students in the transition between school and university. They were more aware of the department, the research and the courses than in previous years. In addition, it had provided a useful channel of communication for the students. Many of the students made comments suggesting that they would find it hard to communicate either their difficulties or their complaints to a lecturer. There was an effective staff–student committee in the department but first year students did not have the knowledge or confidence to use this as a channel of communication. If they had legitimate criticisms, they would tend to discuss them only among themselves. However, the Mentoring Programme gave them an opportunity to air their grievances to someone who, although being in close contact with the department, was not one of their lecturers. Therefore, if the students had complaints about, for example, the course, or the way in which the course work was dealt with, or any other university-related issue, they could bring their dissatisfaction to the mentor and then there was the possibility of the mentor taking action on their behalf, if appropriate, to help to resolve the problem. As Mike put it, 'they're not going to question the lecturer, but they'll question the lecturer to me and then I can find out things like that.' To this extent, the Mentoring Programme acted like a protective 'buffer' for the students – allowing communication, but at the same time protecting the students from any perceived adverse effects of this communication. It had a function as a safety valve for the students, enabling them to ask about, or criticize, aspects of the course, the university or the lecturers without worrying about the consequences. Conversely, the lecturers could explain what was happening to the mentors and know that they were another channel of information to the students. It also started to create an atmosphere where students felt that they could influence the teaching infrastructure. Before students can act they must begin to question, and to legitimize that there must be some channels through which they can initiate change, however small. Educationalists talk about fostering independent learning but for the learner/ teacher model to work students must be given and then encouraged to use their authority. The buffer of the mentoring scheme provided a safe environment in which they could begin to act and explore their authority.

The mentors had tried to explain what engineering was about to their students, and Roger said:

> there was one time we were doing a maths programme and none of us understood a word of it, it was just like double Dutch to us and we went and asked him and he totally explained it and gave us all these examples from engineering and it all suddenly made sense and just things like that, the whole way through.
>
> (Student interview, April 1998)

In addition, the mentors were able to relate the work that the students were doing in the first year to the degree as a whole and that contributed to the students being able to put their studies in perspective. Claire commented that, 'In a sense it can sometimes seem a bit pointless to sit in a maths lecture and learn integration or whatever and you go, "Why, why am I here?" – but when you can see where it's leading to, it makes it an awful lot easier and that definitely worked' (Student interview, April 1998). The mentor's shared experience was useful in giving the students a broader picture of the course as a whole. For instance, Claire explained that she had had no idea about the way in which her course was actually going to progress until her mentor showed her group the sort of things they would be doing in the third and fourth years. This gave her a better idea of her degree structure and how it would evolve.

Mentor learning: 'Designs like these, ye friends of Man pursue'

The benefits for the mentors came as an unexpected result of the programme. When selecting postgraduate and research associates as mentors Steve Beaumont and I had hoped that they would gain in personal development, but how this would happen was not clearly formulated. During the evaluation I realized that the programme encouraged the mentors to reflect on and ultimately evaluate their student experience, to think about group dynamics and team working, to hone their communication skills. There was an opportunity to encourage reflection and even critical action.

The mentors worried about the students and their response to the group. Dan remarked that mentoring had:

given me experience in handling all the different personalities and trying to make sure that, within a group of people, you melt them all in equally ... Those who are quiet and shy, you try and encourage and for those who are taking the leading seat you don't over-concentrate on them [just] because it's easier to.

(Mentor interview, April 1998)

They also reflected on their own personalities and the effect these had on the group. As Alex said, mentoring gave him awareness of working with a group: 'I have learnt the particular traits I tend to fall into and being aware of them has enabled me to feel that I can work better in a group' (Mentor interview, April 1998).

They gave presentations to the students, which turned out to be a very good exercise in simplifying their own research so that the essence of it could be understood by first year students:

I gave one presentation on my research, just as an example. It was incredible because I would start each sentence and think 'God they are not going to understand this' so just trying to present things at a basic level and bring a post doc research project back to student life and reality is, I think, very important.

(Craig, mentor interview, April 1998)

Another mentor commented that he had given the students a 'talk' about his work and 'it wasn't too bad but ... I never realised how far down I would actually have to go ... If you can get things that actually grab their attention. It's focused, it's quite good' (Mentor interview, April 1998). Moreover, unlike in formal presentations to lecturers where they were talking to people who knew and understood their subject, they were challenged to think about the student response. They admitted that the feedback from students was harder and the students did not return if they were not engaged. Dan confessed that he had learned from mistakes what makes an interesting discussion and what does not, 'what facilitates and what doesn't'. He had found that 'visual presentation is the key and I clearly require to sharpen these skills. Perhaps the first session presentation needs to be more dynamic and attractive' (Mentor interview, April 1998). Richard noted that the sessions had 'taught me one important lesson – people will discuss topics they are interested in.'

Not surprisingly, then, mentoring engendered personal reflection, as Mike admitted:

I think, to a certain extent, it might even have forced us to address our own situations and how we came to be where we are. Because you can't, sort of, say, 'Here's my experience and this is what I feel you should do, or this is what you shouldn't do', without actually looking back and evaluating, 'Well, did I do the right thing?' It forced me to learn from my mistakes, because it forced me to go back and acknowledge that I'd made some.

Two mentors took the responsibility to set up training sessions for their students who had misunderstood instructions and not attended a vital workshop. Others drew the attention of staff to problem areas in the curriculum and anomalies in assessments. Mike, who was mentoring electronics with music students, helped to set up a music group and forge contacts with the music industry for them.

As a result of realizing the value of the experience to the mentors, the potential for developing skills in organizing and running teams and personal reflection became one of the areas for evaluation and research. The mentor training was expanded and incorporated ideas from Stephen Rowland (1993) on 'interpretative' teaching and what constitutes an appropriate programme for this kind of professional development.

Second year of the programme: 'a do-it-yourself kit?'

The changes in the second year (1998/9) of the programme were mainly organizational. For example, the mentors had a more central role in the induction day, which introduced them to the students in a relaxed atmosphere and made sure they were an integral part of the initiation process which was designed to be both useful and fun. The training was more focused: for example, besides the initial workshop on small group facilitation, there were short training sessions each week on issues such as peer observation of teaching, communication skills and reflective practice. The sessions with the students were divided between discussions and activities to maintain the students' interest and also fulfil the aims of the programme. The mentors tried to make the sessions enjoyable, as well as useful in terms of the formal curriculum. The bank of source materials was increased with a package of notes for each topic and the materials were discussed prior to the meetings. However, the mentors were still allowed flexibility in the way they used the materials and in the format of their sessions. Where possible the timetabling and group formation were improved so that the mentoring session occurred between lectures and formed part of a 'relaxing break'. Some members of staff and Advisers of Studies[2] supported the programme and recognized the role of the mentors.

The mentors benefited from the experience, coupled with the reflective feedback sessions. In the previous year Craig had reflected on this and said, 'I think it made you think basically, which is not a bad thing . . . I definitely learned from [it] like how you would run a group.' However, one afternoon several mentors had taken their groups in a workshop in the same room. Craig had noticed that, while he talked to his group and was involved with their work, other mentors didn't really try to get their students to talk and those mentors 'never saw themselves as, like trying to teach the group to be a group' (Mentor interview, April 1998). To address this problem of mentor awareness, some of them worked together on peer observation of their sessions. The comments showed that they were using this to develop their understanding of how groups function.

Because there were more formal seminars there were fewer of the wash-up sessions I had held in the first year. Some of the mentors who had been in first year said they missed these and suggested they were useful for sharing information and supporting each other. On reflection I agreed. I had started them for my own sake, because I had no experience of a mentoring scheme and had not taken a mentor group, as it would have been different from the rest, which were run by graduate students or research assistants. However, the evaluation showed how important it is for the mentors to share experiences and learn from each other – dialogue and communication are essential to education.

As the second year progressed, I continued to collect data through reflections and discussions. At the beginning of the year, my perceptions were still fairly scientific and applied, we had identified the organizational problems, incorporated the mentors into the induction day and set up extra training sessions for them. The second phase progressed smoothly, the scheme seemed to be fulfilling the remit, attendance was mainly good and the mentors were enjoying their groups. However, mentoring was still peripheral to the mainstream teaching process. The staff, on the whole, felt it was 'a good thing' but did not bring it into the curriculum. They did not use the reflections of the mentors to discuss the educational process and content or engage in dialogue directly with the students.

My learning and critical professionalism: 'to measure lightning with a footrule'

At this point (September 1998) the Barcelona Group was formed and the subsequent discussions and seminars dislocated my whole approach to learning and teaching.

Melanie, in her proposal for internal funding for the seconded academic staff who would make up the Barcelona Group, had highlighted that:

> collaborative and scholarly action research serves to challenge technocratic approaches to education understanding, innovation and improvement. Such technocratic approaches ('tips for teachers', or skills acquired and reproduced) are akin to the 'surface' learning strategies we wish to discourage on the part of our students.

The Barcelona Group were reading extracts from Barnett's (1997) book, and discussing an academic's responsibility, namely that the university has a responsibility as a university 'to develop the capacity within students to take up critical stances in the world and not just towards the world' (Barnett, 1997: 112). What did this imply in the education of engineering students?

How could the requirements for deep technical knowledge, skills and understanding be interwoven with social development issues? Is it possible to have a mixed approach where some teachers are 'bankers' who, as Freire (1996: 53) writes, believe that the 'scope of action allowed students extends only as far as receiving, filing and storing the deposits . . . [students] are turned into "containers", into "receptacles" to be filled by the teacher', while a critical academic believes with Freire that the 'banking' concept of education is wrong and:

> knowledge emerges only through invention, re-invention through the restless, important, continuing, hopeful inquiry human beings pursue in the world, with the world and with each other . . . education must begin with the solution of the teacher–student contradiction by reconciling the poles of contradiction so that both are simultaneously teacher and student.

Should there be a need for a scheme, part of which has been shown to act as a buffer between staff and students?

Most mentors and students were working together and the excitement of this mode of learning had emerged:

> We had a brilliant laugh, we did some of the most crazy things . . . we were down seeing all about the lasers, the semi-conductor lasers and things . . . You didn't really realize it at the time but afterwards when you thought about what you'd done, you thought 'Oh yeah, I did actually learn something about engineering then'.
>
> (Student interview, April 1998)

The feedback showed that the mentors were both teachers and learners with their groups. For example, the students were concerned about an oral exam they had to take for their mathematics course. Charles, one of the mentors, suggested that in one session they could discuss how to make a presentation. In the next session he would give a talk about his research and they could assess him on the criteria they had agreed in the previous session. This worked very well and the rest of the mentors used the situation. One student described how his mentor:

> gave us a demonstration on one of the things he was doing in his work and it was like an idea of how you could do a presentation instead of forcing you to do it. Because nobody would have done it basically, nobody would have turned up. He did it himself, put himself out, we didn't have to do anything – showed us how to do it and then we commented on it.
>
> (Student interview, April 1999)

Some of the mentors managed to create a robust partnership with their students, as Mike explained: 'One of my hopes was that I could sit back and let them continue without me – this actually happened. Finally it must have worked – they have invited me to the Beer bar next week even though there is no mentoring session' (Mentor report, April 1999). The mentoring scheme did seem to help the mentors to reflect on the relation between students and teachers and consider how both should work together. The evaluation showed that at times the groups fulfilled Freire's dictum that:

> [the educator's] efforts must co-incide with those of the student to engage in critical thinking and the quest for mutual humanization. Her efforts must be imbued with a profound trust in people and their creative power. To achieve this they must be partners of the students in their relations with them.
>
> (Freire, 1996: 56)

We had not read any educational texts in the mentor groups, and the teaching material consisted of tips for learning and careers advice which were gathered from the web or from engineering education handouts. However, as I read further and became concerned about Foucault's (1980) analysis of the structures of power and how groups dominate by 'winning and shaping consent so that the power of the dominant classes appears both legitimate and natural' (Hall, quoted in Hebdige, 1993: 364). I realized that such questions had emerged naturally in the mentors' meetings. For example, the mentors were aware of problems of dominance and wanted to explore them. In his Mentor's report of April 1999, Ian appreciated 'the opportunity to lead a group and excite the group into forming itself. I learned how difficult it is to try and achieve that without dominating', while Alex said, 'even if I'm going to dominate I can at least be aware of it and try and be sensitive to that.' The authority of the teacher was discussed in the group meetings with mentors lamenting that 'it is difficult to make them talk about what they want, they are not used to that', and 'When I was asking them what they would like to talk about the following week, I could almost hear them say, "we don't know, *you* should know, this is your session".'

In terms of the original remit, the mentoring scheme could be viewed as 'successful'. It helped the students to settle in, form friendships and have a forum for discussion of the courses and the course content. Lipton wrote:

> When doing mentoring, I often felt that I was no good at it and it is just not working. But the feedback made me realise that even if it does not help all the students, it helps some of them. For each student that gained from it, that is one more student doing better and it has made a difference. It is worth it.
>
> (Mentor report, April 1999)

At one level the programme worked – the mentors had a good relationship with their students and helped them to settle into the culture of the department. But should this be necessary? I wanted the students to be confident and comfortable within the department and the university but I had not faced Melanie's question:

To what extent is this project consistent with the departmental culture or to what extent is it actually the opposite? What comes through in a lot of different places reading through the mentors' reflections is that they are saying they want more departmental muscle as it were put behind it. They struggle with the fact that it is not compulsory and it is not being pushed by people who have the power... what kinds of things might be going on there?

(Discussion, May 1998)

This brought me back to Mike Gonzalez's comment at one of our group meetings that 'the fact that I am generating knowledge does not actually tell me how I function in the world until I ask a further question which is to what end.'

I began to feel that the mentoring programme was in some sense patching up a system that was technocratic and hence, perhaps, inherently unsound. Mentoring should only be used as part of an educational experience that is based on praxis, not just doing – as Aristotle said, 'Life is praxis, not doing. Mere doing is the action of a slave.' Freire (1996) writes that education is 'always an action either for the domestication of people or for their liberation.' If it is not part of a reflective and critical educational culture, mentoring can help in the domestication of students – was this the result of the programme if the objectives were not incorporated into the mainstream educational priorities of the department?

Year 3, where next? 'Trains have to reach their destination'

During the second year that the programme was running, the Barcelona Group discussed Barnett's (1997: 164) contention that:

teaching, in so far as it contains any hint of transmission of knowledge, of institutional authority or of assimilation on the part of the student has to be expunged not just from our vocabulary but from our practices in higher education ... The development of a human being cannot be taught, but it can flourish amidst an appropriate set of human experiences ... The task of the teacher ... is that of constructing a range of situations where the critical life in all its demands, its forms of action and its discursive competence can be sustained.

There were reservations in the group about this and discussions on the authority of the teacher and his or her role in learning. As a result of the discussions, I began to feel concerned about the effect of the mentoring scheme. I started questioning if such a programme was domesticating the students rather than developing them as critical thinkers. Could the mentoring scheme work if it was just an addition to the curriculum rather than integrated into a system that was based round discussing and evaluating the educational experience? How far could such a scheme change the students' approach to learning if it was part of a predominantly 'bankers' educational system? There was evidence that it was developing the mentors but the value to students was less clear. I wanted discussions and debate in the department about these issues and how we should structure the learning environment.

I had been pleased because I felt that in the mentoring programme we were fulfilling Freire's (1996: 72) vision that 'Founding itself upon love, humility and faith, dialogue becomes a horizontal relationship of which mutual trust between the dialoguers is the logical consequence.' However, looking back I realize that at times during the first year, I felt that I was in the middle of an educational experiment balancing the demands of mentors and students and desperately trying to keep the show on the road. During a discussion, with friends, on my feelings at this time, Di Bumpus, an artist, quoted David Harvey's (1990: 79) statement on postmodernism to me: 'Postmodernism swims, even wallows, in the fragmentary and the chaotic currents of change as if that is all there is.' This quotation illuminated my position. I realized that the canons of other disciplines are sympathetic to and can enhance the development of my own work. We are all influenced by current intellectual concerns and I now felt that, in designing a learning environment for students, academics should be aware of the dominant discourses of our time. Just as the arts have been influenced by quantum and chaos theories, so engineering practice and education are influenced by the discourses of modernism and postmodernism. I wanted the students to enjoy the intellectual 'pursuit of difficulty' (Ryan, 1999: 164). This does not mean that engineering students should study Derrida or Baudrillard but that, perhaps, an aim of the mentoring process should be to create a love of discussion and argument which makes students aware of the culture of other disciplines. Part of the philosophy employed in designing the MEng degree was that, while engineering students could not be experts in finance, law, marketing or business management, they would have a broad introduction to these disciplines. As practising engineers, they should be aware of the background and concerns of professionals in these fields. It seems to me that, similarly, all students should be exposed to cross-disciplinary ideas that can illuminate their present condition.

I had tried to suggest ways of changing the approach to the first year curriculum to develop the teacher/learner rather than the banker model, to create an intellectual, exciting, vibrant learning environment for the students. However, for 1999/2000, the Director of Undergraduate studies for the department did not wish to consider changing the approach to learning in the first year. Without some critical reappraisal, I did not feel the mentoring scheme was viable, but he believed that it was fine and should be continued in the present format. As a result of this divergence of views, I was not involved in the third year of the scheme. Mentoring continued with only minor changes to the organization. The format of the induction day meant that the groups did not form until the afternoon and were made up without ensuring the students shared the same courses or would meet in labs or tutorial groups. An emphasis was put on understanding the research in the department, with formal tours round the laboratories rather than through the mentors sharing their enthusiasms with the students. A preliminary evaluation suggested that fewer than half the students attended the sessions and, although the new mentors were enthusiastic, students did not see the relevance to their curriculum.

The issues raised in the organization and implementation of a mentoring scheme illustrate the debate in educational circles. Recently, Blake *et al.* (1998) have discussed Barnett's view that 'higher education is being locked into a Weberian cage of prescriptive rationality, of given ends and of operationalism' (p. 56) and Dewey's premise that 'through democratic, open relationships, as opposed to autocratic and authoritarian ones, however benign, we learn from and with one another' (p. 100). Mentoring is an opportunity to develop such relationships but, to work, it needs to be part of the educational process, to be embedded within the context of the critical experiences and situations within the curriculum. My personal development and reflections on both the mentoring scheme and the first year curriculum in the department made me realize that, although it had positive benefits in terms of giving advice to the students, it was essentially helping the existing practice to continue. It is very difficult to provide a learning environment that is supportive, reflective and critical if there is not a strong departmental ethos with shared values and approach. The three domains of engineering education – the technical, the social and the industrial – can only be joined by a Freirian web of love, humility and faith.

Notes

1. Highers are taken in Scotland usually at the end of the fifth year, a year after the standard grade, which corresponds to GCSEs in England and Wales. A new Higher Still syllabus is being introduced in 2000 which will be taught over two years. Scottish students tend to take three or four Highers and are broader based than English students. Sixth Year Studies are more advanced and tend to be taken in the specialization, so are more akin to A levels.
2. An Adviser of Studies' principal function is to help with appropriate subject choices at the start of each session. They also provide advice throughout the year to students who experience any kind of difficulties which might impinge on their studies.

References

Baillie, C. (1999) First year experiences in engineering education: a comparative study. Unpublished report, Imperial College, London.

Barnett, R. (1997) *Higher Education: A Critical Business.* Buckingham: SRHE/Open University Press.

Blake, N., Smith, R. and Standish, P. (1998) *The Universities We Need*. London: Kogan Page.

Cowan, J. (1998) *On Becoming an Innovative University Teacher*. Buckingham: SRHE/ Open University Press.

Crichton, T. (1990) The Library. In T. Leonard (ed.) *Radical Renfrew*. Edinburgh: Polygon Press.

Edward, N. and Middleton, J. (1997) Induction – A contextual approach to the start of the Engineers' formation Proceedings. SERA Annual Conference, Dundee, September.

Engineering Council (1997) SARTOR Standards and routes to registration 1997. Unpublished report, Engineering Council, London.

Engineering Professors' Conference (1991) *The Future Pattern of First Degree Course in Engineering – A Discussion Document*. London: Engineering Professors' Council.

Engineering Professors' Conference (1993) *Developments in First Degree Course in Engineering – A Discussion Document*. London: Engineering Professors' Council.

Entwistle, N. and Hounsell, D. (1989) *The Performance of Electrical Engineering Students in Scottish Higher Education. Final report to the Scottish Education Department*. Edinburgh: University of Edinburgh.

Finneston, M. (1980) *Engineering Our Future: Report of the Committee of Inquiry into the Engineering Profession*. London: HMSO.

Foucault, M. (1980) *Power/Knowledge: Selected Interviews and Other Writings 1972–1977*. New York: Pantheon.

Freire, P. (1996) *The Pedagogy of the Oppressed*. London: Penguin Books.

Harvey, D. (1990) *The Condition of Postmodernity*. Oxford: Blackwell.

Hebgige, D. (1993) From culture to hegemony, in S. During (ed.) *The Cultural Studies Reader*. London: Routledge.

Institution of Electrical Engineers (1999) *Response to SARTOR 1997*, www.iee.org.uk/ SARTOR/sartor97.htm

MacCaig, N. (1993) *Collected Poems*. London: Chatto and Windus.

Moore, R. (1995) *Student Retention Rates: Final Report*. Sheffield: Division of Access and Guidance, Sheffield Hallam University.

Rowland, S. (1993) *The Enquiring Tutor: Exploring the Process of Professional Learning*. London: Falmer Press.

Ryan, A. (1999) *Liberal Anxieties and Liberal Education*. London: Profile Books.

Wilkinson, J., Walker, M. and Rolfe, L. M. (1998) Evaluation Report on Mentoring in the Department of Electronics and Electrical Engineering, University of Glasgow. Unpublished report, Teaching and Learning Service, University of Glasgow.

5

Using Debates in Developing Students' Critical Thinking

Chris Warhurst

Introduction

This chapter explores my interest in developing university students' capacity for critical thinking, through the use of debates as a method of teaching in one of my undergraduate courses. It outlines my perspective on the importance of critical thinking as part of: an individual's personal development and contribution to society; a university's educational purpose; and a skill now being increasingly demanded by employers. The chapter further considers how innovations in teaching, of which the action research reported here is a part, are occurring within structural changes to university education (see also Chapter 1), changes in the organization of the economy and political imperatives to foster 'good citizenship'.

The research reported here is drawn from a small-scale project in 1997/8 in which I examined the use of debates as an integral part of my teaching of one of my undergraduate honours courses. My research suggests that the use of debates in the classroom setting: first, enabled students to accept the validity of their own ideas, in other words that they themselves could offer substantive positions on issues; and, second, gave them the confidence to challenge the accepted or existing positions of others. As a result, students were able to contribute to the body of ideas on particular issues. In so doing, these students were imbued with a capacity to contribute to innovation (what used to be called 'change') beyond the ivory tower, thus creating a situation in which teaching strategies, workplace innovation and 'active' citizenship are linked together. The context in which the research was undertaken was, first, developments in higher education over the past decade and, second, changes to the structure of the economy – the emergence of the so-called 'new economy' and types of employees, and new concerns about the need to develop citizenship. The chapter assesses how higher education 'delivery', through the use of debates at the micro level of classrooms, might respond to those changes.

The following section briefly outlines discussion about critical thinking in higher education. The next section then describes and critiques changes in expectations of citizenship, the nature of the economy and higher education, indicating the new 'thinking skills' said to be required of individuals that enable their experimentation and expression. The research methodology and methods are then briefly outlined, and my research focus is described. The main section presents and discusses the research findings, exploring the contribution made by debates to students' learning in general, and the development of critical thinking in particular. The final section offers some concluding remarks on the efficacy of using debates for encouraging and facilitating the development of critical thinking among students.

Critical thinking

Teaching 'thinking' and in particular 'critical thinking' has been a key feature and objective of Western education for the past 2000 years. In medieval universities, where disputations were a form of training in the use of rhetoric in preparation for entry to such professions as law and divinity, critical thinking developed the ability to think 'on one's feet' (Barnett, 1997). Whether through offering specific courses in critical thinking or infusing whole curricula with it, there is now a body of literature concerned with suggesting ways in which lecturers might develop students' capacity to learn to think critically (see, for example, Gent *et al.*, 1999).

One of the catalysts in my own teaching for the introduction of the class debates reported here was my introduction to Perry's (1979) model of intellectual development. As student counsellors in the 1950s and 1960s, Perry and colleagues began examining students' learning experiences at Harvard and Radcliffe Universities in the United States. From this longitudinal study, Perry noted that students' intellectual development appeared to follow a logical progression. He identified nine positions that formed a 'map' of such development, and clustered these into four broad developmental categories: dualism, multiplism, relativism and commitment (to relativism).

Put simply, students intellectual development moves along a continuum. First year students typically employ simplistic right–wrong positions (dualism), in which 'truth' exists, with the role of the lecturer being to impart knowledge to receiving students. Basic information acquisition is the aim. As a consequence, student peers are not seen as legitimate authorities of knowledge. Later students come to appreciate that much knowledge is unknown and that a process of discovery exists towards 'truth'. The role required of the lecturer is to direct students along that path of discovery. Students now learn how to learn. Student peers, while not sources of authority, can support the search for truth, helping in distinguishing between the multiple perspectives that they now acknowledge. (More sophisticated students at this stage might play the 'academic game', which involves strategically providing answers that students believe the lecturer considers correct, rather than answers they themselves believe to be correct.) Finally, students come to accept that knowledge is complex and contextual, so that no absolute truth exists; right and wrong only make sense within specified contexts. These students know that they must exercise judgement, and in doing so modify and expand existing knowledge. The lecturer now becomes source of expertise guiding students, and student peers become sources of learning and diversity (Finster, 1989, 1991). Perry's original model is complex; the main positions outlined above have usefully been simplified into three types (A, B and C students, respectively) by Gray (1997) in his own research into learning chemistry at the University of Glasgow.

This is not to say that these three 'types' map uniformly over each student's development, or that they correspond neatly to levels of study. Broadly, however, according to Perry the desired progress along the continuum for student thinking is clear: towards type C, from a typical first year undergraduate student type A. Type C students can be recognized by their ability to interrogate practice, to evaluate information, and their preparededness to question received authority, not passively receive and accept it. Such students also recognize the contributions that they themselves can make to the development of existing knowledge.

Despite some important methodological criticisms of it,[1] Perry's general model has been widely applied. Moreover, it does resonate with the task for the lecturer, as Barnett (1997) argues, not simply to wean students away from their secure adherence to one authority, but to present them with multiple authorities and make them comfortable with that multiplicity. The model further supports facilitating students' acquisition and development of the resources through which they themselves might produce authoritative knowledge. As with Perry, Barnett (1997: 22) advocates that students be familiar and comfortable with 'an education of multiple frames'. Where Barnett parts company with Perry is in his perception that critical thinking as a requisite of higher education is 'a means to a greater end – better life, emancipation, greater understanding' (p. 3). For him, there are three good reasons for higher education to promote critical thinking. First, it is potentially emancipatory, as students become 'free . . . from dependency on their former taken for granted worlds' (p. 4). Second, it is educationally radical, requiring a jettisoning of didactic teaching in favour of greater classroom participation. Third, it is socially and culturally radical, conceiving higher education as a formative agency 'of critical persons who are not subject to the world but able to act autonomously and purposively within it' (p. 4). The result, argues Barnett, is a possibility of changing the 'universe' and the person who inhabits that universe.

Thus Barnett suggests that critical thinking is not enough. Instead, he advocates higher education's purpose as the development of the 'critical person', the distinction being between the 'reflection' that characterizes the former, and the *action*, or rather 'transformation', that characterizes the latter. The distinction is more than semantic, but it does cast critical thinking as a 'lower order' activity, equating it with single loop learning: that is, a 'focus on continuous improvement of current processes but not on developing new knowledge for alternative . . . possibilities' (Ahanotu, 1998: 182). In practice, critical thinking has to be a prerequisite of students becoming critical persons, and the two cannot be easily decoupled in practice. However, Barnett's emphasis is clearly on the wider purpose of critical thinking. Although both Perry and Barnett would see the development of type C students as desirable, for Perry that outcome is intellectual development. Barnett regards such intellectual development as a means to an end, that end being 'brave acts' (p. 22) by students, so that 'higher education cannot be seen as purely cognitive, but has to be seen as experiential'. Such practice thus encourages students not only to learn about their world and about themselves, but to develop themselves and contribute to their world.

This requires opportunity. For Barnett, 'critical spaces' have to be constructed through higher education pedagogy to encourage students' development of self, knowledge and action. One of the key shifts recently in discussions about teaching students to learn to think critically has been moving the emphasis from being on what the lecturer does to facilitate this learning, to what the student does (Ramsden, 1992). It is not enough to tell students what critical thinking involves, while the lecturer continues to do the 'critical work' in the classroom. Students have to be involved in it; in other words, they must learn by doing. As Gent *et al.* (1999: 514) argue, 'the teacher must approach learning situations as complex webs of student support and challenge, activation of prior knowledge and utilization of cognitive tools, exposure to materials etc., aimed at meaning construction, rather than knowledge transmission, memorization and examination of recall.'

To develop type C students, course design needs a structure that encourages independent learning, encourages student participation, allows students to define problems and develop solutions and includes space for students to argue the merits of these problems and solutions. As outlined below, these features were incorporated into the classroom debates reported here. Hence the introduction and perceived importance of those debates as a learning tool.

The context of the research

The issues outlined above – the need for critical thinking that encourages both reflection and transformation in order to develop both the self and the world – have clear resonance with current debates and developments both within and outwith higher education. Three developments in particular are significant: those related, first, to the political approach to citizenship, second, to the nature of the economy and, finally, to higher education.

David Blunkett (2000: 4), UK Secretary of State for Education and Employment, reminded us recently that during the 'dark days' of Thatcherism 'we were told that "society" itself was merely an outdated ideological concept'. He might also have said that with the pronounced death of the 'social' and the drive towards the marketization of relationships, 'citizens' have been reconfigured as 'customers', consuming 'efficient' services provided by the (quasi-) state for instrumental reasons, education being an example (Levacic, 1993). Here individual rights and not social responsibilities are paramount. With the political changes arising out of the 1997 general election, debates about the relationship between education and citizenship have been renewed, especially in relation to the role that the former contributes to developing the latter. A functionalist approach regards the purpose of education as the inculcation of societal values and norms. Education thus provides the link between the individual and society, providing, for Durkheim (1961), the essential similarities that generate homogeneity and so enable cooperation and solidarity for the maintenance of the social system. For more radical writers, such as Bowles and Gintis (1976), the purpose of education is the reproduction of labour power by preparing the consciousness, behaviour and personalities of students for exploitation in latter employment.

While these debates are beyond the scope of this chapter, it is interesting to note that a functionalist approach appears to inform recent government initiatives in education – although education's role in the reproduction of an apposite labour power is still stressed (see, for example, Department of Trade and Industry, 1999). The government is currently championing the work of the Committee on Education for Citizenship and the Teaching of Democracy in Schools, which seeks to encourage active citizenship as a set of rights, responsibilities and skills that can be taught. Given the declining rate of electorate participation[2] and cynicism among the electorate about the political process, such an initiative is laudable. Park (1999: 53, 55–6), for example, argues that in 'a cohesive and healthy society' students must be able to 'learn about themselves' and become emotionally literate if they are 'to reach out and grasp new forms of knowledge, and to experiment with creative solutions to the challenges that confront them as members of our society.' It is important, one teacher commented, that 'children ... understand that they have a voice and that their opinions can make a difference' (quoted in Crace, 2000: 2). Such endeavours ought not to be confined to schools. All education, Finlayson (1999: 47) has argued, should aim not simply to instil 'fixed blocks of information into their students but to produce autonomy, responsibility and creativity'. Higher education in particular is very well positioned to develop students as 'critical thinkers', a Fabian Society pamphlet notes, because of its capacity to train these students 'to question accepted truths, construct wider principles from evidence, and ask penetrating questions' making them 'fit citizens for a democratic, free thinking polity' (Johnson and Mitter, 1998: 7). Such views resonate with Barnett's (1997) notion of 'critical being' and 'critical persons', that education ought to be producing students who are active citizens familiar and comfortable with experimentation and expression that challenges the status quo in an attempt both to improve society and to enhance democratic participation in it.

The same experimentation and expression are key issues within the changes in economic organization that are now occurring. Many argue that the same capacity for critical thinking that will make students 'fit citizens' will also make them highly attractive to employers because the needs of those employers has now changed. As Warhurst and Thompson (1999a) note, there is a remarkable consensus among the advanced economies' policy-makers, business writers and serious academics that a 'new' economy has emerged driven by information technology, in which the key asset for national economies and firms is knowledge. Creativity and ideas now become the engine of economic growth (see, for example, Reich, 1993; Blair, 1998; von Krogh *et al.*, 1998; Byers, 1999; Castells, 1999; Scottish Office, 1999; Vickery, 1999). 'The future', suggests Barley (1996: xvii), 'will depend more on brains than on brawn.' Consequently, the new skills to be developed by government are the 'thinking' skills used by those working in research, sales, marketing, management and information technology (see, for example, Scottish Enterprise, 1998). This work will focus on problem-identification and problem-solving, and strategic brokering between the two processes.

Ironically, changes to higher education over the past decade or so seemingly undermine the capacity of universities to develop critical thinking among students. Student numbers have risen rapidly and dramatically without commensurate increases in funding to provide the necessary resources to enable this expansion. In Scotland, for example, there is to be an increase of 2,000 higher education places by 2002, with the aim of having 30 per cent of the population with a degree. Thereafter it has been suggested that this target should be raised to 40 or even 50 per cent (Wyllie, 1999). With 'productivity' and 'cost centres' entering the higher education lexicon, it has been suggested that the collegiate governance of universities has been recast along the lines of a 'company model' (Black, 2000: 17); that higher education delivery has become a Fordist mass production process (Parker and Jary, 1995) or simply a manufacturing process (Elliott, 1999); that managerialism has emerged in which financial constraints have led to the adoption of new public sector management (Walsh, 1995); that education in higher education institutes has been usurped by vocational training; and that there is an emerging deprofessionalization of academic labour (Wilson, 1991), compounded by publication requirement constraints (Rowbotham, 1999). It has even been suggested by Parker and Jary that these developments have created the 'McUniversity', with standardized, bite-sized modules served up by 'have a nice day' automatons to increasingly instrumental customers.

Pronouncements of the arrival of the McUniversity are probably premature (although they make for good knock-about conference discussion and group therapy among stressed academics). Other work has been more cautious, pointing out that there is much resistance to these developments on the part of managers, academics and administrators (Prichard and Willmott, 1997; Clark *et al.*, 1998). Nevertheless, concerns continue about the associated 'dumbing down' of higher education, and the need for higher education professionals to be more assertive in taking responsibility for guiding and developing the intellect of students (see, for example, Fox, 1999).

Jettisoning a preoccupation with developing a 'marketable product', higher education should again become 'mind-expanding, generating self-fulfilled, curious citizens, able to question received wisdom and to think and act autonomously' (Black, 2000: 17).

A kind of common ground is thus emerging. As a consequence of changes in higher education, the economy and expectations about citizenship, academics, business writers and policy-makers alike make much of the need to develop 'thinking skills' and more 'critical thinking' among students. These skills would provide for students' engagement in problem-identification, problem-solving and brokering between the two processes, which in turn rely on these students' capacity actively to intervene, experiment and express themselves for the purpose of social, economic and political amelioration. It would be easy to be cynical about the commitment that policy-makers, businesses and even universities might have to such needs: for example, is the goal *obedient* or *enquiring* employees? At issue is how narrow or wide the parameters are around the end purposes of what it means to think critically. However, a more positive approach might strategically capitalize on these shifts as a springboard for initiatives that develop critical thinking among students in higher education.

An outline of the research methodology and methods

An action research approach was adopted, more general and specific details of which can be found in Walker and Warhurst (2000) (and see Chapter 2). Suffice it to note here that this approach integrates self-evaluation through systematic reflection with professional development through planning and practical changes. The research partnership here involved a dialogue between myself as lecturer as practitioner/researcher and Melanie as a higher education practitioner/researcher. Our partnership was intentionally emancipatory in intent, inasmuch as it attempted incremental though modest change, the aim of which was the creation and maintenance of spaces in which students speak back to power, reflectively and critically, and in doing so generate alternative voices. Such an approach encompasses a repositioning of the relationship between students and lecturer, with the students learning to question received authority not just in course content but in method of content delivery. The students were also asked to reflect on the research issues and participate in dialogue about those issues.

A flexible and responsive research design integrated action and research within the frame of the project in an iterative process of deepening reflection. The research evidence presented here includes the reflective conversations between myself and Melanie during the planning and implementation of the debates during the course, the latter consisting of two terms of direct lecturer–student contact. Three of the four debates (see below) were videotaped, students' written evaluations of each debate were collected and nine of the students completed a detailed course evaluation with questions on their own preparation, presentation and peer assessment skills, their own learning and the lecturer. In addition, group interviews were conducted by Melanie with eight volunteer students. Two students also made a short video called *Debates as a Teaching Format*, in which they questioned students on their thoughts about the debates as a teaching method. An email list was also set up, although only one, albeit very thoughtful, submission was made. Because 'voice' was regarded as important by both of us, in terms of education and politics, and also as a form of representation, the words of students feature in the description and evaluation of the project.

Finally, the Barcelona Group provided a critical forum and research-led professional dialogue to discuss the innovation. This group of colleagues formed a small but critical mass of individuals with similar concerns and ideas about the importance and dynamism of teaching practices and assessment methods. They provided research partnerships for members (especially, in my own case, with Melanie), as well as more general benefits of cooperation and support. On one level, Barcelona provided a quasi-focus group (to use fashionable terminology) for each of us through which we could explore our own research and practice-related ideas. Focus groups usefully enable concepts to be clarified, particularly in the early stages of research. But Barcelona provided much more than a sounding board: it involved the sharing of a common purpose. Through this group we sought to develop a critical professionalism in our higher education work, we exchanged ideas, initiated genuine dialogue and established a community of practice that provided 'the interpretative support necessary for making sense' (Lave and Wenger, 1999: 25) of the practice and research of its members. In this respect, Barcelona was a sensory as well as knowledge-enhancing opportunity.

My action research focus

International Management was an undergraduate honours course for students with three or four years' attendance which I taught at Glasgow until the end of 1998. In the year of the research (1997/8) the course attracted 40 students, of whom 23 were fourth year students, nine were third year students and eight were foreign students, the last attending the university for a single year of study. Most of the foreign students were from the United States or from German-speaking countries of the European Union. Of the total cohort, 26 were female and 14 male.

The department is located within the university's Faculty of Social Science. As is normal within Scotland, the department offered a four-year undergraduate degree programme. The first two years of this programme consist of pre-honours courses, intended to provide students with knowledge of the inter-disciplinary study of management and managers within private and public sector organizations. During these two years the aim is, first, to provide students with a theoretical and practical understanding of the key activities comprising management and undertaken by managers and, second, to furnish students with a similar understanding of the range of management activities. Throughout these two years, students were assessed through traditional essays and closed-book, time-constrained examinations. To progress to honours study, students had to achieve a final assessment mark of at least 60 per cent (identified with 'good' or 'excellent') in the second year of assessment. With honours study, students had to take courses from across the functional areas of management: for example, in financial management or human resource management (HRM). The International Management course was part of this latter area.

Business and management studies are now among the most popular university courses in the UK. International management courses emerged first in the USA to provide US managers working overseas with the skills to manage and negotiate with host country nationals. A perennial topic, for example, has been the selection and training of expatriate managers. This practical 'how to deal with foreigners' approach still persists (see, for example, Hickson and Pugh, 1995). The Glasgow course was determinably different. In terms of course content, it sought to provide students with conceptual rather than practical skills. The course content focused not simply on managers as an occupational group, but on management as a process of the international economy. The aim of the course was to examine management of the international economy, to analyse the management of firms within that economy and to understand the relationship between these. Examples of this approach are highlighted in the class debate topics below. The debates were, however, also expected to be useful for other practical skills, such as presentation, communication and team-working.

As with other honours courses in the department, International Management consisted of 40 hours of contact time, divided between lectures and seminars. My introduction of debates in this course was novel within the department. No pre-honours or honours class included such debates. Debates were introduced in the third year of the course to complement the lectures and seminars, and it was this year which became the focus of the research reported here and was also the first year in which class debates were systematically included. During the previous year (1996/7) I had experimented with *ad hoc* debates for the first time. As with all honours courses in the department, course assessment required a 3,000 word essay and an end of course examination. Weighting favoured the examination. I had hoped that, in addition to enhancing their critical thinking, debates among students might also provide an opportunity for introducing peer assessment. Melanie's and my thoughts, experience and research findings in this latter regard are reported in Walker and Warhurst (2000).

Seminars consisted of individual or paired presentations requiring not only a summary of a case study illustrative of the lecture but also the highlighting of key points to be noted from that case study. A typical case study would be a 6,000–8,000 word book chapter or academic journal article which offered an empirical example of the conceptual issues raised during that week's lecture. After the seminar presentation, students questioned and commented on the content and interpretation of the presenter. As a consequence, students were required to defend their particular reading of the case study before their peers. These presentations were compulsory for each student but not part of the formal assessment of the course. Their intention, instead, was to develop students' capacity for summation and critique, initially as an aid for the formal assessment of the course but later also to complement the skills required for the class debates. Thus, prior to each debate, every student in the class had experienced four weeks of lectures and seminars related to each debate topic, which were themselves integrated into the overall course design. Within that design, the four sequenced topics I chose for debate were:

- This house believes that a global economy now exists.
- This house believes that competitive advantage is generated by firms through their internal structures, practices and strategies.
- This house believes that in the transition from a command economy to a market economy 'shock therapy' rather than 'gradualism' is the best strategy.
- This house believes that regulation of the international economy is not desirable.

These debates centred on key issues and received thinking about the management of the international economy. For example, that a global economy now exists has become a mantra of policy-makers of every hue, pop business writers and academics across a range of disciplines – see, for example, Blair (1998) and Wood (1999), Ohmae (1994) and Drucker (1986), Sklair (1991) and Waters (1995), respectively. Drawing on the previous weeks' supplementary readings from lectures plus the seminar material, one team of four or five students argued in support of the motion, another against it. The aim was to convince a third group of the legitimacy of their particular argument. The 'audience' group of students listened to each argument in turn and were then required to adjudicate. Having read the relevant material prior to the debate, these students were also required to offer questions and comments to either or both of the debating teams. Following a discussion among themselves, the audience group then decided which argument was the more convincing. Debating for and against a motion, and adjudicating, was rotated among the groups. The students were schooled on critiquing, analysing each argument on the basis of, for example, internal inconsistencies and contradictions, configuring the same material to produce different conclusions and identifying omitted or additional material that might support or refute the claims being made.

On a scale ranging from one for 'unconvincing' to five for 'excellent', the adjudicating group had to consider the persuasiveness of the argument, the competence of the debating teams' efforts and the quality of the presentational skills of each team. The first dimension was concerned with the content of each team's argument, the second with assessing the collective effort and coherence of each presentation and the third with the communicative skills of each team. There was also space on the assessment forms to note 'additional comments' should they have wished. Members of the adjudicating group noted their own individual mark first, and then a collective mark derived from the group discussion. Although not contributing towards a formal summative assessment, each debate topic was explicitly linked to questions set in the end of course examination.

The debates were intended to offer students the opportunity to engage as learners, while also developing their subject knowledge of the course. Importantly, they were intended to enhance the critical thinking of students. Students were encouraged to challenge existing thinking on a range of key issues, in a way that sought to develop their own 'thinking skills'. In addition, the debates offered the students an opportunity to develop simultaneously other more practical skills also regarded as increasingly useful beyond the university: presentational, communication and teamwork, for example. It is the development of the students' critical thinking, however, that is the focus of this chapter and that will now be explored further.

Research findings

For every debate, students were provided with a general overview of the topic and suggested readings. No opinion on the topic for debate was offered by me. Using lecture, seminar and reading list material, students would research and present their argument as a team. They would then be exposed to counter arguments from the team against whom they were debating, and face evaluative comments and questions from the adjudicating team.

Learning, preparation and being prepared to debate

At a general level, all the students believed that the debates were a good learning tool; they were, one student (Christina)[3] asserted, 'a key factor in helping us learn'. Because the debates involved public performance, it forced the students to undertake the preparation that they knew was required of them as learners but which, ordinarily, they could avoid through anonymity: 'with the debates, because you have to stand up, you have to do the work so it forces you to do it', said one student (Kate). 'You didn't want to stand up in front of anyone and act like you knew nothing', another student agreed (Christina). As a consequence, the students felt that they learned more, as these two (anonymous) written evaluations confirm:

> I think debates were really good for my own learning. I know I can otherwise be lazy about reading material . . .

> You had to do the preparation and therefore you absorbed the material more.

Having to prepare for the debates resulted in students acquiring more of the base knowledge of the course: 'There is a need to do a great deal of background reading which is obviously helpful in understanding the course as a whole' (Anonymous, debates evaluation). Similarly, Uta stated that 'It's really good because we had to look at the materials and the books and of course if you didn't like the pros and cons we had to look at it, to the other groups as well, if they were in favour of it and we were against, so we really had to look at it, really helped to learn about the subject.' Preparation with wide reading was a key to being effective in debates: that is, knowing more and more of the different perspectives provided students with the necessary tools not only to acquire base knowledge, but to be able to present and counter arguments.

Those students listening, rather than debating, offered comments and questions and so also participated in the debates as well as adjudicating them. The debates thus encouraged all students to participate in the discussion. As Uta stated, 'It was a good course because it really helped me to take an active part or if you really had a question, you asked. It's not in [other courses] like this, you only sit there and don't ask because otherwise you probably feel ashamed.' For some of these students, simply listening to these arguments was therefore productive, 'help[ing] me to get a greater understanding of the issues . . . Even if you did the reading or not, as soon as you go to the debate and come away, your level of awareness almost reaches the extent as if you had read anyway because you still get this holistic understanding of both sides of the argument' (David). However, for others, not being part of a debating team actually lessened their learning because there was less compunction to prepare. Nevertheless, the debates compared favourably with more conventional learning tools, such as the seminars and lectures, according to the students, because in contrast to these forms of learning, debates encouraged more preparation from greater numbers of students.

Students were also able to identify and appreciate the instrumental benefits of class debates for their post-university employment, in terms of the development of both their personal and interpersonal communication skills. 'You can't only focus on the topic itself, you also have to know how to present it. I mean it's really useful for your working life later on I think and team work', explained Oskar. Debating with teams necessitated students having group discussions on the issues and planning their respective roles in the presentation and argumentation. The debates thus also contributed to the development of their capacities 'to deal with people', as one student put it (Christina). On a personal level, Oskar continued by saying that he 'learned . . . in a very short time to analyse things and . . . to prepare for the questions that might come up.'

In this respect, students certainly learned to think and talk on their feet, resonating with the disputation training that formed the critical thinking noted above as having been developed in medieval universities. One anonymous submission summarized this capacity: 'Did a fair amount of reading for the research and preparation to make sure that I could speak without much reference to my notes.' In addition to being an 'effective learning tool' according to one student (David), debates also required students to communicate their comprehension of the issues in a coherent and convincing manner: 'It demands that you're lucid and it demands that you know what you're talking about because if you don't, when it comes to the head to head, you will be questioned and it will be quickly ascertained, you know, the level of your comprehension.'

However, debate involves not just forwarding but also countering arguments, a requisite that the students quickly recognized and pursued: 'To be effective in your argumentation you have to understand both sides of the argument', said David. 'When I argue a particular motion, before I even begin to argue it, the first thing I think about is the fundamental flaws of my own argument, what are the strengths of the other person's argument and therefore I build up this, this sort of holistic awareness of all the different aspects of the argument.' Students were thus developing a capacity to reflect on their and others' understanding, to construct arguments, deconstruct those of others and reconstruct the argument as a form:

> I only chose one argument . . . for my presentation. I subdivided it into different parts, which I built up again like a wall . . . The disadvantage of this strategy is that it is quite logical and people in public seldom ask 'why' but more 'what'. In consequence they don't pay attention to the quality of the argument. They only count how many arguments seemed probable to them.
>
> (Oskar)

As for the team against whom his own was debating, he noted how they tended simply to list authorities rather than use that information to develop their own coherent position: 'The problem with the other group was that they only named arguments . . . repetitions, contradictions and unclear arguments were the consequence.' Another student (David) revelled in his newly developed capacity strategically to counter or subvert other teams' arguments: 'I think this is quite a key skill, whether or not you can win your argument by focusing on the material or whether you should try and get them, get the opposing team to go off on a tangent and attack them on the premises of the tangential argument rather than the principal argument which they're arguing for.'

As the debates progressed and they reflected on past performances, the students became more confident in their own abilities and the development of those abilities. One student (Christina) said that she was extremely nervous for her first debate but that 'the next one was even more challenging because you were used to what you needed to do . . . Okay, last time I didn't do this very well, so I must concentrate on this. So it gave you a variety of skills, not only in presenting but in learning.'

While it was not a specific focus of my initial concern around critical thinking and peer assessment, in her observation of the debates, it struck

Melanie that there appeared to be gendered differences in the responses of the debating teams. She explained in one of our discussions:

> I started to think, gosh are none of the women going to ask questions and are none of the women in either team going to respond? But much later they did, and I was struck by the fact that both the questions and the responses were very thoughtful. I got the impression that the women had been listening to what was going on, so it was less the immediate kind of jumping in, more a considered response.

When she raised this in the student interviews, the students agreed: 'Women listen', said one (Christina). 'Men will be quick to give their opinion where I will listen to what other people say before I form my opinion, which doesn't mean I'm forming it because of what you say, it means I just want to hear what all the different ideas are before I say something back.' Interestingly, the students did not express stereotypical gendered responses. On the basis of their experience of different cultures, they suggested that this gendering could be nationally or even organizationally specific. As Christina noted, 'in the States you actually hear more women speak first and I think there it's competitively situated, where you have to do that. I think here [Scotland] it's still more of a male dominated world.' David suggested that from his experience 'Women have a much stronger voice at university, young females are very strong in their opinions and they have no sort of reservations about expressing them . . . in, you know, a different environment, a lot of young women tend to more or less suppress what they think and just go with the male opinion.' While only touched on here, the relationship between the development of critical thinking and 'critical persons' in universities and gender would be an interesting issue to pursue.

Towards type C students?

Stimulating preparation, generating understanding and communicating that understanding by thinking and speaking on one's feet are clearly significant outcomes in terms of student learning. However, they do not in themselves equate with critical thinking. With debates, a space was clearly provided that encouraged and facilitated the development of critical thinking among students. Following Perry (1979) and Barnett (1997), this critical thinking should involve students accepting the multiplicity of knowledge and being able to engage that knowledge in ways that are not just evaluative but also innovative. For these students, peers become sources of learning and diversity, and existing authorities such as that of the lecturer become sources of guidance rather than judgement.

The evidence here suggests that debates clearly exposed students to a multiplicity of knowledge. As one student (Jane) stated:

When you went to the debate you listened to both sides of the argument, which I thought was the main strength of the debates, that you see both sides rather than just seeing it from one point of view. Lecturers do tend to have their own opinion, so in this way Chris [Warhurst] made sure we heard both sides of the argument.

For some of these students the array of ideas and information was confusing: 'after a debate you felt like you were left with lots and lots of information, lots of different details and you felt like not knowing anything any more . . . sometimes you felt like "I don't really know what's true anymore, what is "globalization"?', said Jörg. It seems, therefore, that for some students progression from basic information acquisition quickly turned into information overload with the debates, and these students became disoriented, desiring a return to more simplistic right–wrong positions, with the lecturer signalling 'correct' knowledge. One student put it this way: 'He [the lecturer] obviously wanted to make us get to know every single point . . . he was really ambitious with us, so it was a bit too much at times I think.' These students wanted a distinction to be made between sufficient and advanced learning processes and outcomes. For example, with preparatory reading, Jörg suggested that the lecturer should still provide a comprehensive reading list but then indicate 'These one, two or three books are important and the rest, just for those who are a bit more ambitious and want to know a bit more.' The lecturer is here regarded as an authority on the knowledge, able to determine for the student not just what is required to be known, but also the level of necessary understanding.

These students wanted confirmatory or otherwise feedback on the ideas and arguments that they prosecuted in the debates. As Jörg commented, 'He [the lecturer] could give more sort of feedback . . . about the content. Just say "This was really wrong what you said, it was just not true." I mean, just to improve people.' This position did not seem to involve any reconstruction of the existing student–lecturer relationship, as this student continued, 'Let the students do it and then leave five or ten minutes for himself in the end and give feedback as lecturer . . . give some kind of solution or something like that; "You could've said that, you could've put that into the question" or whatever.' Another student (Oskar) agreed that 'Sometimes we went out of the class debate and said to ourselves "OK, we present something, either we were convincing or not for the group but what should we believe in?"'

Other students were more comfortable with the array of ideas and information generated by the debates. For these students, the debates, in terms of both process and outcome, facilitated greater not lesser comprehension and allowed them to develop their own understanding, as two anonymously written submissions indicate:

[The debates] helped you prepare topics more in depth. Heard different viewpoints on certain topics – gained greater insight and helped you formulate your own ideas.

You had a chance to hear both sides of current debates and then form an opinion.

Such developments were confirmed by other students. When researching and developing an argument for the debates, 'you got to, you know, get your own opinion', said one student (Margaret). Exposed to the various arguments, those not debating also developed their own opinion by evaluating 'whose argument was stronger', said another (Jane).

Students demonstrated considerable capacity to evaluate their peers' debates. One student was firm on the performance of even her friends: 'I think they were pretty awful actually. I think they were quite bad today. Obviously no preparation at all.' The whole group then provided an assessment of the debating teams. Their comments continued in a fairly critical vein as they castigated one team for lack of effort, for poor delivery and for lack of a coherent argument. They graded their peers in that team as unconvincing and weak, providing reasons for that assessment among themselves and in the public feedback later to the debating teams as part of their adjudication.

Settling upon an opinion did not always mean accepting knowledge offered by the existing literature or the derived arguments of their peers. Developing divergent understanding resulted in attempts to forge new ideas, even if those ideas were composite: 'At the end it's always not yes and no, it's always to find a middle way', suggested Uta. The debates thus not only provided students with a broader awareness of the range of knowledge on any particular topic but also facilitated their developing of new forms of understanding.

There was some indication that students were progressing towards type C. This possibility was confirmed by the other comments from the students. These students were developing critical thinking; able to acknowledge multiple authorities, evaluate the value of each and then develop their own reflective understanding. One such student was David:

> You can argue a point and then someone comes up with a better point and I feel that if you're gonna be involved with, in debates, you can be opinionated to a degree, but I would say to someone, 'Be flexible, be able to retract your opinion because you can be right a lot of the time but you won't be right all of the time. If someone else is more right, take their viewpoint.' I think the most important thing is not whether you win, it's developing this awareness, understanding the material and that comes through being flexible in your own opinion.

In addition, in a class with students from other countries, students quickly began to realize the limits of their own knowledge: 'they [the international students] had a huge knowledge about international things and we'd be sitting there going "Didn't know that, didn't know that".' Moreover, these students from other countries had 'different perspectives on certain issues' (Christina) and thought that exposure to these different perspectives was good, 'creating a different learning experience in itself'.

During the course, some of these students did become engrossed in the debate topics beyond the classroom. Engaging their peers (often flatmates not attending the International Management course) in 'full blown debates' over the weekend preceding a debate had become a 'prerequisite', said one student, not just for purposes of rehearsal but because his household had become interested in the issues of the debate topics to the extent that they were now 'discussed regularly' (David). This increasing awareness of issues related to the world around them resulted in some of the students developing, in their words, a 'sociological' or 'philosophical' world view. For others, it raised their political – with a small 'p' – consciousness. 'I mean for me it's seriously, politics used to be, I used to, even when I think about them, I don't want to know, I don't want to hear and now I actually know what's going on in the world and it's been seriously probably the best course I've done here yet because of that simple fact, that it's actually taken an interest upon me where I had no interest' (Christina).

These students acknowledged the possibility and desirability of developing innovative understanding, and taking and applying that understanding beyond the classroom. It was interesting that, even with the opportunity for developing more collaborative learning with their peers, students are still aware of lecturers as the bearers of academic authority and disciplinary power, especially in terms of assessment. 'I always think they're right', said one (Jane). 'It's just because they seem as this high and mighty kind of power thing, they know so much.' As undergraduates, they were still keen to hear the opinion of the lecturer. However, and resonating with the sophisticated type B student outlined above, such students did note that the lecturer divulging an opinion might result in students skewing their arguments towards that opinion. Even among those students who were progressing towards type C, there was some evidence that reassurance was being sought from the lecturer, although the lecturer now represented an expert guide rather than sole arbiter. This need for reassurance was again rooted in concern about the assessment role still maintained by the lecturer:

> Sometimes I'll ask the lecturer what his opinion is, because he always seems to take an impartial viewpoint so I'll try to gauge what's his opinion and see whether my understanding is similar to his understanding. I think that's so effective because you can quickly gauge to what extent your, how well . . . you understand the material.

A dilemma thus emerges for any lecturer using debates as a learning tool to develop critical thinking among students. On the one hand, there is my own intention to encourage students to challenge existing, and so generate new, understandings and, on the other hand, a necessity, particularly in relation to students' assessment, for me as the lecturer to maintain a position of expert authority on any understandings. This dilemma became the subject of discussion between Melanie and me. She was sanguine, recognizing both the limitations and benefits of the use of class debates:

I think sometimes we've got to be careful that we don't move so much in the other direction that we lose sight of quite valid expectations on the students' part. They know that you [the lecturer] know more. They know that you are an authority and they're quite clear about the power that you have in the system and they're probably limits to the extent to which you can actually transfer or relocate that power towards the students.

. . . there's absolutely no sense that I got from the [research data] that they in any way felt disempowered or excluded from their own learning processes in your classes. . . .

At the end of the day . . . if you had [given them your opinion] it would almost have been sort of 'play acting' or guessing game. It really would have been about 'Well let's guess what the lecturer wants because that's what it's really about. He's going to tell us the right answer at the end.' You never did that. So they were pushed back onto their own resources and their own thinking.

Discussion and concluding remarks

This chapter has examined my attempts to use debates as a learning and teaching tool to develop critical thinking among my undergraduate students. Drawing on the work of Perry (1979) and its application by Gray (1997), my aim was to use this method to encourage and facilitate type C students. Such students are able to appreciate knowledge and the truth it offers as context bound rather than absolute; they are able to evaluate competing truths to derive their own understanding of this knowledge; and they are comfortable with a reconfiguring of the relationship with their peers and lecturer. Their peers becoming additional sources of learning and diversity, and the lecturer is seen as an expert guide rather than a final arbiter of truth. The purpose of developing this type of student is, according to Barnett (1997), to free them from dependency on a 'taken for granted' world, to create more participative learning about that world and to affirm higher education as a formative agency of persons able to act autonomously and purposively within that world. The result is the possibility of transforming both that world and the students as persons who inhabit it.

It is for these latter two reasons that critical thinking has become an issue. Recently government and employers have become concerned that higher education should be providing enquiring rather then obedient, engaged rather than disengaged employees, and citizens capable of experimentation and expression within work and society. In short, both government and employers desire an instrumental production of type C students. It has to be recognized that higher education is a state-funded service, and that for tax payers' money, higher education should be contributory to the state. However, this recognition means that universities should be sensitive to, but not driven by, the needs of the state, in this case an appositely developed citizenry and workforce. Moreover, and importantly, these needs resonate with the concerns that a number of academics (myself and the Barcelona Group included) currently have about the nature of changes to higher education. In our view we need to wrench higher education from the potential abyss of 'McDonaldization', and affirm higher education as mind-expanding rather than mind-numbing, generating curious individuals, able to question received wisdom and to think and act autonomously.

Debates, I had hoped, would provide an appropriate learning space for the development of type C students. Debates potentially encourage independent learning, facilitate student participation in the learning process, allow students themselves to conceive of problems and solutions and provide opportunity for students to argue the merits of these problems and solutions. My action research reported here assessed whether or not the use of debates as a learning tool as part of an undergraduate course could, in practice, encourage and facilitate the development of critical thinking among students.

My findings offer mixed evidence on the development of critical thinking using debates. Some students found the process of preparing for debates too demanding and the outcomes too discomfiting. For these students, basic information acquisition remained a priority and they continued to look to the lecturer as the arbiter of required knowledge and understanding. It might even be that the debates regressed these students towards type A. Other students appreciated that the necessary preparation enhanced their understanding of both the debate topics and the course overall. Besides stimulating their preparation and providing them with greater understanding, the use of debates, these students felt, enhanced their argumentation, communication and presentational skills. They still desired a directive role from the lecturer, although, with contributions from their peers, they were comfortable utilizing both as sources to help them distinguish which knowledge might be more legitimate. These students were clearly type B. However, and interestingly, these students also recognized and utilized their peers as sources of learning and diversity, as type C students might. There is some evidence, then, that type C was emergent. This emergence was evident not just in the use of peers but also, and importantly, in the way that some students not only felt comfortable with a multiplicity of knowledge but were able to evaluate this multiplicity and use it to generate their own reflective understanding and even new ideas. Moreover, these students were taking these skills and ideas outside the classroom and university and applying them to their engagement in the world beyond. On balance, therefore, most students appreciated the use of debates as a learning tool and the use of debates did enhance the 'thinking' skills of most students, with some clearly developing 'critical being'.

Even for these type C students, however, there remained issues which arose and remained unresolved with the use of class debates. One such issue was the role of the lecturer as assessor, not merely teacher. On the one hand, the lack of formal assessment of the debates by the lecturer led some students to limit their efforts, especially when faced with the pressure to submit essays and reports for other classes. This limiting of effort irked these students' debating team members. For various reasons, including their expectations of lecturers and the quality of their social relationships with their peers, no students were willing to engage in formal peer assessment (see Walker and Warhurst, 2000). On the other hand, a tension exists in the lecturer wanting students to generate their own understandings, and students wanting directed understanding, even if the understanding offered by the lecturer is only confirmatory. The issue is about encouraging and facilitating students' critical thinking, which involves the lecturer not imposing correct or required answers/solutions, in this case to class debates. Imbuing students with critical thinking implies providing them with a capacity to challenge and so innovate.

This capacity to challenge and innovate potentially creates further tensions beyond that of assessment within the university. On the one hand, employers, for example, might want enquiring employees who are able and willing to contribute, through their innovative capacities, to the solutions to managerial problems, but it is extremely unlikely that these employees would be encouraged to challenge management itself. Similarly, governments might want engaged citizens who are able and willing to contribute, again through their innovative capacities, to government policies and programmes, but do not want citizens who challenge the legitimacy of the government itself. In other words, there are limits to experimentation and expression implicitly (if not explicitly) set by those who call for the development of critical thinkers. On the other hand, if the development of critical thinking is a requisite of creating the critical person, then the purpose of that creation is, Barnett (1997) argues, to provide for persons able and willing to undertake 'brave acts' that lead to transformation. However this transformation might be *of* as well as *in* work and society. We would suspect that, despite the rhetoric, neither government nor employers would advocate a strong version of the former, although a weaker version characterized by evolution rather than revolution might be acceptable. It is more likely to be transformations *in* society and work that are desired by government and employers.

In this respect, the reflection that Barnett suggests characterizes critical thinking becomes salient. Barnett acknowledges and accepts that critical persons will act critically within whatever context they find themselves, and that critical thinking allows those persons the ability to reflect on what is to be transformed and why, and why any particular action is better at that point than any other action. In other words, those persons can, through reflection, distinguish between 'in' and 'of' and apply themselves accordingly. It would be instructive to apply Barnett's schema to some of the government's new active citizenship programmes, as well as employers' initiatives to encourage workplace problem-identifying and problem-solving by employees.

Similarly, because of the need for longitudinal analysis and my own departure to another university, it was not possible to evaluate the effect that the use of debates had upon students' formative assessment. Moreover, any

assessment of those effects would have to be appreciative of the characteristics of each year's cohort of students; for example, the number of foreign
students, the mixture of third and fourth year students or the ratio of
English to Scottish students attending the course.[4] While Melanie and I
certainly hoped that the students' knowledge and understanding of the
course had been enhanced – and the students' comments reported above
would suggest this to be the case – and that this enhancement would be
reflected in examination performance, for example, the purpose of the
debates was to develop capacities which are non-measurable in terms of
formative assessment within universities – critical thinking. Moreover, this
capacity to encourage and facilitate critical thinking was not solely as a
means to improve students' university career outcomes but more their contributions beyond the university, to their work and society.

The use of debates as a learning tool should be pursued and researched
for longer than was possible here. There is some indication from our research that the use of debates within university courses can encourage and
facilitate the development of critical thinking among students. Introducing
debates as a learning tool into undergraduate courses enables a university
education that is able to contribute to individual personal development as
well as the needs of work and society, without being subordinated to those
needs. In fact, given current concerns about the changing nature of higher
education, the use of debates might provide for a mutual gains agenda for
higher education, business and government. As for the students, the majority seem to benefit personally, in terms of a range of skills enhancement,
from the introduction of the debates. So satisfied was one anonymous student about the debates that she advised students in the following year:
'Make good use of them. They will help.'

Acknowledgement

I would like to thank Melanie Walker for her support, encouragement and participation in the research reported here.

Notes

1. It has been suggested that Perry's study is gender blind if not biased, with its
   subjects being predominantly male, though its results extrapolated for both men
   and women (Gilligan, 1982). However, that differences exist between men and
   women in terms of intellectual development remains a contested issue (for example, see Belenky *et al.*, 1986).
2. See Crace (2000) and Mooney and Davidstone (2000) for examples of the
   appallingly low turnout in recent elections within the UK.
3. All student names are pseudonyms.
4. Two points are worth noting here. First, Scottish students can attend university
   from 17 years of age, but students from England and Wales from 18 years of age,

and they experience different school regimes in their respective countries. Second, the department operated a single diet of examinations for honours classes: that is, regardless of which year students attended a class – in their third or fourth year – they sat the examination for that class at the end of their fourth and final year.

References

Ahanotu, N. D. (1998) Empowerment and production workers: a knowledge-based perspective, *Empowerment in Organizations*, 6(7), 177–86.

Barley, S. (1996) *The New World of Work*. London: British–North American Committee.

Barnett, R. (1997) *Higher Education: A Critical Business*. Buckingham: SRHE/Open University Press.

Belenky, M. F., Clinchy, B. M., Goldberger, N. R. and Tarule, J. M. (1986) *Women's Ways of Knowing*. New York: Basic Books.

Black, J. (2000) It reflected an ideology that higher education was just another marketable product, *Herald*, 25 March.

Blair, T. (1998) *The Third Way*. London: Fabian Society.

Blunkett, D. (2000) Influence or irrelevance: can social science improve government? *Secretary of State's ESRC Lecture Speech*, 2 February.

Bowles, S. and Gintis, H. (1976) *Schooling in Capitalist America*. London: Routledge & Kegan Paul.

Brewster, C. (1995) National cultures and international management, in S. Tyson (ed.) *Strategic Prospects for HRM*. London: Institute of Personnel and Development.

Byers, S. (1999) People and knowledge: towards an industrial policy for the 21st century, in G. Kelly (ed.) *Is New Labour Working?* London: Fabian Society.

Castells, M. (1999) Flows, networks, and identities: a critical theory of the informational society, in M. Castells, R. Flecha, P. Freire *et al.* (eds) *Critical Education in the New Information Age*. Oxford: Rowman & Littlefield.

Clark, H., Chandler, J. and Barry, J. (1998) Between the ivory tower and the academic assembly line. Paper presented to the Sixteenth Annual International Labour Process Conference, UMIST, April.

Crace, J. (2000) The new citizens, *Guardian*, Education supplement, 15 February.

Department of Trade and Industry (1999) *Building the Knowledge-driven Economy*. London: The Stationery Office.

Drucker, P. (1986) The changed world economy, *Foreign Affairs*, 64(4), 768–91.

Durkheim, E. (1961) *Moral Education*. Glencoe, IL: Free Press.

Elliott, L. (1999) Still stuck in the machine age groove, *Guardian*, 12 April.

Finlayson, A. (1999) Revisioning the economic: new Labour, democracy and markets, *Renewal*, 7(2), 42–51.

Finster, D. C. (1989) Developmental instruction. Part I: Perry's model of intellectual development, *Journal of Chemical Education*, 66(8), 659–61.

Finster, D. C. (1991) Developmental instruction. Part II: Application of Perry's model to general chemistry, *Journal of Chemical Education*, 68(9), 752–6.

Fox, C. (1999) Picky, coddled students? Make them read Beowolf, *Times Higher Education Supplement*, 26 February.

Gent, I., Davidston, B. and Prosser, P. (1999) Thinking on your feet in undergraduate computer science: a constructivist approach to developing and assessing critical thinking, *Teaching Higher Education*, 4(4), 511–22.

Gilligan, C. (1982) *A Different Voice*. Cambridge, MA: Harvard University Press.

Gray, C. (1997) A study of factors affecting a curriculum innovation in university chemistry. Unpublished PhD thesis, University of Glasgow.

Handy, C. (1995) *The Future of Work*. W. H. Smith Contemporary Papers 8.

Hickson, D. J. and Pugh, D. S. (1995) *Management Worldwide*. Harmondsworth: Penguin.

Johnson, E. and Mitter, R. (1998) *Students as Citizens: Focusing and Widening Access to Higher Education*. London: Fabian Society.

Lave, J. and Wenger, E. (1999) Learning and pedagogy in communities of practice, in J. Leach and B. Moon (eds) *Learners and Pedagogy*. Milton Keynes: Paul Chapman/The Open University.

Levacic, R. (1993) Education, in R. Maidment and G. Thompson (eds) *Managing the United Kingdom*. London: Sage.

Mooney, G. and Davidstone, C. (2000) Scotland divided: poverty, inequality and the Scottish parliament, *Critical Social Policy*, 20(2), 155–82.

Ohmae, K. (1994) *The Borderless World*. London: Harper Collins.

Park, J. (1999) The politics of emotional literacy, *Renewal*, 7(1), 52–9.

Parker, M. and Jary, D. (1995) The McUniversity: organization, management and academic subjectivity, *Organization*, 2(2), 319–38.

Perry, W. G. (1979) *Form of Intellectual and Ethical Development in the College Years: A Scheme*. New York: Holt, Rinehart and Winston.

Prichard, C. and Willmott, H. (1997) Just how managed is the McUniversity? *Organisation Studies*, 18(2), 287–316.

Ramsden, P. (1992) *Learning to Teach in Higher Education*. London: Routledge.

Reich, R. (1993) *The Work of Nations*. London: Simon & Schuster.

Rowbotham, S. (1999) Locked in the ivory tower, *Times Higher Education Supplement*, 19 February.

Scottish Enterprise (1998) *1998 Strategic Review Consultation Document*. Glasgow: Scottish Enterprise.

Scottish Office (1999) *Skills for Scotland*. Edinburgh: The Stationery Office.

Sklair, L. (1991) *Sociology of the Global System*. London: Harvester Wheatsheaf.

Thompson, P. and Warhurst, C. (2000) Ignorant theory and knowledgeable workers: myths and realities of workplace change, in D. Robertson (ed.) *The Knowledge Economy*. London: Macmillan.

Vickery, G. (1999) Business and industry policies for knowledge-based economies, *OECD Observer*, 215, 9–11.

von Krogh, G., Roos, J. and Kleine, D. (eds) (1998) *Knowing in Firms: Understanding, Management and Measuring Knowledge*. London: Sage.

Walker, M. and Warhurst, C. (2000) 'In most classes you sit around very quietly at a table and get lectured at . . .': debates, assessment and student learning, *Teaching in Higher Education*, 5(1), 33–49.

Walsh, K. (1995) *Public Services and Market Mechanisms*. Basingstoke: Macmillan.

Warhurst, C. and Thompson, P. (1998) Hands, hearts and minds: changing work and workers at the end of the century, in P. Thompson and C. Warhurst (eds) *Workplaces of the Future*. London: Macmillan.

Warhurst, C. and Thompson, P. (1999a) Knowledge, skills and work in the Scottish economy, in G. Hassan and C. Warhurst (eds) *A Different Future: The Moderniser's Guide to Scotland*. Glasgow: Big Issue/Centre for Scottish Public Policy.

Warhurst, C. and Thompson, P. (1999b) Why the McJob and not the iMacJob threatens to dominate our economy, *Sunday Herald*, 21 November.

Waters, M. (1995) *Globalization*. London: Routledge.

Wilson, T. (1991) The proletarianisation of academic labour, *Industrial Relations Journal*, 22(4), 250–62.

Wood, I. (1999) Chairman's foreword, *The Network Strategy*. Glasgow: Scottish Enterprise Network.

Wyllie, A. (ed.) (1999) *Dynamic Security: Skills and Employability in Scotland*. Edinburgh: Scottish Council Foundation.

6

Engaging a Large First Year Class

Quintin Cutts

Aside

As I sit to write this chapter, I have just leafed through a draft of Alison's chapter. Nightmare of comparison. Witty, clever, articulate, deep, scholarly – any number of judgements can I make against my own rather scientific writing. Yet, as my stomach settles, I realize that my whole narrative is intimately related to this one reaction. For myself, my students and perhaps academia as a whole, I am looking for increased personal responsibility – an awakening to acceptance of self, and the consequent energy that flows when we choose and create from such a standpoint.

A 'constellation of fragility'

Academics for me seem to be living in fear of the whims of their paymasters, or of one another:

> Depressing conformity has infected the normally bolshie higher educa-
> tion community. What is missing is the spirit of challenge, of argument for
> argument's sake. Have we all given up and surrendered our intellectual
> vigour, independence of thought or potential challenge to authority?
> (Peter Knight, *Times Higher Educational Supplement*, 1 January 1999)

My students conform to a system of which they clearly disapprove. On the topic of excessive time spent sitting in front of computers, my level 3 students commented:

> *T*: If the whole lab is sitting up to like twelve o'clock at night, you're
>   not going to turn round and say but it's only 20 per cent [of the final
>   mark], I'm going home at five.
> *S*: We can't not do it, know what I mean, because everyone else around
>   you is doing that.
> *B*: It's a peer pressure thing.

And, most significantly for a Glasgow student: 'And going to the lab after I go to the Celtic game . . . I went to the lab after I went to Parkhead'[1] (Focus group, February 2000).

All of the above speaks to me of a succumbing to our fears of what will happen if we don't live up to the expectations of others: for me about how I would be judged by others; for academics about how rebelliousness would be viewed; and for the students about how they would fare if they voiced their honest opinions about the teaching and learning environment and this early induction into a 'long hours' working culture. In short, we appear to be unwilling to take a stand for our own views on education.

In this chapter, I am aiming to illuminate my view of the inherent *messiness* and complexity of education, for both providers and receivers, a view shared by the Barcelona Group. Messiness for me relates strongly to Barnett's (2000) 'constellation of fragility', constituting challengeability, contestability, uncertainty and unpredictability as the fundamentals from which we can begin to define modern university education. Messiness requires university educators to accept that there is no formula for the *right* delivery or receipt of an education. We are called to recognize ourselves as agents of change for the students, in every fresh instant, rather than mere receptacles for and dispensers of knowledge. In accepting this agency, we ourselves must be willing to be educated, to recognize and embrace the need for change and to take a stand on and argue for what is fundamentally true for us. Education can never be neatly packaged; it is fundamentally unruly!

At the same time as highlighting messiness among students, the chapter presents my own shifting evolution as a university academic: from a starting point as a product of the scientific research 'machine', to the position I now find myself in, where I am optimistically questioning many of the ground rules by which most academics seem to operate. Crucially for me, this position is both within the system, and critically reflective upon it.

The chapter is based around the research project that I took on as a result of joining the Barcelona Group: the analysis of a first year computer programming module with an intake of around 450 students of varying ability, for which I am the module coordinator. The messiness of education is embodied in a series of dilemmas facing both staff and students when they are considering module content, communication and prevailing attitudes, and upon which we are called to adopt a position and to act from it:

- *Innate ability versus teaching and learning techniques.* Among computer scientists, the belief has long been held that the ability to write computer programs is largely innate, rather than learned. Against this, the more experience students have of practising their program writing skills, the more successful they generally are. The opportunity to practise in a supportive environment, however, is expensive to provide. My belief is that programming is a learned ability, and so the dilemma for me here is whether to take a professional and ethical stand for students and against the prevailing attitudes within the discipline, or simply to accept standard practice. In taking the former position, I am called to develop a sound and graded teaching methodology that will deliver improved results, but that is also tenable with increasingly large class sizes.

- *Content versus engagement.* While I have been teaching this course, there have been many moments when the students are fully engaged, most often when the application of programming to the students' world is evident. However, in my view, learning the nuts and bolts of programming requires significant and less obviously relevant study for success. The dilemma here involves finding the balance between using techniques that include all-comers to the module, and ensuring that sufficient core subject material is covered. A related dilemma is the balance between subject content and more generic skills. Students are called to decide whether to engage with the subject, staff to decide how to encourage this engagement.
- *Safety versus sharing.* The development of a community of learners requires a commitment to open communication between and among students and staff, permitting all parties to express opinions, desires and fears. A lack of awareness of the need for this commitment or a fear of exposure, however, often prevents this kind of communication from taking place. One dilemma here is again around resourcing – balancing investment in the encouragement of dialogue with investment required to learn the subject matter. A second dilemma for both staff and students is whether to cross the safety barrier in order to deepen learning.

I have presented the dilemmas in the order in which I encountered them while evaluating and adjusting the programming course. My initial concerns were largely technical, around the subject matter. Subsequently, the difficulties of gaining and retaining motivation became clear. Most recently, I have realized that neither of the earlier stages is really of very much use unless honest, open communication between all parties is possible. This communication starts with each one of us being as honest as it is possible for us to be with ourselves.

The module coordinator

Before I continue, some truths about me. I am a scientist by training, unaccustomed to writing in this style. Indeed, the very idea of placing myself in my writing is anathema to that training. Nevertheless, I am also the fifth child of a general medical practitioner and a general practitioner's daughter, brought up instinctively to view people as individually important, to read and to argue, usually simply for the sake of a good argument.

My family background lies in stark contrast to my education and career. I was restricted at the age of thirteen to O-levels consisting of languages and sciences only, and at fifteen to all science A-levels. These subjects tended towards a right/wrong concept of knowledge, to *certain* knowledge. The spirit of argument and discussion was absent from much of my education, which after a very competitive primary school start, was for me more about scoring highly than about the joy of learning. The end result was what mattered, not the ongoing process, hardly surprising since that process consisted more of straightforward knowledge acquisition than the messy business of learning alluded to earlier, which encourages the self to stand by individually constructed views of the world.

My undergraduate education in the sciences did little to change this view. I clearly remember one of my professors berating the class for not rioting in the streets or at least demonstrating against university cuts, as he had done in the sixties. Yet the teaching and assessment styles of the university were as much the cause of our apathy as was the cultural training we had received to date. While our training in the science of computations was as good as any other university's, our training in critical and reflective thinking was extremely limited.

For me, this limited training is a key failing in the current science education framework. The following quote from Neils Bohr epitomizes the issue:

> There are two kinds of ideas in our universe and they are represented by two kinds of statements: those whose opposites are obviously false and those whose opposites are obviously true. The first form the basis of most publications and are intrinsically unimportant. The second can point to truth and must be cherished.
>
> (Quoted in Smith, 1996: 33)

In my research training, the game of certain knowledge, of gathering these first kind of ideas, was played to some extent. However, for me we also examined areas that were more about challenging our curiosity than about the necessary delivery of academic publications. 'As long as there are fresh new ideas to work with every morning' was a maxim by which I lived.

My first attempt at formal university teaching, while still a post-doctoral fellow, was based largely on the models I had experienced as a student. The course in question was offered for political reasons, to placate various members of the department while at the same time allowing another course, to which they objected, to remain in place. The aims and objectives of the new course, set by the department, were hopelessly ambitious. I remember expressing my astonishment to a colleague at how little of the material was being absorbed by the students. A summary of his response was 'You'll get used to it', a depressing induction into the low expectations that many academics have of their students.

As a full-time lecturer at Glasgow University, I received early advice from many quarters pointing at teaching as a dead-end activity, with research grants and research students being the path to promotion.[2] The content of lecturer training courses was viewed by new lecturers such as Alison and myself as both useful and interesting. We were generally aware that existing teaching methods inspired neither ourselves nor the students and yet, because of a perceived requirement to be highly active in the research arena for progression, most of us knew that we did not have enough time in our everyday teaching to use the ideas proposed in the courses. Of concern here is the ability of academic institutions to define, beyond vague generalities, the characteristics and behaviours of excellent teachers. With such a definition in place, it would be possible to reward a teacher who chose to be highly active in the education arena, reusing and creating innovative teaching methods.

Conscious attempts to reflect on my teaching were confined primarily to lunchtime sessions with Alison and one or two other colleagues, where we considered, among other things, the potential similarities between spoken and computer language teaching. In an unfocused manner, I was beginning to realize my frustration at a teaching and learning regime that was largely a waste of our time, most particularly because we did not appear to be serving the students at all well. Why use valuable lecturing time conveying information that could be transmitted using a host of other techniques? At last, the values involving respect for individuals, inspired by my family background, were consciously contradicting the values of my scientific training.

Late in 1997, I joined a course run by Vicki Gunn and Melanie Walker of the Teaching and Learning Service that focused on 'reflective practice'. This was my first introduction to any significant literature on education research. The course and the literature awoke me to the possibility of self-acceptance for my student-centred views. A report I wrote for this course on a critical incident helped me to start unpacking the way I viewed myself as an educator. Reflecting on the incident, I wrote:

> I can see that I am becoming very involved in what it is that the students like, perhaps losing rather what it is that is best from a teaching/ learning point of view. This is a common problem – people should like me, rather than my taking a stand on what I believe is correct/appropriate. Additionally, I take the views of those who disapprove more strongly than I do of those who approve.

This speaks to me of a lack of clearly defined purposes around my teaching, other than that the students should like their lecturer. It is also clearly a sign of someone who is easily swayed by the expectations of others. Yet it is a surprise to me how many colleagues make similar comments about the effects upon themselves of disengaged students.

Returning to my own development, as I started the Barcelona secondment I was awakening to my concerns around student learning and about the importance of acknowledging each student individually. My own position as a professional in academia was still barely examined. The following sections discuss the module under study, students, subject matter and teaching techniques in detail. Towards the end of the chapter, I return to my own professional development in the light of my secondment.

Module basics

The Introductory Programming module (IP1) is the first module that students encounter in any of the computer science related degree courses at Glasgow University. Additionally, as part of the Scottish degree structure, any student admitted to the university may take the module, even if they do not wish to continue on to a computing science degree. The lack of specific entry requirements results in a very wide range of abilities among the students on the course, from those who have no programming experience at all, to those who have written programs at home, school or even work for many years.

The class size has grown from around 300 to over 450 during my four years as module coordinator. The module runs for 12 weeks. There are 24 one-hour lectures given at the rate of two per week, alongside six one-hour tutorials and six two-hour laboratory sessions running in alternate weeks. A team of around 20 tutors staff the tutorial and laboratory sessions. For those sessions, the class is divided into groups of around 20 students each.

These are the bare facts about the module. Understanding more about the students, the material to be studied and how to make use of the resources at hand is the focus of the following sections. Methods used to gather data about the students and their progress with the module included focus group sessions, staff-student meetings, email exchanges and discussions with tutors.

The students

I start with the students themselves. The vast majority of the students in the module, over 97 per cent, are school leavers who have just started university – the first IP1 lecture is on their first day of formal lectures. The disruption to learning behaviour due to the school/university transition inevitably takes months or even years to be fully overcome. Four weeks into the course, Andy had this to say about his Higher[3] course compared to the IP1 course:

> There was ten of us [at school] with one teacher and we're getting really close attention . . . a machine each available all the time. You could do whatever you want whenever you want and you're having to adjust to three hundred punters with one lecturer. I think university is really impersonal whereas school is quite personal.
>
> (Focus group, November 1998)

On top of the academic transition, many students are away from home for the first time, although this effect may be less strong compared to that in other institutions, since Glasgow University has a high proportion of home students. Fees and loans inevitably affect students' conditions as well; one of the students was working for over 50 hours per week outside the university to support himself.

The majority of the students have some previous experience of programming, varying widely from those who have used computers and even written programs from the age of four or five to those who have taken introductory school classes only. Despite Andy's earlier comments, he and others were ambivalent about the teaching of programming at school. For example:

> *Andy*: You got held back in Higher. I think probably throughout, teach-
> ers are marking the marking scheme. It is treated as a science and
> not an art.
> *John*: Definitely. It's so bureaucratic . . . if there's more than one equally
> good way to do things, as you've shown us, at school we would only
> have had the option to do it one way and if you'd done it the other
> way then we'd have it given back with red ink all over it.
>
> (Focus group, November 1998)

Analysis of student progress at university also suggests that more than simply previous experience is at play. Of particular interest is the group of students who start the module with significant experience of programming. Some of them gain from the module, and yet a proportion also fall back. The following comments are from students with very similar previous experience levels. Their very different attitudes to the learning process are likely to affect their progress significantly.

> *Nigel*: I think if anyone's done a significant amount of programming,
> they probably realize that they're going to have to change the way
> they do things here. You know if [the programs] get any bigger then
> [school techniques] just won't work.
> *Peter*: I thought the programming bit would seem to me to be going a
> bit slow, but to be completely honest I find it painful going.
>
> (Focus group, November 1998)

Nigel can see that although he is an experienced programmer for a particular class of relatively simple problems, the university course is ultimately aimed at problems of a larger magnitude and so he is willing to learn the new techniques on offer. Peter, on the other hand, appears to be unaware that there is new material for him in the course, instead falling back on his existing techniques to solve the early, simple, problems of the course.

There is an indication here that the attitude and previous experience of students will shape their ability to access new knowledge and their success on the course. This is examined in more detail in the final section of the chapter. For the moment, the subject matter itself is the focus of examination, in order to tease out some of the skills required to master it, and to show that these are, to a large extent, generic skills. The conflict within me between training in computer programming and university education in the wider sense becomes apparent in these two sections. My language in this next section has veered back towards a scientific presentation, in stark contrast to that of the final section on student and staff attitudes. The gap across to that section is bridged with a middle section discussing teaching methods, in which the human aspects inherent in education cannot fail to become apparent.

Breaking down the skill of computer programming

Even before the Barcelona Group started to meet formally, I had worked with Judy on the relationships between her teaching of mathematics to engineers, reported in Chapter 8, and my teaching of programming. There are many similarities:

- Both classes contain non-specialists – the mathematics class consists of engineers, while around half of my class does not intend to continue with computing.
- Both subjects involve solving problems.
- The problems are solved using combinations of a set of *tools*: in Judy's case, mathematical formulae, equations, proofs; in programming, the set of computational concepts that can be expressed using a programming language.
- Use of the tools is expressed using *languages*, either formulae, equations and algebra in mathematics, or a programming language in my subject.

The implication of these similarities suggested to us that we might, first, be able to share teaching methods across mathematics and computer science in the areas of student motivation and problem-solving and, second, be able to adopt existing teaching methods more commonly associated with modern language teaching.

In our discussions, Judy and I searched for the individual components of these disciplines as a starting point to develop a better understanding of what was happening in our classes. In particular, we wanted to determine whether the ability to program was largely innate, or whether we could find a simple enough set of steps that anyone could learn. We examined problem-solving and language/tool use independently.

In his seminal book for mathematics educators, *How To Solve It*, Polya (1957) defines key steps for problem-solving, familiar to most of us from our everyday experience of the process:

1. Understand the problem.
2. Construct a plan for solving the problem.
3. Carry out the plan.
4. Examine the solution obtained.

In programming, the problem-solving aspect is usually thought of as consisting of only steps 1 and 2 of Polya's scheme. Step 3, *Carry out the plan*, is the translation of the plan into formal programming language code and its subsequent execution on a machine. These stages are shown in Figure 6.1.

Problem-solving

Understanding a problem fully, or grasping its essence, requires questions to be asked about any uncertainties or ambiguities in the original problem

Figure 6.1   The programming process

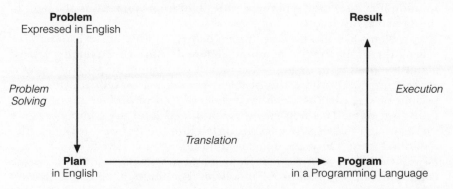

statement. A problem solver must be able to formulate such questions and be willing to ask them.

The next step is to construct a strategy for solving the problem, probably the hardest stage and the least well understood. This is a possible reason why the ability to find solutions is often thought of as innate. In essence, it involves designing a set of steps that when carried out will produce the desired solution to the problem. How are these steps determined?

An understanding of the available tools, and how they may be used, is required. In programming, some tools are built into the programming language, and some are fragments of code written by another programmer and made available for reuse. Compare this with a chef, who may use some raw ingredients and some processed foods, a wooden spoon and some complex machinery in order to 'solve' a particular culinary problem. An understanding of the way in which tools may be combined is required. Tools may be used in various ways – in a sequence, as an optional action or repeated many times. These methods of combining tools are regarded as fundamental concepts of computation.

An ability to visualize the program's behaviour during execution is necessary. The plan that embodies the strategy and the corresponding program are static descriptions of a dynamic process. When the program is executed, data values are created and the steps of the program are followed, causing the data to be changed over time. Most programs will create tens or hundreds of data values that are adjusted in complex ways to follow the real world situation they are attempting to represent. Writing plans and programs requires us to be able to breathe life into these static forms, to see in our mind's eye how the world embodied by the data values inside the computer will be changed as successive program statements are executed.

Crucially, previous experience of solving problems comes into play. When a new problem is faced, the solver may be in one of three positions:

- Exactly the same problem has been seen before. In this case, the previous solution may be reused – perhaps with slight improvements in the light of the previous results.
- No problems like this have been seen before, in which case a strategy for solving the problem must be found. There are various techniques known about for finding strategies – a common one taught in programming is *stepwise refinement*, where the problem is *analysed*, or refined, into component pieces, each of which is considered to be a problem to be solved in its own right. This refinement is continued until the components are small enough to be easily solvable, or fall into the first or third categories described here. Once the smaller components are solved, they are *synthesized* back into a single complete solution. Analysis and synthesis are common features of all problem-solving techniques. One of the hardest aspects to master here is the decomposition of the tasks into pieces that can be solved with the tools at hand. A strategy for fixing a car that used a spanner would only be any good if we actually had a spanner, and knew how to operate it.
- A problem *similar* to this has been seen before. This is the most interesting position of the three. Experienced problem-solvers have a repertoire of previously solved problems. Fast solving comes from an ability to *abstract out* the essential similarities between a new and a previously solved problem and so pick out the reusable parts of the previous solution. These parts constitute a reusable template or *pattern*, which may be specialized to the new problem. For example, if I have previously solved the problem of playing a game of patience, I will be aware of the strategy of repeatedly taking a move until a winning situation is reached.

From this discussion, it appears that the skills required of a successful problem solver are largely not specific to programming, and consist of the following:

- an ability to question, to be inquisitive;
- a thorough understanding of the set of tools available for problem-solving, and how to combine them;
- an ability to visualize complex models and changes to them over time;
- analysis and synthesis skills;
- an ability to abstract out key features from a description to form a template, and then to specialize that template for use in other situations.

Problem-solving skills alone do not appear to be sufficient for successful programming, however. In addition, an ability to understand and manipulate languages is also required.

Using a programming language: translation

The plan developed using the problem-solving process can be expressed informally, in steps written in English, before being translated into the syntax of the programming language. The intention is that the plan is written at a similar semantic level to that which can be expressed in the programming language, and so translation is straightforward provided the syntax of the programming language is well known. However, for novices, the vocabulary and grammatical structuring of a programming language, as well as the precise semantics of the language's phrases, are rarely well understood.

Alison and I considered the relationship between modern language and programming language teaching. We found interesting correlations by considering *communicative* and *structural* teaching methods. In brief, a communicative style encourages swift application of the language to our lives, particularly listening and speaking, at the expense of perfect understanding of the language's grammatical structure. The underlying objective is to practise communicating with the language as soon as possible, to increase fluency and creativity. By contrast, the structural view encourages deeper understanding of the underlying mechanics of the language, which in the long run will ensure that translated sentences have the right 'feel' in the target language. In the short term, however, the structural view is epitomized by teaching and drilling grammar, with scant attention to the real world concepts being conveyed in the process.

Programming languages differ from spoken languages in that the computer requires exact adherence of a program to the language's syntactic and semantic rules. There can be no sloppiness – the program will only run once all errors have been removed. Anyone learning to program twenty or more years ago knew no other way of using a computer and accepted that learning to use a programming language would be largely a structural matter.

However, advances in recent years have brought us *wizards*[4] of all descriptions, the World Wide Web and the HTML language, all of which encourage us to think that the computer will sort out any inaccuracies for us. For example, in the HTML language used to describe web page layout, a web browser will make the best interpretation of the HTML code it can. Usually something reasonably close to the author's intention is displayed.

The relationship with spoken languages is that wizards and HTML encourage a communicative style of learning. We look at what someone else has done, make a few adjustments to match our own requirements and hope or test that it works. Frequently, the full underlying semantics are poorly understood. This may be acceptable for web pages. However, when writing software to control aeroplanes or power stations, such an approach is entirely unacceptable, and no mainstream programming languages follow it.

Overall, the case is neither for nor against either method. Instead, both are required. For example, correcting errors and maintenance of a program over time depends on being able to read and understand thoroughly the precise meaning of each statement of existing code, while at the same time being able quickly to get a feel for what large chunks of program code are intended to do with respect to the entire application. Gaining these skills requires a mix of both educational methods.

Requirements for understanding and writing programming language code include:

- understanding/appreciation of grammars in general;
- ability to pick out grammatical structures in a program;
- acceptance that the computer cannot understand incorrect code, contradicting existing views formed using wizards and HTML;
- ability to map the language structures on to their underlying semantics.

I hope that I have highlighted the many aspects involved in the subject, both in problem-solving and in language manipulation. Personally, I think that there are a number of skills to master and that collectively this makes for a challenging subject. Rather than saying that programming ability depends on some innate quality of the practitioner, a teaching and learning strategy must cover each of these skills.

Development of teaching techniques

My analysis of the subject demands was mostly complete by the start of the 1998/9 teaching session, and had highlighted a number of crucial content components required in the module. The focus of this section is the teaching methods used to convey these components in a manner which aimed to engage the students.

To reiterate, the aim is to provide a module that is of value to *all* registered students – those with no, and those with significant, previous knowledge. Additionally, a secondary aim has been to maintain the primary aims and objectives of the module, and the module structure, set as it is within an existing degree and staffing infrastructure. These two aims have created a number of dilemmas in the choice of appropriate teaching methods.

Practical subject versus lecture-based module

Programming is a skill and therefore requires repeated practice for mastery to be achieved. As a successful student put it, 'Lectures are good, self-study sheets are helpful to see what you are after, and the laboratory is what it is all about' (email, February 2000). By this, the student meant that the time actually writing and playing with programs was the most beneficial time. Supervised laboratory time for large classes is expensive to supply, however, while lecturing to a large group is relatively cheap. The challenge for me has been how to maximize the limited laboratory time available to the students. I have addressed this in two ways.

In the first session I researched (1998/9), I broke each lecture into periods of teaching and of practical exercises. In the latter, the students were encouraged to practise what they had just seen and heard on a small exercise. As well as helping to embed the material for the students, this ideally gives me a mid-lecture opportunity if most students were having difficulties. In practice, I found this latter aspect hard to realize, as the layout of a 300-seat theatre prevented personal contact with the majority of the class in order to assess their development. Nonetheless, many students found the active style of the lecture beneficial, and made these sorts of comments:

> The interactive approach was excellent, helped to keep you focused and concentration levels up.

> Getting people involved by putting up programs to hand-execute was good and brought forward any problems with understanding.
>
> (Course questionnaire, January 2000)

On the other hand, I saw many students not attempting to engage in any way in the exercise sections. Student attitudes to learning, discussed in more detail in the final part of the chapter, are strongly in play here. As one student said, 'In-lecture work was not very good because no one concentrates on work and would rather wait for the answer. Good only if you concentrate' (Course questionnaire, January 2000).

As well as active participation in lectures, I am also keen for students to make effective use of their own time. Observations of tutorial and laboratory performance indicated to me that many students had difficulty bridging the gap from relatively passive lecture material to active engagement in practical work, either on their own or at a machine. To counter this, in the second teaching session (1999/2000) I introduced a series of guided exercise sheets, one for each lecture. Known as self-study sheets, these were an optional extra for the students, intended particularly to assist those students with little or no programming experience. They consisted of relatively easy material similar to the exercises used in lectures, along with fully worked up answers.

Reading student feedback on where the students directed their energy, I can see a real confusion about the role of the self-study sheets, and how to make best use of them in the context of course components viewed as mandatory, such as the assessed laboratory exercises. The strongest link that was *not* made during the course by students was that completion of self-study sheets would reduce the overall time required on the assessed work. Here are a number of responses of different kinds:

> Most of my time was spent on assessed laboratories, I did not do enough SSS [self-study sheets].

> I tended to ignore SSS, didn't feel they were of any worth. Not sure why. Probably due to previous experience, i.e. done it before. [SSS are not really intended for a student of this level.]

> SSS were useful and didn't take too much time. [From a beginner.]

> SSS useful, but get neglected when more pressing things in other subjects arise, i.e. coursework, exam revision – can lead to difficulty in laboratory work.

I found that about 90 per cent of my time was spent on laboratories. I never did the SSS as I felt other things I had to do were more important and could be more beneficial. The fact that marks in the laboratory were what would help me pass the course, I concentrated heavily on these.

(Course questionnaire, January 2000)

This concentration on marks is discussed below. Overall, however, the comments on the self-study sheets and lecture exercises were positive. The following comment from one student indicates that they encouraged product-ive use of a student's time:

Since I had no programming experience before, I'm happy to have a little knowledge now. But I think it's not much. But I know the things covered by IP1. In Germany I don't normally know the things after a lecture. I need much more time to repeat and repeat . . . I liked IP1 because this repetition was covered by the lecture (and SSS, lab).

(Course questionnaire, January 2000)

My reading of this response is that the student was able to keep up with the course as it progressed, an essential requirement in programming, where each new piece of knowledge builds on what has gone before.

Problem-solving versus language learning versus concept learning

Initial analysis of the course with staff in the department indicated that problem-solving was the aspect that students found most difficult. I addressed this issue in the first teaching session by spending significant time on this aspect early in the course. I had made two assumptions: that the basic tools or con-cepts of computation, such as repetition, sequence and state, were relatively easy to absorb; and that translation from a plan to a program was easy. These assumptions were shown to be incorrect during the course. One student said:

I think for people who have had no experience whatsoever, one of the main difficulties is going to be coming to terms with another language altogether, because it was a bit of a shock to me. Learning that there is a new language and how to use that new language to get what you want, that's going to be quite difficult.

(Focus group, November 1998)

A mid-term surprise test asking the students to show the outcome of execut-ing a simple program demonstrated very clearly that many of them had not grasped the basic concepts behind the language. Interestingly, many students who stated that they had 'reasonable' programming experience fell into this category.

Nonetheless, the staged planning of a problem solution is still a large hurdle for beginners and experienced students alike. A student with Higher and SYS[5] computing qualifications said in a focus group discussion with Melanie and myself:

> The most difficult part about it, the tutorial questions and the exam and stuff is that you are expected to actually put a plan down and I just wasn't used to doing that. I was just used to, because of what I'd done in school, I was just going straight to the computer and just going, like *ad lib* again basically, so my mind is more tuned into sort of looking at a problem and then going straight to code rather than going, sort of pseudo English but I'm getting better at that now. So it's easy to do that for like small problems but it's not very easy to do it for bigger ones unless you actually, sort of break it up into procedures and then you can do it. That was the hardest part I found with the tutorial questions, that you quite often, you were supposed to say right, why did you do it that way rather than this way and to me it was just kind of instinctive.
>
> (Focus group, April 1999)

At issue is that the student does the task, but does not know why or how he has succeeded – he has no explicit structural rules on which to draw the next time. Yet elucidating the process is of key importance for successfully working in teams of designers and programmers, and an essential end skill of the degree program, if not of this module.

In the second teaching session (1999/2000), on the basis of observation and feedback, I introduced the computational concepts first by getting the students to concentrate on examining small programs and making changes to them to embed understanding of the concepts thoroughly. Later in the course, I introduced problem-solving, believing that the building blocks for programming were in place. The early part of the course was well received, but then the step up required for solving problems came as a surprise to students. The early part was not in fact thoroughly embedded. Responses from several students echo the following email from a student:

> I think when we were faced with it [the first major problem-solving exercise], it came as quite a shock as the lectures hadn't really made it clear that we would be expected to write programs like this. I am sure that many beginner programmers who had gone to (and listened to) all the lectures really felt that they had missed something when the assignment was handed out.
>
> (January 2000)

Although I had covered it in lectures, students could not see how to link the two stages of work, resulting in a core belief in many that the course was designed for those who had programmed before. Such a belief could be used by the students as an excuse for opting out, a situation discussed in more detail in the final section of the chapter. Being clearer about the course structure and expectations will also help to reduce the potential for unconsciously adopting this excuse.

Motivational versus curriculum material

The final dilemma for me in this section concerns the need to balance course content that is engaging to the students with concepts and techniques expected in future courses in the degree program. Having thoroughly analysed the requirements for programming, I am amazed at how much we expect of our students. As a result, I have been attempting to hone down the content to an essential minimum, while making the remaining material as relevant to the students' lives as I can. Little is learned when the connection between new and existing knowledge cannot be made. A course where the content is viewed as irrelevant is quickly classed as boring and completed only through requirement, not choice.

Traditional programming courses have centred on programs that interact with the outside world using text. A common early program might read in a name typed at the keyboard and then write out to the screen a message welcoming the person with that name. This is useful for learning programming, but hardly relevant in an age where students have WAP-enabled phones, and have been playing virtual reality video games and using highly interactive windows-based computer systems for years.

My initial attempt to tackle the obsolescence of text-based systems has been to work with graphics-based programs, effectively programs that have more in common with video games. Students can much more easily grasp the effect of their coding on the graphical output, and respond more positively. I am caught, however, by a need to introduce the text-based interaction techniques for further courses. This need seriously unbalanced my course, coming in the middle section, and overloading many students.

Judy and I found we had similar concerns in this respect. Lecturers, specialists in the subject, often view a large core of material as essential for those wishing to become specialists themselves. Both Judy and I have large numbers of students who have no expectation of becoming specialists. We have been looking, therefore, at the minimum detail required to gain understanding of the fundamental subject matter, suitable for potential specialists and non-specialists alike.

The dilemma here is for me to take a stand in my department for large-scale reorganisation of the syllabus in order to accommodate the change in focus that I think is required. I am very aware of the resource cost of significant course retooling. Yet I am also aware that the current balance is serving our students poorly.

Reflection, questioning, safety, sharing

Bound up in the dilemmas discussed so far in this chapter is the requirement for students to be able to reflect on the processes unfolding within and around them. For students to engage fully with course content, they need to reflect on their purpose for studying the subject and on their own learning processes. Students who are able to see how their own beliefs, fears and values interact with course material and methods are likely to be able to make necessary adjustments more quickly when the two are in conflict compared to those who react automatically. Additionally, reflection by and particularly between students and staff is likely to involve participants' crossing habitual safety barriers in order to reach new understanding about self and others.

A thread running through many of the conversations within the Barcelona Group has concerned students' ability to ask questions, as a means to reflect on their progress and to strengthen engagement with the material. This question-posing skill is arguably the most important learning 'skill' for students to acquire.

In one of our early meetings, I had explained to Alison my teaching methodology, which at that time involved taking a problem, analysing its major components, writing a plan for the program and then translating that plan into a program using a programming language. Alison said:

> When you've tried to get me to understand programming languages, you've put [a program] on the table and said, 'This is the programming language, ask questions about it'. I haven't been interested in the planning and I haven't been interested in the sort of generalization and translation and all the concepts stuff and I wasn't quite sure where it was going or why it was even important, but what I'm saying is OK, well those colons are obviously there for a reason, they're in a pattern, that pattern of work is obviously there for a reason, why is it there, and then starting to ask the questions.
>
> (Group discussion, November 1998)

On another occasion, Mike commented on a session which I had recounted to the Barcelona Group, one where I felt I had fully engaged the students. He said, 'You were saying that there's this incredibly extraordinarily interesting set of questions we should ask, and once you've asked the questions which are fascinating, there's the small matter of how the hell, what do you need in order to answer them' (Group discussion, January 2000).

I had in fact asked the class to write down any questions they had about the module so far, after that session. They were all at a very high level, not a single one at the level of the subject content I was currently covering in the module at that time. Examples are:

1. Why are we learning Ada and not a cross-platform programming language like Java?
2. Why does the course suddenly jump from something we can all understand to something which appears able to be done only by people with computing history? Did I miss something?
3. Can I connect my programs to colour graphics output?
4. In school you learn a language and then at uni you learn a new language, so it is a bit confusing. So why do languages differ?

5. What relevance does IP1 have outside the computer science course?
6. Why do we need maths?
7. What will knowing computer science give me over an ordinary Windows user?
8. Where is the Internet?
9. Will I get a good job having taken this course?
10. What will be in the exam?
11. Do you ever brush your hair?

Note that with both the students and Alison, the questions relate directly to whatever fascinates the questioner – another example of teaching needing to attach to the existing hooks of knowledge in order to engage the students' interest. From the above list of questions, numbers 1, 5, 7 and 9 relate to issues around career prospects, 2, 6 and 10 to passing the module, 1, 3, 4 and 8 to the general subject area and number 11 to the lecturer. This one experiment highlights the heterogeneity of a group of students, from those who want to know what it will take to pass the exams to those keen to find out more about the lecturer himself! Yet many still hope to find a 'one size fits all' educational model.

All this opened up explicitly for me the inherent complex messiness of university education. Associated issues of fear, reflection and engagement are illustrated in two crucial critical incidents that occurred in the lecture theatre. The first occurred as a result of two student emails and some student feedback about the course so far. An email from Tim suggested that, 'The assignments are good, but as you keep emphasizing in lectures, since this subject is a "doing" subject, why on earth is the coursework only worth 20 per cent of the module mark???? Surely, given the amount of time I and others spend on these assignment then surely it should be more like 40–50 per cent' (email, December 1999). A second email, this time from David, expressed the student's frustrations: 'this whole course is a joke how the hell are u ment to go from moving a stupid wee man across a room to a complex program like sun earth moon. U just keep on adding bits to the assessment and people cant even do the bits before it. Its not fair on the people who haven't done programming before. THIS IS MENT TO BE INTRODUCARY PROGRAMMING' (email, December 1999). Finally, a third anonymous comment as part of feedback on the lecture said simply: 'Kill John Smith [one of the other level 1 lecturers]' (Lecture feedback, December 1999).

All of these speak, in quite different styles, of confusion with the course structure, and certainly in the latter cases of extreme disengagement. The second email was a whole critical incident for me in its own right. Aware of how damaging these views could be to students' willingness to tackle the material of the course, and to wake up students to the processes and reactivity in which they were immersed, I summarized my thinking around these comments in two slides presented at the end of the next lecture, and shown here in Figures 6.2 and 6.3.

Figure 6.2   Student and staff attitudes to the learning process

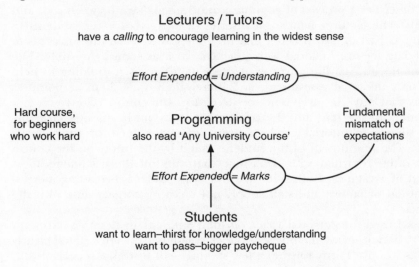

Figure 6.3   Communication barriers between staff and students

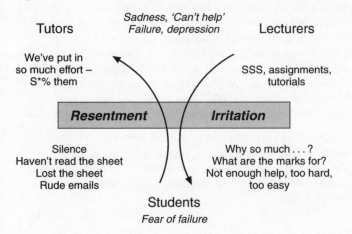

The slide in Figure 6.2 primarily answers the question posed by the first email, by making clear the differing viewpoints that staff and students have of the effort expended by students during a course. In most cases, the staff are keen primarily for the students to gain understanding about a particular subject, and the fact that assessment is required at all is only as a test of that understanding. The students, however, often consider that effort expended deserves marks, and hence a pass in the course, with little connection to the appropriate understanding expected by staff. There is a mismatch of expectations here, which leads on to the second slide in Figure 6.3, which describes a process of communication breakdown between staff and students. The lecturer hands out a series of exercises for the students to attempt, as part of a firm belief that the only way to learn the subject is to consolidate lecture material with practical work as soon as possible. The students do not see the purpose of these materials as scaffolding to help them pass the final assessment, and increasingly view them as pointless hurdles that must be overcome to succeed in the course. The result is a resentment of the staff and the course that leaks out in disengaged behaviour: silence in tutorials, lack of preparation and terse or rude emails to staff. The resentment of the students is felt by the tutors on the course and is often returned with behaviour that cuts off those students most in need of assistance. Both sides lose out, with students becoming increasingly afraid of failure and staff simply not enjoying contact time with the students.

When I used the personal attack on John Smith as an example of resentment/irritation, many members of the class laughed. When I stated clearly that this was not funny for me, a few still giggled. It took a repeat of this, and an enquiry as to whether they really thought this was constructive feedback, before the class as a *whole* engaged with the issue, and examined their response. As Alison commented, 'It's interesting to reflect on how is it you know that you've got them, what are they sending out, and it's actually silence.' Indeed, I could hear a pin drop in the 300-seat lecture theatre at that moment, but in addition there was a tangible increase in energy.

The final slide of the lecture, shown in Figure 6.4, encouraged students to view university education in a manner most likely different from any they'd had before – exploring in an environment of uncertainty but safety under the watchful eye of the teacher (the messy view of education). The following excerpt from a student's email is typical of responses to the lecture:

> Personally, I think that you should carry out that type of lecture, not periodically but occasionally – because it's very important to keep the link between us the students and the lecturers/tutors. I only realized this myself today when you showed the slide on what you thought was happening between the two.
>
> (December 1999)

The connection generated by this kind of interaction has been very compelling for me, and there has been a danger of valuing it above the course content to be covered. Yet at heart is my own passion to teach *all* the students this more universal material, to wake them *all* up to their reasons for being present in my lecture theatre. At a practical level, the learning for me from the incident is the crucial importance of keeping the students informed of the purposes of my teaching strategies, and to make them aware of the way that internal fears can lead to anger and resentment.

The second incident, and ensuing discussion with the Barcelona Group, illuminates this passion. On another occasion, I had asked a noisy contingent

Figure 6.4   The messy view of university education

Designed to make you wrestle with ideas – *to think*	*You* learn. We light the way, but do *not* teach	Encourage you to explore your strengths and weaknesses

University courses are hard

Expect you to work independently and from your own motivation	Clean yourself up when the s%$t hits the fan	We are not here to *tell* you how to think (or to program for that matter)

'*Too hard*' and '*too difficult*' are not in the university's dictionary. Anything goes – either you want this, or you should be elsewhere

You require a large dose of *personal responsibility*

of students at the rear of the theatre to be quiet, suggesting that since they had a choice to be there, no lecture being compulsory, it was unhelpful for them to sit in the theatre and talk their way through the lecture. This was not the first time that the work of the class had been impeded in this way, as I recounted in a Barcelona Group discussion:

> *Quintin*: I asked them quite passionately to be quiet and then as I went down the steps I heard this giggling from the back of the theatre and I just absolutely lost my rag; I had never done that before. That was another case where my passion about 'why are you here, what is this all about?' [came out.]
> *Mike*: What was their reaction?
> *Quintin*: Well, connection again, absolute connection like, you know, to me it seemed like I'd contacted right down to something that got them questioning, 'Why am I here?'

Some of them may have been plain embarrassed, of course. We continued to explore what seemed to have been going on:

> *Mike*: All of this is attached to a need or a desire to teach something. So you don't explode because you're in a bad mood, you explode because something un-named is interfering with your ability to do the teaching business and that something which is interfering is not a technical problem, it's a much deeper one. It's about your relationship with a group of people, a diverse group of people.
> *Melanie*: And it's inclusion into the structures of knowledge. So it's inclusion into getting a sense of being part of a community of learners.
> (Group discussion, January 2000)

My overriding sense here is of the importance of authenticity. My most committed moments with the students are when I am authentic, right to my toes. Once I had 'lost the rag', I owned my feelings in my chest at that moment, apologized for the outburst and explained about my passion for them to be in my lecture for a worthwhile reason, to tackle their university education with that same reason. Somehow, in seeing my humanity, the students are able to engage with their own deeper purpose.

The following email from a student underlines the importance of an inclusive approach. The student writes: 'At today's lecture you brought up some issues that were desperately needing attention. It pisses me off when people start talking . . . you must have extreme will power not to shout abuse at these individuals as I know I have fallen out with a few students doing just that' (email, January 2000). I am sad that I have not received any response from those at the rear of the class. Judging from the following email excerpt from a student, I should guess that they are thoroughly disenfranchised from the learning and teaching process and chose to demonstrate their frustration with their non-participatory presence in the class. I expect others demonstrate it with simpler non-attendance. In passing, the student said to me:

> This is on a different subject but I tried sitting in the back row a few lectures ago. They all seem to think they are rebels and they really have no cause. I wonder why they turn up in the first place. They just sneer at everything said in the lectures. There is a palpable sense of utter ignorance there, a place where I shall not be visiting again I think!
>
> (email, January 2000)

In these critical incidents, I am inspired to act out the kind of reflection that I am looking for from the students, perhaps most particularly from those in the back rows. In the first incident I received feedback, polite and rude, from both students and staff, then reflected on what was happening in my module and presented my findings back to them. I opened a channel of communication. In the second incident, I had also opened a channel of communication to let the students know my real feelings in that instant. The Barcelona Group commented:

> *Mike*: You've said, 'Hey, I'm reflecting on what you're doing to me and this is my reaction to it', so you're enacting what it is you want the students to do but equally you're doing it in a way that is trying to include rather than divide. So you've got this diverse group, some of whom are behaving well and some of whom are behaving badly and what you're doing by turning round at that moment, is actually embracing the whole theatre and bringing them all together and including them.

Melanie: Your story, more than any of the others, is about not having the ideal group necessarily to work with. It's a very large group with very different aspirations and expectations and that's why the notion of the inclusivity of the teaching is so important because your aspiration, your value position is to try and find a way to teach all of those students.

(Group discussion, January 2000)

Conclusion

To put into perspective what programming teachers are trying to do, Alison exclaimed while comparing German courses with level 1 programming courses, 'That's like trying to teach the whole of German grammar and a large chunk of literature in one semester!' In another conversation with colleagues, one commented that in modern language terms, programming teachers were perhaps putting together in a single course native English-speaking students who had no knowledge of foreign languages with those who had widely varying degrees of ability in some or all of French, German, Italian and Spanish, and then teaching them all a beginners course in Greek.

As the middle sections of the chapter indicate, I have been trying during the Barcelona secondment to discern a *right* way to teach programming in a short module. The truth is of course that, in line with messiness and uncertain knowledge, there is probably no right way. In each new teaching session, I match available resources with my current understanding of the discipline and the environment, and teach as best I can to every member of the class. The realization about uncertainty, about which I have told my students often, comes home once again. I take full responsibility for my actions and my life and in the same breath release myself from the demand for some unattainable perfection. In recent years, by contrast with my early reflective writing, I notice that I care less about whether the students like me. Indeed, I find that the students write less about the qualities of their lecturer and more about what they have gained from the course itself. In the role of teacher-expert to the novice, I have been modelling a *way of being* with the challenges around us, while at the same time teaching masterful programming, as far as I know what this means.

Whether we like the currently popular phrase 'lifelong learning', we are confronted by it. Everything we do changes us and requires an openness to the new learning available. The students, whose cycle of change is the most evident, are challenged to adopt responsibility for themselves and their learning beyond that of their schooldays. My colleagues, my department, academia as a whole are all challenged to accept the changing nature of higher education and to make a stand for our fundamental beliefs. And myself? I am challenged repeatedly to learn that there is no right answer to the many dilemmas in life, and to acknowledge my ability to search for a worthwhile path nonetheless.

Notes

1. Celtic is one of the football clubs in Glasgow, and Parkhead is the name of its stadium.
2. This is an attitude that is slowly changing as university policy changes.
3. The Scottish education system has an exam classification known as Higher, used to examine students on study from the age of 16 to 17. Students usually take around five Highers and may enter university on the basis of these qualifications at the age of 17.
4. A tool provided in a software package to assist the user to perform some operation. The wizard requests key information from the user about the operation and then performs it without further intervention.
5. SYS is a further grading level for Scottish students who choose to stay on for an extra year after their Highers, from the age of 17 to 18.

References

Barnett, R. (2000) *Realizing the University in an age of supercomplexity*. Buckingham: SRHE/Open University Press.
Polya, G. (1957) *How to Solve It*, 2nd edn. Princeton, NJ: Princeton University Press.
Smith, T. (1996) *The Ideas of the University*. Sydney: Research Institute for the Humanities and Social Sciences/Power Publications, the University of Sydney.

7
Measuring Performance:
Some Alternative Indicators

Alison Phipps

In the middle of a Ceilidh the student who was helping me to dance 'Strip the Willow' asked breathlessly over the music: 'Dr Phipps, do you think about Adorno when you are dancing?'

This chapter will not give an answer to that question: sometimes answers are those of delighted laughter and surprise; answers of wilful secrecy; answers that keep students guessing and puzzling over the stories and movements and shapes that their teacher embodies; answers that have an erotic power, that compel, that dance and desire dancing. But this chapter does seek to investigate other questions this question raised. What are the conditions that make such a question possible? What is the role of the teacher 'Dr Phipps', of knowledge, of 'Adorno' and of 'dancing' in bringing a student to formulate such a question? How do students gain access to esoteric knowledges and come to apply them with such embodied ease? What is lost in the process when only measurable performance indicators are used?

The data that I examine in this piece are taken from an honours level course in the German Department at Glasgow University. Over the course of two years, using an action research methodology, I have engaged with my own teaching practices and the learning experiences of my students. I have collected data in the form of focus group transcripts, retrospective narratives, video tapes of student performance, audio transcripts of class plenaries and student group discussions both in and outside the classroom. The data are rich and compelling and through them I will seek to critique and juxtapose the traditional structures and assumptions about learning in higher education with alternative structures and principles which I have identified through this research project.

I explored my stories, sought interpretations and found some tentative answers to these questions with the group of researchers drawn from different disciplines who came together to investigate the different disciplinary qualities of teaching and learning and whose work is integrated into this book. This group provided a space for evaluation and critical reflection on the teaching process and on the learning of the students on my course. The reflections of this group were key to the development of the course and to a recognition of the importance of curricula, i.e. of the specificity of practice to the discipline and to the embodiment of that discipline in the body of the teacher. But this group also served to discover common elements of alternative practice. The group was particularly concerned to create spaces and offer support in an institutional environment where, in McGrath's words, all too often teaching and learning were competitive, individualistic, lonely endeavours: 'Pedagogics is the art of passing down information and judgements, the art of the superior to the inferior. Distance, in place of solidarity; pseudo-scientific 'objectivity' in place of frank admission of a human, partisan and emotional perspective – coldness, in place of shared experience' (McGrath, 1982: 40–1).

Box 7.1   Case studies in popular German culture

Honours option, 15 students, 20 contact hours
Classes run fortnightly, seminars last 2 hours

Assessment: One written assignment of 3,000 to 4,000 words, two final examination questions

Mode
Classes are participatory. Students work together in small groups of five and in the plenaries to discuss task-based questions and problems which relate to popular German films and texts and to theories of popular culture. Each seminar sees the introduction of a different theory of popular culture and of a different case study. Students are expected to read the theoretical background and to work on the case study before each class. They will meet in their small groups between classes to discuss questions which relate the theories to the case studies. The first hour of each class takes the form of a plenary, with each of the groups feeding back in turn on their task as it relates to the case study and the theory. Others ask questions, make notes and add their opinion. The teacher's role here is as chair, trouble shooter and devil's advocate. As the course develops, the questions, tasks, presentations and discussions gain in complexity. Theoretical questions are addressed in a variety of ways and revisited in tasks and discussions throughout the course. The second hour of the course is in two parts. The teacher introduces the next theory of popular culture, supplementing material that the students have already engaged with, with examples and discussion and critique. The students then discuss this new theory in their groups and begin to apply it to the case studies. Recursion is an important element of the course, as is space, in small groups and in plenaries, for open questioning and exploration of ideas. The teacher engages informally with all the small groups in the classroom as their discussions unfold.

This is, sadly, also the dominant view expressed of teaching in higher education by many of the students who were invited to contribute their opinions on good learning and critical practice as part of our action research project. Alan Read's ethics of performance asks 'what makes for good theatre?' I wish to ask, again and with others, 'what makes for good pedagogy?' I want to demonstrate the importance of the rootedness of pedagogy in everyday relations and to transpose the theatrical metaphor into the classroom in order better to understand the 'epiphanal nature' (Read, 1993: 11) that pertains to good pedagogy as well as to good 'performances'. Action research, for me, has been about knowing and viewing the everyday experiences of student learning and of my own practices more critically, and to do this I have needed the critical relationships, collegiality and support that the Barcelona Group offered. This group has helped me to see my limitations and to dance beyond them. Ben Okri's 'Flamenco Dancer', where 'A flamenco dancer, lurking under a shadow prepares for the terror of her dance' (Okri, 1996: 9) is one that has haunted my work and challenged my assumptions in much the same way as the group's relations, my relations with my students and with my disciplinary home have been haunting, inspiring and challenging. I shall use extracts from Okri's piece throughout to illuminate those relations. This dancer inspires me to try out some steps and to teach those moves that I know to others. The understandings I have reached about my own practice and my students' learning, the increasing reflexivity that informs my work are not my own but are the work of a mesh of relationships, of understandings and counter-understandings that helped me to prepare for and participate in the 'dance'.

Dr Phipps

> I want to dwell for a little while on this dancer. I want you to dwell on this dancer because, though a very secular example, she speaks well for the power of human transcendence.
>
> (Okri, 1996: 9)

In a discussion of an earlier draft of this chapter, one that focused mostly on the student voices and on metaphors of Artaud's plague, the group offered comments and in particular pointed to my absence from the story of the course. So, awkward as it may be, I offer the following reflection on Dr Phipps. I offer it in the third person because Dr Phipps is a representative of a critical professional and because, through this rhetorical move, I am attempting to gain a critical distance and facilitate reflection. 'Dr Phipps' is a creature of the academic classroom. She is thought to be young. She has studied German and, it would appear from the courses she teaches, theatre studies too, and some anthropology. Her students think she teaches 'cool stuff' – Popular German Culture is one of the special subjects that her

Glasgow honours students take. It requires students to watch contemporary German films and read contemporary best-sellers – it's a 'sexy' subject. It also requires students to read, understand and apply theories of popular culture, such as those from the Frankfurt School, most notably those of Adorno. And her options classes are usually quite big, relative to others. Melanie asked the students in a focus group session why they had chosen the course:

Melanie: Did it have a short reading list?
Lisa: Yes, but it wasn't that, it was more the content of the reading list. I could sit down and read it quite easily although it was in a foreign language and that doesn't happen very often.
Jon: I think one of the most important things was the books themselves because they were sort of up-to-date and quite modern, whereas a lot of things we do are, you know, most of the people we've been studying have been dead for like a hundred and fifty years or something, so I found it quite good in that way.

(Focus group interview, 21 January 1999)

Reflecting back on the course, another student, now a postgraduate, made a similar observation, in a separate taped discussion with Melanie: 'I don't think most people that do her courses are aware of how hard they are going to be when they start, especially with a title like 'Popular Culture'. It sounds much lighter than something like studying Lessing or Middle High German or something like that' (Interview, 19 March 1999).

Dr Phipps is somehow different, in curricular terms. Her teaching sets her apart from the traditional German literature and language courses that the students encounter more commonly in the department. She is angered by the implications of articles such as the one by Claire Fox in the *Times Higher Education Supplement* (26 February 1999) entitled 'Picky, Coddled Students? Make them read Beowulf':

The key task now is to make courses attractive to more students. Students have become consumers and lecturers forced into selling their wares. Courting student approval is seen as a necessary marketing strategy . . . Accepting student-centredness means adopting a focus group approach to what happens in universities . . . Take pick and mix modular, interdisciplinary degrees: How can students choose when they do not know how to construct a meaningful syllabus? They need leadership and guidance.

There is an issue here. The popularity of a course with students can suggest that a lecturer has sold out to the market and is making life 'too easy'. It is, after all, a commonplace that those who teach cultural studies are 'trendy-lefty pinkos' who are 'student-centred' and who are heading up the race to 'dumb down' higher education and drop standards in the name of 'access'. Such accusations bring their own pain to critical professionals, pointing, as they do, to a supposed lack of academic integrity.

Somebody has wounded her in words, alluding to the fact that she has no fire, or duende. She knows how to dance her way past her limitations, and this may destroy her forever. She has to fail or she has to die . . . I want you to imagine this frail woman. I want you to see her in deep shadow and fear.

(Okri, 1996: 9)

The Dr Phippses, the Barcelonans of this world, can thus become easy game in the scramble to blame. Asking the 'picky' students what they think, 'coddling' them in a focus group (heaven forbid), when they are clearly devoid of any valid opinion on the subject of learning, becomes a bogus activity and the hallmark of anti-intellectualism and market ideology. The problem with stereotyping teaching approaches – from whatever ideological position – is that stereotypes are stupid, they can't think, they aren't critical, they are just Aunt Sallies or straw men, put there by those who need to fight a dummy to show the power of their argument.

And so these 'picky, coddled students', who may not be reading Beowulf but who are reading Adorno, wonder about the subtlety of what has been happening to them as a result of having a particular body of knowledge, embodied, in part, by their teacher in their particular learning context. In fact they begin to discover other questions they have about Dr Phipps, activating their own desire to understand the transformations that their learning has brought about. In the safe, structured space of the reflective focus group with her and Melanie, they question her and reflect with her:

Lisa: I think there was one class in particular, I can't remember what it was and we were all were like, 'sorry, explain that in simpler terms' . . . And then you put it into something really simple. I can't remember the example now, but I was like, 'Oh, yeah, right, OK!' Now I don't get that from group work, I don't get that from my own sitting with the book for five hours or whatever long it took me.

Jon: Lisa said earlier that you need to have a leader there to sort of guide us through it all and I think that's the most important role that you play in the class.

Peter: But I think in a way you're trying to bring us to a certain sort of way of seeing things and answering questions and things like that but it's more subtle than just being here and saying, 'Right, this is what I'm teaching you and this is what you learn and that's it.' I think it's different. I think it's much more that you're trying to see how we react and I think that what's more interesting really in the teaching is how we sort of receive what you're giving and what we give back. I think we still respect the power but it's different I think.

Jon: Do you think that your role is to make us more able to think by ourselves? Because that's what I think. I think that's more what you're trying to get at.

Peter: Do you sometimes feel you're doing something subversive?

Alison: (whispers) Surely not. (All laugh.)

(Focus group interview, 21 January 1999)

In her inaugural lecture *Being Naughty: a Play for Justice?*, Griffiths (1998: 12) highlights the potentialities for play – naughty play, subversive play – for tackling injustice and, for women in particular, for focusing on 'the difficulties faced by dealing with difference'. Being gently, ironically naughty is one of the strategies Griffiths advocates for illuminating structures that repress difference. And for Dr Phipps there is something risky, naughty even, in crossing this honesty boundary with students, and letting them in on the secret:

> *Alison*: Yes I do, yes. I find it quite painful at times, if I'm really honest, when I hear your stories of other courses or when I see comments that students bring to me in floods of tears, or when I see how devalued and frightened and angst ridden you can become, then I feel . . . if I can go a small way to just reversing that a little bit and give you a positive experience and show you what I think university education is about, then yes, it is subversive.
>
> (Interview, April 1998)

When the music starts she begins her dance, with ritual slowness. Then she stamps out the dampness from her soul. Then she stamps fire into her loins. She takes on a strange enchanted glow. With a dark tragic rage, shouting, she hurls her hungers, her doubts, her terrors, and her secular prayer for more light into the spaces around her. All fire and fate, she spins her enigma around us, and pulls us into the awesome risk of the dance.

> (Okri, 1996: 10)

But 'subversive' Dr Phipps is still 'Dr Phipps'. There is an apparent incongruence here – one that surprised Melanie and others in the Barcelona Group particularly. The other Barcelonan staff were not, as a rule, addressed formally by their students. Alison was: 'and I said to Dr Phipps', and, 'I'm used to Dr Phipps' teaching.' Indeed, noticing this pattern emerging in the early stages of a focus group, Melanie modified her address too: 'What are the sort of things that Alison is doing, Dr Phipps is doing?'

She is taking herself apart before our sceptical gaze.

> (Okri, 1996: 10)

This highlights the particular discourse that is at work in the course and the ambiguity involved in the need on the part of the students for safe, clear rules when other cultural norms were being subverted in their learning experience. According to Gee,

> [Discourse] is not language, and surely not grammar, but *saying–doing– being–valuing–believing combinations* . . . Discourses are ways of being in the world; they are forms of life which integrate words, acts, values, beliefs, attitudes, and social identities as well as gestures, glances, body positions, and clothes.
>
> (Gee, 1989: 6, emphasis added)

When *saying* 'Dr Phipps' the students are unconsciously situating themselves in a tradition that articulates the power relationship of students and
lecturer, and, in earlier education, of pupil and teacher. They are *doing*
distance, difference, awareness of an authority, even fear of that authority's
power to do good and ill. They are *being* students, learners, respecters of the
institutional rites of passage that set them at different stages on a scale of
development. They are also *being* what students before them have been and
have taught them. They are *valuing* their space, their peers' conventions,
the safety of the culture of the department they are a part of, but also their
distance from the work that leads to such titles as 'Dr'. And they are *believing* in the processes of knowledge and learning in whatever form they encounter them, because of the guise they come in. Dr Phipps, aware as she is
of the liberal, humanist ethics on the left of equality and equity in relations,
tried to enable her students to call her by her first name. They resisted, they
felt uncomfortable, awkward, it wasn't a discourse they wanted to be part of,
at least not until after they had graduated and power relations had been
transformed by the examination rites. Dominic, her former student and
postgraduate, reflected on this critically with Melanie:

Melanie: Why do you think the undergraduate students hold fast to, or
    particularly like the boundary between themselves and Alison? She is
    always Dr Phipps to them . . . I mean she wouldn't mind at all if they
    called her Alison, but the students want to call her Dr Phipps.
Dominic: They have respect for her. She's their teacher and they need
    to know that she is the possessor of the knowledge and they need to
    believe that . . . I think it's a lot to do with the whole way that univer-
    sity is set up and that's the way universities traditionally have been.
    There's always been this distance between the knowledge holder and
    the knowledge receiver and you know . . . Alison might be happy to
    be called Alison but I don't think that would necessarily be true for
    a large portion of other staff.

(Interview, 19 March 1999)

The discussion above about Dr Phipps is an example of what Griffiths has
termed the theory of the 'patchwork' self – 'neither a unity nor fragmented'.

It is a patchwork in which new patches join, adjoin or obscure what is
already there, changing it in the process. It is never possible to throw
away the whole construction and start again . . . The idea of a patchwork self sheds light on the relation of self-identity to questions of
justice, since some of the patches are formed precisely by the nature of
the society as a whole: its power structures with their accompanying
dominant stereotypes.

(Griffiths, 1998: 9)

The patchwork self here, in the body of this teacher, is one that is striving to
find ways of being a critical professional, reflecting on practice, refining
approaches, collecting stories and discovering a creed of values and principles.

The neo-liberal values that dominate the context of higher education, the existential angst that prevails in modern languages, the fear and frustration of students and the critical hope of the Barcelonans make up part of the patchwork as it turns, changes and grows in shape, structure and dexterity through the teaching experience and through the critical reflection upon the questions the experience raises.

'Do you think?'

She is disintegrating, shouting and stamping and dissolving the bound-aries of her own body. Soon she becomes a wild unknown force. Glowing in her death, dancing from her wound, dying in her dance.

(Okri, 1996: 10)

It is within the context of notions of the patchwork self that I find myself questioning views of professionalism, even if critical professionalism is about engaged, politicized teaching and learning. Professionalism, as a static noun, a state of being not doing, suggests only one piece of cloth in the patch-work self. Critical, intellectual engagement, whether of the learner or the teacher (and the teacher in my experience is often the student), demands a more vocational, demanding view of the life it challenges us to live. Barnett's (1997: 179) coinage of 'professing-in-action: that form of professional life in which professionals live up to their professional calling by engaging critically with the world' is perhaps more pertinent. The language carries overtones of Romanticism and of religious calling. This is not as big a problem for me as the careerist, technocratic discourse that sees me as a functioning, reliable instrument of tortuous teaching and which seeks to deprofessionalize my role by replacing my autonomy and judgement with targets, aims, objectives and benchmarks. All language is slippery and com-promised by history. All engagement is slippery and compromised and part of the process of history. Critical engagement, or 'criticality' as Barnett terms it, is about much more than a clean, safe, rights-protected contractual obligation that professionalism suggests. It is more than legal idolatry and docile compliance: 'A more adequate and serviceable version of ethics would focus less closely on the institutions (obligations etc.) or morality. It would make room for consideration of the virtues, and of what constitutes a per-sonally fulfilling life, including concern for self alongside concern for others' (Blake *et al.*, 1998: 97).

Engagement, in this context, is about working critically to give students a chance to shine, not through threat but through careful nurture, or, to quote Gee (1989: 7), through 'enculturation ("apprenticeship") into social practices, through scaffolded and supported interaction with people who have already mastered the Discourse.' It is about providing opportunities for students to experience the building of learning communities and about showing them alternatives and ways of critiquing the dominant discourses and structures that make up the flow of the status quo.

Why do I dwell on this dancer? I dwell on her because she represents for me the courage to go beyond ourselves. Whilst she danced she became the dream of the freest and most creative people we had always wanted to be, in whatever it is we do. She destroyed us because we knew in our hearts that rarely do we rise to the higher challenges in our lives, or our work, or our humanity.

(Okri, 1996: 11)

Doing this work is about knowing that teaching transforms and not trying to stifle this: 'The liberal classroom that avoids overt talk of form and superficialities, of how things work, as well as of their socio-cultural political basis, is no help' (Gee, 1989: 13).

In this respect I also believe that engaged criticality is about performance indicators. I am not interested here in the dominant discourse of perform-ance indicators, the discourse that Blake *et al.* (1998: 4) criticize when they review the Dearing Report on higher education:

This is not a picture that asks for the transformation of students into flexible mathematicians, flexible linguists or flexible social scientists. On the contrary, it calls for graduates to be ideally no particular kind of person at all. The ideal graduate is not assumed, in this picture, to be one who can draw on her deep knowledge and understanding of one area of knowledge to extend it, sideways or in depth, by analogy or reapplication to new ideas. Unencumbered by bodies of knowledge, she becomes the adept of information access and the dubious beneficiary of 'transferable' skills.

This is the discourse that fills the web sites of staff development and quality assurance. It is a deprofessionalizing discourse of standards that assumes practitioners are failing to do their jobs 'effectively' and that students have to learn to learn 'effectively'. In the functionalist literature on teaching and learning in higher education effectiveness is a virtue. What is 'effective' practice is 'good' practice (see Ramsden, 1992). The Institute of Education, University of London, produced a special edition of its research news letter entitled 'Effective learning' (*SIN Research Matters*, no. 5, 1996), which is a handy guide to practice, using Kolb's 'effective' active learning model and present-ing readers with useful learner characteristics – models that are 'effective' and will produce 'effective' learners, helped along by an increasing army of counsellors that 'effective' lecturers and 'oh-so-desperate-to-be-effective' learners may draw upon, namely 'effective' learning advisers. The problem here is that what is effective is all very well, but it is only the beginning of the story, because what is good, graceful, considered, what is wise, sparky, 'cool' and elegant, what is disciplined, synthesized, creative and intelligent never is primarily and obviously 'effective'. The effectiveness of such qualities in a learner or in a teacher is a very minor and rather boring part of the story. The discourse or 'default language' (Blake *et al.*, 1998) of effectiveness turns teaching and learning into a technical exercise in individualized managerialism, for both the teacher and the learner. Or, as McWilliam and Palmer (1996: 165) put it, 'Desire is collapsed into motivation, pleasure becomes performance indicators, eros is rendered excellence.'

Thankfully, the humanities and human beings have recourse to a much older tradition of performance – that of mimesis. Live performance, dramatic transformations, epic stories, comedies and tragedies are all actively at work and struggling 'to drain colossal social and ethical abscesses', to quote the surrealist man of the theatre, Antonin Artaud, to lance the poisonous boils of systems, structures and practices (of whatever ideological persuasion) which do not produce education but products, which produce graduates who are 'employable', 'flexible' and most of all unthinkingly compliant. As a critical being I have sought, modestly at times, and with fierce arrogance at others, within the limits imposed on practice, to create spaces in the courses for performance, for group-based, problem-based learning, for playing with ideas and for creative confusion as values-in-action of critical professionalism. My own view of student performance has often been wilfully at odds with the paucity of notions of performance indicators, aims and objectives, yet the students have been successful, many gaining first class marks. The students taking this course have also been successful in other ways – ways they value, ultimately, more than their assessment gradings.

When asked how their experience of a different approach, an approach that understood itself to be 'doing criticality', matched up to their normal expectations they gave a variety of replies:

> *Kate*: There's also the fact that I don't feel as if I've got to know this because I'm doing an exam. I get the idea that it's more a learning thing than actually looking forward to a degree and I like that fact that it's kind of, just go in and enjoy learning some things and not worry about the fact that I've got to sit finals.
>
> *Heather*: And just the way we all responded to each other, like when we watched a different group perform, we all, you know, responded to them, the way that we knew they wanted us to respond . . . You feel like you're all doing everything together, whereas in other classes, it is just one little person standing all by themselves.
>
> *Kate*: I don't ever feel like we've finished . . . all these ideas, no one has got the answer to them. Its just so good to be able to think about it rather than having to just accept it, listen to what the lecturer's saying and write an essay on it.
>
> *Heather*: I think also the fact that we all know each other's names. I find that in lots of classes there are people in the classes that I do not know their name at all, which is awful, but you don't hear it all the time, whereas Dr Phipps always says your name and there's always references to your name everytime you say something 'Yes, Heather, Yes Judy'.
>
> (Focus group interview, 15 March 1999)

This view of life, this paradigm for university teaching, is one that sits uncomfortably with notions of effectiveness. What is interesting is how *ineffective* the 'effectiveness' discourse is in practice; how little content it appears to have. The managerialist discourse on effective learning is rather like the Emperor's New Clothes; there is nothing there. The student focus groups provided many examples of the everyday experience of learning and of encounters with professionals in the university context. John McGrath's (1982: 40–1) view of pedagogy as the art of superiority was affirmed by the students as a normal experience of learning:

> *Lisa*: I would be more willing to cooperate with someone that's going to, not say I'm right all the time, but make me feel as if I'm being right, than someone that is very condescending. You know that they're there and you're here, put it that way.
>
> *Jon*: And they make it very clear 'This is what I think, so obviously . . .', well I get the impression sometimes, 'This is what I think, so this is obviously what you should be thinking as well'.
>
> *Lisa*: 'I'm much cleverer than you.'
>
> (Focus group interview, 21 January 1999)

Their examples and stories of bad learning experiences versus good learning experiences did not include encounters with models of 'effective' learning or with anything that just 'worked', at least not in the humanities. Models do not teach and learn. Effective models do not teach and learn. People do. Relationships and respect within the learning context were the key elements for the students. Learning occurred if they had been confident enough to speak and to engage with the material and with their tutor, if they had been relaxed enough to learn, if they had experienced desire and thirst for knowledge and for time to play with ideas as well as an environment that nurtured and supported their work:

It is relationships that form the focus for Blake *et al.* (1998: 100, 98):

> The relation between teacher and taught is a dialogical one – quality of experience is what counts . . .
>
> Unable to form any real personal relationship with lecturers and tutors whose name they may barely know (and are seldom known by), they are correspondingly less able to experience and internalise the norms, value and methods of the subject or discipline of study . . . or they find it difficult to make connections between their own individual lives and modules 'packaged' in such a way across faculties.

Hot air expended on effectiveness on the one hand or on ineffectiveness on the other masks the real issue: the values, attitudes and relationships that come together in classrooms, in corridors, in tutorials and lectures, and most especially in the curriculum. It is these values that produce desire, respect, rapport, effort, reflection in all who are critically engaged. Evans and Abbot (1998: 57–8) highlight the importance of positive relationships in the learning process:

Yet our findings revealed our tutors to be, for the most part, unaware of the level of anxiety which some students, albeit a minority, experienced in seminars. Since they were unaware of this, tutors were, therefore, also unaware of the extent of their potential for boosting or lowering students' self confidence and of their capacity for enhancing or damaging students' self esteem . . . Tutors' qualities as teachers, it appears, not only determined what students learned but also how they felt about what they learned.

In the same way, McGrath is critical of the 'superiorizing' of certain teachers. The bigger problem for these critics and for myself is precisely the way certain pedagogic practices fail to inspire. Where values, principles, thoughtless or unreflective practices are instrumental, weary, neutralized or condescending, where the relations don't spark, for whatever reason (and many of the reasons are very good), exclusion occurs. The burden here should be not only on the teachers, but on the learners too, but the burden should be a shared one, one which is acknowledged, one through which all can relate:

Dominic (reflecting back): I suppose being completely non-threatening, showing obviously genuine interest, an interest in people outside the classroom and not just in the classroom . . . that element of being, you know, human interaction . . . You are a human, I'm not just your teacher and that's the way that she teaches and I think that's the way that she has to teach and I think she wouldn't feel comfortable teaching any other way.

(Interview, 19 March 1999)

That spirit of the leap into the unknown, that joyful giving of the self's powers, that wisdom of going beyond in order to arrive here – that too is beyond words.

(Okri, 1996: 12)

'Adorno'

'To escape boredom and avoid effort are incompatible', wrote Adorno. The content of the Popular German Culture course demanded effort and consequently demanded that students escape from boredom. Key pedagogic relationships are relationships to material, in its textual form and in the form it takes as it becomes embodied in the learners and is presented in the body of the teacher. It is tempting not to let students loose on theoretical models and difficult texts. Students do complain about lectures and seminars that are 'too difficult', 'go over their heads', but not because they are questioning these aspects of the curriculum, as Fox would have it (see earlier), but because they haven't yet found a way of establishing a relationship to the material, of forging a dialogue with a demanding text. University is the place of the 'too difficult'. If the 'too difficult' is not tackled in the academy then it will not be tackled: the space to think and to play with ideas *with others* and *through material* is the very privilege of intellectual work. And there are no 'effective' ways of approaching Adorno, or the subject of postmodernism, or Saussure's theories of language, all of which have challenged common-sense assumptions about culture and language and meaning in the context of modernity, other than through the effort of forging and nurturing a critical relationship with them. Such critical relationships are transformational, they add perspectives to life. The students experienced this from their own reading and by observing the effects of their new-found knowledges:

Lisa: Right at the very beginning in the first chapter I think, although it was a bit extreme the theory, but it was literally about how the masses are just totally taken in by the whole mass media thing and I could see it happening and I could see me going home and doing the things that it was saying I was doing.

Peter: It makes you really aware of what you're doing and what's happening.

Anna: Does that mean that you change what you are doing? Does it stop you doing what you're doing or does it make you do things differently?

Jon: It makes you recognise what you're doing. It's not so much, I don't know, that it makes you change what you're doing, but it makes you recognise what you're doing and makes you think about why you're doing it. It goes back to like sitting watching this film where I knew what was going to happen at the end anyway. I'd never seen it before but it's just that it's so predictable and things and it's because I've seen fifty or however many films that follow these patterns.

Peter: I think it could change your vision of the world if you really want to, it might change that. It's obviously quite, that's why I find it sometimes scary.

Nancy: It didn't stop me going home and sitting watching the TV or reading magazines or wanting to be interested in what film's coming out or what I should go and see, so it didn't change it like that but I think that it did change my views about feminism and make them a bit more together because it straightened a few things out in my head.

Kate: It's quite good when you realise why you think that . . . It's really helped me think better, I think, in general about everything and applying it.

Jon: The point is I don't think I actually had a view of society before. Society was there it was what I lived in but I didn't really have a view of why it was like that. I think that's what gives you a sort of different way to look and see, you know, why things are the way they are and why are people the way they are. Whereas before I don't think I really thought a lot about that. I probably moaned about certain aspects of society but I never really had any idea what society was.

Kate: I almost think more of popular culture now than I did before.

Marie: But it sounds like your choices are much more conscious.

Jon: I feel as if we are all sitting here saying, you know, this changes the way I think and so on.

Lisa: No I think it has, I think it's changed my opinion of university even, because of the confidence thing as well. Before the course I probably wouldn't have spoken much in the tutorial because I had the impression that anything I said wasn't good enough, you know, I was frightened to come out with something that would sound good and I couldn't do it and I think it has really built up my confidence a lot as well and that's only in a very short space of time.

(Focus group interview, 21 January 1999)

Dominic: I mean I obviously learnt a lot about cultural theory and it was a completely new area for me and personally fascinating . . . it was like what's going on outside, what's going on outside the window and for me that was wonderful. I just really really could, you know, get my teeth into it.

(Interview, 19 March 1999)

'Metaknowledge', writes Gee (1989: 13), the kinds of knowledges that these students have experienced working in their lives, 'is liberation and power'. Kramer-Dahl (1995: 31) sees critical consciousness as language consciousness and is as scathing of neo-liberal discourses as of liberal humanist ones for their part in the politics of exclusion: 'At worst it [liberal humanism] generates an illusion of agency and empowerment which helps conceal the extent to which this dominant discursive formation validates certain ways of knowing and marginalises others.' The students were aware of being excluded from discourses of power and were also aware of the way the relationships they had forged with the material had enabled them to participate:

Heather: I remember about two years ago, I was sitting with my friend and his dad, who are both really sort of hyper intelligent, sitting in the pub and they were talking about some picture that was postmodern and I just sat there completely silent for about an hour, thinking 'God, I'm so stupid, I don't understand any of this at all' and now you hear people say something and you actually do know, you notice things that people say all the time and suddenly they have a lot more meaning to them.

(Focus group interview, 15 March 1999)

The effort, that makes a mockery of the notion of performance indicators and returns performance to its rightful, playful, mischievous place, is the enjoyment of difficulty for all engaged in this learning process. It led Melanie to 'push' the students on their reactions to the difficulty of the tasks set:

Melanie: I mean why don't you just rebel and say to Alison, 'How do you expect us to answer this question?'

Jon: 'Cos its interesting.

Marie: Right.

Jon: It's difficult but it's something that you enjoy, especially in the groups.

Nancy: I think the main difference is that most lecture courses or any courses we've done for German so far, you get told all the time to think for yourself and when you write an essay we want your own ideas as well, but all you get in lectures is the lecturer's thoughts on it and then somewhere you've got to make up your own ideas.

Jon: There are aspects of all the theories as well that you think, you know, that you think you don't agree with, like the idea that all, you know, that popular culture is there to dupe people and the people can't notice this because basically they're too thick to be able to or whatever. There are things that you say 'I don't agree with that' as well and that's what I like about it in that you take the bits out of it that you think that you can agree with and things, but there are bits in almost every theory that I think that I don't agree with.

Peter: That's the playful element. You're going to have this assignment and you're going to choose some theories that you like or find interesting and then you're free to do what you want, you know, that's what I like.

(Focus group transcript, 21 January 1999)

Critical approaches to a difficult curriculum, on the basis of these student data, may be seen to have transforming effects on the social experience of learning and of building community in higher education. In response to questions about their course on Popular German Culture and their experience of learning in problem-based, yet critically motivated, group sessions and plenaries, Melanie asked: 'So what's all that got to do with university education?' The response:

Jon: It's what it should be.

Kate: A lot more than some of the things we do.

(Focus group interview, 21 January 1999)

'What it should be' for the students is neither neutral nor gently violent, to use Foucault's term. It is a time for nurture – both of over-wintering after hard, disciplined pruning, and of the fecund blossoming of spring. It is charged with the force and effort of life, embodied life, not just rational life, and it calls for allowing what bel hooks (1994) sees as the presence of 'eros in the classroom as a motivating force'.

Dancing

We seldom try for that beautiful greatness brooding in the mystery of our blood.

(Okri, 1996: 11)

As part of my professional duty to take student 'performance' seriously, the students were expected to produce an assignment that was fully assessed as coursework, and a class presentation. The remit for the presentation was to prepare a celebration of the course, in their own fun performances. The students were given free rein to dress up, write their own scripts and perform, but most of all to embody the theories and the content of the course they had been studying. McWilliam (1995: 106) writes of a similar enterprise in her discussion of a lecture as a postmodern event: 'Role play or dramatic performance is not a pedagogical product here, but a postmodern perform-ance or event generated by and generating new processes and forms of engagement with educational ideas.' My own use of performance had similar aims. I wanted to see what the new knowledges could look like inside student bodies, not only on paper in their assignments. I wanted to see the playfulness and potentialities of criticality in the students and I wanted them to see this in each other, to see the new discourses in critical action.

The presentations were group presentations, the assignments individual, but informed by group discussions and a common sense of action. Through-out the course learning had occurred in groups as well as in individuals. As a result of the group discussions and learning projects micro 'communities of practice' (Lave and Wenger, 1999) had taken shape. Lave and Wenger (1999) see communities of practice as places where the circulation of know-ledge among peers or near peers means knowledge spreads rapidly and effectively – engaging in practice rather than being its object allows learners to make the culture of practice their own. It was Vygotsky (1978: 85) in *Mind in Society* who drew attention to this social dimension of learning: 'Over a decade even the profoundest thinkers never questioned the assump-tion; they never entertained the notion that what children can do with the assistance of others might be in some sense even more indicative of their mental development than what they can do alone.'

The students certainly had a sense of community, of practice and of owner-ship with regard to the group processes and their own group's performance:

Alison: Do you think that the groups that you're working in have a knowledge, a kind of social knowledge or level of knowledge that they reach that is different to your personal knowledge?
Jon: It's like adding all the personal knowledges up.
Nancy: Yeah it's like all the mixture of knowledges.
Jon: Everybody comes with their own and thinks 'That's it, that's what I got out of it and I can't get any more out of it' but then someone else will say 'Yeah, well, but you've not got this or what did you think about that?' and I'd be like 'I don't get that at all out of it.'
Peter: I'm actually surprised to see how well it works. I mean it's quite amazing when you think about it, because we are so different. I know we might come from different backgrounds and have different experi-ences and eventually it works and I'm amazed to see what others do.

Lisa: I think for this particular course, the group work is now, after having participated, it is essential, I don't think you could have a course like that without the group work, because I really don't think you would get anything out of it at all.

Jon: I just think that it's because people apply it so much to experience.

(Focus group interview, 21 January 1999)

Both performances caused excitement and panic and pushed the students beyond the safe confines of effectiveness models. The essay, a question designed to be open and to make the students take a stance and form a critical opinion *vis-à-vis* the subject, became a highly charged activity, with students regularly dropping by as the deadline approached to ask more questions and explore more ideas as they began to find a way of articulating beyond their normal limits:

Dominic: I think the essay's amazingly important and I think what's fascinating about Alison's courses is the amount of panic, you know, that surrounds the essays and I felt it personally . . . It was a very, very scary thing to do because there was so much knowledge and there was so much information and there were no right answers and people aren't used to that. I mean I wasn't used to that and I was like, 'That's not fair', you know, 'There's no right answer.'

(Interview, 19 March 1999)

Lisa: I don't think I've ever put so much of myself into an essay and it was really, really scary.

Jon: When we got the essay question I remember, well, at least everyone in our year running to Dr Phipps' office . . . and once you realized that you could make up your own ideas and you took the theories and you took your data and you just decided yourself what you thought, then you could go away and do it.

(Focus group interview, 15 March 1999)

By the time the students had written their assignments, practised and polished their steps, they were dancing. It was the performances that made them 'think about Adorno when they were dancing'. Reflexivity is embodied practice, not some kind of reverent moment's pause, it is acquired through reflection and relation but is observed, assessed in the widest sense, in action.

Box 7.2   Performance, play, presentations

A student walks into the classroom dressed in a smart, burgundy silk suit and holding a hair brush as a microphone: 'Hello, my name is Janessa and I'm your host today as we investigate opinions on German popular culture.' Music plays, the theme music for *Vanessa*, the TV agony aunt show, and a panel of students in assorted attire take up their positions. A student in tweeds and brogues with a pencilled

> moustache bemoans the scandal of mass culture, a Karl Marx lookalike
> discusses the legacy of Marx, an angry young woman in combat gear
> attacks the way popular culture represses women and a student with a
> mobile phone, loud shirt and walkman enacts the postmodern condi-
> tion. The audience are given a vote for the most appealing opinion
> and they hold up their red or green cards to demonstrate their views.

Their performances were presented in cabaret style. They dressed up
as characters from the books or films they had studied or as theorists they
had encountered. They took models from British popular culture to show
the relationship between their course and their everyday experiences of
life. The scripts they wrote and the acting they produced were polished
and very funny. A former member of the course from a previous year
attended to give peer comment: 'What was specially marked with all of
them really, was the fact that they had started off, they'd understood the
theories but they weren't standing up and explicitly reeling off details,
you know, reeling off the theories just to show that they'd learnt. They
were applying it to culture' (Interview, 19 March 1999). Students from the
groups reflected on the effort and, for them, on the surprising quality of
what they produced:

> *Melanie*: Can I say one thing about the presentation . . . I mean I thought
> they were awfully clever. I mean they're very multi-layered and very,
> very clever. What do you think of them watching them on tape some
> time after. I mean how do they strike you?
> *Lisa*: I think they look a lot better than we thought when we were
> doing them.
> *Heather*: It's actually very good. (Laughter.)
> *Ellie*: I was surprised how good they were.
> *Heather*: We spent hours on ours.
>
> (Focus group interview, 15 March 1999)

Conclusion

Giving students a chance to perform and to experience power in performance was informed by my own reading of the anthropologist Victor Turner
and his theories on ritual and performance (Turner, 1995). Turner sees
communities as sustained by both structure and anti-structure, by periods of
clear social hierarchy and periods when those hierarchies are inverted,
periods he terms 'communitas': 'Communitas, with its unstructured charac-
ter, representing the 'quick' of human interrelatedness, what Buber has
called *das Zwischenmenschliche* . . . has an existential quality that involves the
whole man [*sic*] in relation to other whole men' (Turner, 1995: 127). Performance, in the way we experienced it, was humbling, ludic, transforming
and passionate:

'What forms of passion might make us whole? To what passions may we surrender with the assurance that we will expand rather than diminish the promise of our lives?' The quest for knowledge is one such passion. To the extent that professors bring this passion, which has to be fundamentally rooted in a love for ideas we are able to inspire, the classroom becomes a dynamic place where transformations in social relations are concretely actualized and the false dichotomy between the world outside and the inside world of the academy disappears. In many ways this is frightening. Nothing in the way I trained as a teacher really prepared me to witness my students transforming themselves.

(hooks, 1994: 195)

The comments made by the students about my role in enabling this to happen are intimate and touching and make student feedback forms pale into insignificance. They are hard to share and to display here. The action research leads me to understand that they are about something good, not something beyond critique, but something that has no welcome place in the neo-liberal, standardized cultures we inhabit:

Dominic: She gives everybody a role and everybody feels they have a role and I don't know how she does it but I'm convinced that that is the key to the success of the course. I'm really absolutely convinced it's the community you have in that classroom. Nobody feels frightened to talk, to contribute . . . there really is a sense of community, yeah, the desire to exchange information, exchange experiences, sometimes quite personal experiences . . . She's definitely an enabler . . . She's a listener, she's a listener as well, very much a listener . . . and she's the encourager, that is an amazingly large part of Alison's success, is the listening and the encouragement that go on and they go on in terms of the essay, giving essays back but they also go on in the classroom all the time and she really does listen. Sometimes you think 'She can't be interested all the time, it's not possible for her to be interested in everything that everybody says', but you know, she is and she's genuinely interested and encouraging in what anybody has to say, but not in a totally uncritical way . . . and she's an enthuser as well.

(Interview, 19 March 1999)

What I have shared here was an experience of teaching and learning as bel hooks (1994: 198) questions and envisions it: 'When eros is present in the classroom then love is bound to flourish. Well-learned distinctions between public and private make us believe that love has no place in the classroom.'

If we could be pure dancers in spirit we would never be afraid to love, and we would love with strength and wisdom.

(Okri, 1996: 12)

'Dr Phipps, do you think about Adorno when you are dancing?'

Acknowledgements

I am indebted to those students of the Popular German Culture Honours course at the University of Glasgow who have participated in this action research project with such enthusiasm and willing, trusting openness. I am also indebted to all members of the Barcelona Group for their constant support and critical friendships.

References

Barnett, R. (1997) *Higher Education: A Critical Business.* Buckingham: SRHE/Open University Press.
Blake, N., Smith, P. and Standish, P. (1998) *The Universities We Need.* London: Kogan Page.
Burwood, S. (1999) Liberation philosophy, *Teaching in Higher Education,* 4, 447–60.
Evans, L. and Abbott, I. (1998) *Teaching and Learning in Higher Education.* London: Cassell Education.
Gee, J. (1989) Literacy, discourse, and linguistics, *Journal of Education,* 171, 5–17.
Griffiths, M. (1998) Being naughty: a play for justice? Unpublished inaugural lecture, Faculty of Education, Nottingham Trent University.
hooks, b. (1994) *Teaching to Transgress: Education as the Practice of Freedom.* New York: Routledge.
Kramer-Dahl, A. (1995) Reading and writing against the grain of academic discourse, *Discourse: Studies in the Cultural Politics of Education,* 16, 21–38.
Lave, J. and Wenger, E. (1999) Learning and pedagogy in communities of practice, in J. Leach and B. Moon (eds) *Learners and Pedagogy.* Milton Keynes: Paul Chapman/The Open University.
McGrath, J. (1982) *A Good Night Out: Popular Theatre. Audience, Class and Form.* London: Methuen.
McWilliam, E. (1995) Seriously playful, playfully serious: the postmodern lecture and other oxymorons, *Taboo,* 1, 31–43.
McWilliam, E. and Palmer, P. (1996) *Pedagogy, Technology and the Body.* New York: Peter Lang.
Nicol, D. (1997) Research on learning and higher education, *UCoSDA Briefing Paper,* 45.
Okri, B. (1996) *Birds of Heaven.* London: Phoenix House.
Ramsden, P. (1992) *Learning to Teach in Higher Education.* London: Routledge.
Read, A. (1993) *Theatre and Everyday Life: An Ethics of Performance.* London: Routledge.
Turner, V. (1995) *The Ritual Process: Structure and Anti-Structure.* New York: de Gruyter.
Vygotsky, L. (1978) *Mind in Society.* Cambridge, MA: Harvard University Press.

8

Designing a New Course

Judy Wilkinson

A landscape with one fence, and that for deer.
Yet though it's seven feet high, and seems so fit
In winter snows they walk right over it.
    (Norman MacCaig, 'Boundaries')

Introduction

Teaching mathematics to first year engineering students is beset with difficulties. The students claim they do not like mathematics, the lecturers claim the level of mathematics in schools has declined and the administrators worry about the use of calculators, plagiarism and goodness knows what else. There has been a lot of work in recent years on addressing this situation with the development of computer-aided learning packages (for example, Mathwise) and the use of software packages (such as MathCAD, Mathematica and Matlab). The reality is that students have to be engaged and encouraged to struggle with the concepts and technical skills required in order to reach the level of confidence and ability they need as engineers.

This chapter describes the philosophy behind the first year course in mathematics for engineers in the Department of Electronics and Electrical Engineering at the University of Glasgow. Although the course was designed over several years, the first year of teaching it in the present format coincided with the start of the Barcelona Group. Throughout the year (1998), Quintin and I analysed the similarities and differences between basic computing and basic mathematical skills; we agonized over the student responses; we discussed with Alison the philosophy of teaching the languages of mathematics, computing and German; we explained to Melanie the complex interaction between patterns, symbolic representations, graphical display and numerical evaluation. Then the web became more complex as we discussed what is meant by the practice of reflection and critical action. I reflected on what kind of mathematics engineers need, how students learn, the ways they should be assessed and the agenda for the curriculum. As usual this has led to more questions than answers, more hopes than solutions, but a deepening respect for Freire's (1970: 77) position that:

> The starting point for organising the program content of education or political action must be the present, existential, concrete situation reflecting the aspirations of the people. Utilising certain basic contradictions, we must pose this existential, concrete, present situation to the people as a problem which challenges them and requires a response – not just at the intellectual level but at the level of action.

Freire's work was based on building on the students' prior experience, engaging them in the subject and presenting them with problems and situations which require a response that is not only intellectually challenging but also develops them as critical thinkers. The following sections trace my unfolding thinking and practice as I attempted to develop the course design, teaching strategies and student development to exemplify these educational theories and values. What relevance do they have for a course on engineering mathematics taught in a Scottish university to mainly 18-year-old male students?

How should students learn mathematics in an engineering context?

When my colleagues and I first thought about redesigning the mathematics course, we were influenced by the findings of the Cockcroft Report (Cockcroft, 1982), which outlined six styles of teaching mathematics:

- exposition by the teacher;
- discussion between teacher and student and between students themselves;
- appropriate practical work;
- consolidation and practice of fundamental skills and routines;
- problem-solving, including the application of mathematics to engineering situations;
- investigational work.

This report became the starting point for our course design, because although it was based on work in schools it is equally valid for university practice. We also considered the advice listed in Backhouse *et al.* (1992) on planning a course. These included aims, teaching strategies, groups, selection of materials and formative assessments. Originally we took an intuitive approach to the balance and timing of the different methods. The students were to be encouraged to learn by using the techniques and support best suited to their needs and abilities. Easily said, but in practice difficult to produce.

During the past two years I have become more aware of several issues which arise in taking a holistic view of teaching mathematics to engineers

and these should be considered, together with the Cockcroft recommendations. As Green and Kennedy (2001) write, the real need of engineers is 'to
deal with uncertain, conflicting and often unique problem situations', and
to develop this ability students must learn a reflection in action that goes
beyond 'statable rules' (Schon, 1987). Schon discusses two modes of operation within a teaching environment: telling and listening, or demonstrating
and imitating. Telling and listening is, of course, exposition by the teacher.
In her report on 'mathematical experiences and mathematical practice in
the higher education science setting' the main recommendation for effective
teaching made by Molyneux-Hodgson (1999: 9) is for 'supporting existing
structures (e.g. lecturers) to reconceptualise mathematics as ideas-in-use
within science learning situations.' This approach puts the lecturer at the
centre of the learning experience. It may help in the acquisition of basic
science knowledge but, as our end of year questionnaire (Wilkinson, 1999)
showed, many students find the skills exercises, assessed tutorials and class
tests more helpful than the lectures. Only by practising examples and
becoming confident in the discipline can students grow to understand the
use and power of mathematics in the design and analysis of engineering
products.

Demonstrating and imitating requires the learning modes of 'follow me',
where the tutor demonstrates a technique and the student imitates, and 'joint
experimentation', where the tutor and student work together on solving an
open-ended problem. Many engineering departments have incorporated
such an approach into their teaching, particularly in design courses. For
example, Kappraff (1990) has incorporated a broad spectrum of knowledge
in his course on design science. The product design course at Glasgow
University (Green and Gerson, 1999) was designed to address many of the
educational practices advocated by Schon. However, mathematics courses
rarely provide the learning environment and culture which Schon (1991)
deems necessary for effective professional learning. These courses tend to
concentrate on technically rational analysis rather than 'inquiry into messy
problematic situation of manifest importance where, however, we are unable
to be rigorous in our studies in any way we know how to define' (Schon,
1991: 10). To avoid this dilemma requires postulating a clearly defined
problem and also making clear what we mean by 'rigour appropriate to the
reflective study of practice'.

I came to believe that in designing a course for engineers we must weave
together three strands of action for the students. First is the reflection-in-
action approach of Schon. There follows the responsibility of the students
for their own learning, exemplified by Barnett (1997: 112), who emphasizes
that the role of the educator is not only to compile:

> an agenda of issues that draw upon multiple frameworks, structuring
> tasks, getting students to collaborate on projects, positioning imagina-
> tion and intellectual range as criteria, and drawing students' attention
> to a range of relevant literature . . . Strategies of this kind, rather than

teaching *per se*, are necessary elements in producing critical persons. But they are not sufficient: for that students have to take on their responsibilities for their own continuing explorations.

Finally, the structures and material should be designed to respect the experiences and aspirations of the students. In Freire's (1970: 74) words:

> For the anti-dialogical banking educator, the question of content simply concerns the program about which he will discourse to his students; and he answers his own questions by organising his own program. For the dialogical, problem-posing teacher-student, the program content of education is neither a gift nor an imposition . . . but rather the organised, systemised and developed 're-presentation' to individuals of the things about which they want to know more.

The lecturer works to create dialogue, taking into account who the students are and what they bring to the course, while the students must also take responsibility for, and reflect upon, their own learning. As we have discovered during the past three years, this is far more difficult than composing lecture notes and exam questions.

Nonetheless, I believe that our first year engineering mathematics course goes some way to addressing these issues, certainly by providing a well designed scaffold to support the students and perhaps beginning to move them into the realm of critical action. However, is concentrating on the practical, technical specifications a sufficient scenario for designing a course, albeit mathematics for engineers? If we are educating engineers should we also consider the pragmatic and social constitution of the discipline? Barnett (1997: 73) exemplifies this dilemma by posing the question, 'is engineering largely a matter of solving technical problems or does it introduce a sensitivity to the people whose lives are likely to be affected profoundly by its practices?' At issue is whether teaching mathematics to engineers should include more than just inculcating technical skills in mathematics. Should a holistic approach which values the ethos of the engineering discipline be woven into the academic course, or should the main driving force be to teach the students to give a mechanical response to set problems?

What are the components of engineering mathematics?

Arguments, such as those presented above, about the format of a mathematics course for engineers have raged in the Faculty of Engineering at the University of Glasgow as well as in many other places. There are strong differences between lecturers who believe that a mathematics course should concentrate on students developing a basic tool kit in mathematics, based on straightforward manipulations, and those who favour an approach starting from engineering problems (Scott and McGregor, 1996).

The fundamental issue is whether students should be taught only basic manipulations and traditional problem-solving in the mathematics course, with all applications left to the specialist courses where the technique is then used and discussed in the context of the technical examples. On the other hand, should the mathematics courses start from the applications, with manipulations and theory introduced and explored as part of specific problem-solving? Our course follows a mixture of the two approaches, providing a structure in which the students are encouraged to develop their manipulative skills, while also giving engineering examples that are solved using the mathematical techniques. Student interviews suggest that they respond well to this approach, saying, for example, '[it] teaches you how to work at university . . . helps you to learn what you should know' (Focus group interview, March 1998). However, it is difficult to find practical examples that the students understand and which do not cause further problems because the engineering concepts in such examples are outside their competence. Understanding engineering concepts has always been considered a pyramidal process, depending strongly on building on previous skills and understanding, of which mathematics is part. Mathematical techniques have been used to develop physical models but, until they understand the mathematics and the engineering principles, the practical situation may not be clear to the students. The lateral thinking and ability to apply ideas from one discipline to another, which is one of the strengths of a good engineer, also militates against application-based teaching unless the fundamental underlying patterns of the mathematics are brought out clearly.

A lot of the review time on this course was spent in developing and discussing proposed projects and questions for the assessed tutorials. We tried to find suitable applications for which the student had the necessary background to appreciate the mathematics involved without being bogged down in other concepts. We believe that the difficulty of finding such examples is the reason why, even in textbooks on engineering mathematics which purport to have many applications, there are very few good examples (e.g. James, 1996; Croft *et al.*, 1998). One of the ways we tackled this problem was to liaise very closely with the other first year lecturers so that some examples were based on the materials the students were meeting in their electronics, physics and computing courses. Awareness of when this joint material is being taught ensures that the learning can be reinforced.

Teachers also debate the use of technology as a component of a mathematics course. This discussion ranges from whether to use calculators in the primary school classroom to using computer packages in a university course. Modern technology enables engineers to use software to solve mathematical equations without the need to perform the analysis for themselves. It has changed the way in which students use mathematics because, instead of giving them problems to solve which have analytical solutions obtainable with a pen, paper, slide rule or tables, they can tackle more realistic open-ended problems with numerical solutions. They can investigate these using computer software with algorithms written by mathematicians and computer scientists. Most engineers no longer have to solve differential equations, manipulate matrices or compute Fourier series, but they do need to understand and use the solutions to differential equations and the results of manipulating matrices, and to interpret Fourier transforms. They must be able to select the relevant software package and criticize the results, they should be able to scale results and use transforms. Even algebraic manipulations can now be performed on a computer and, like the skills of sewing, spinning and weaving that are unnecessary for the modern housekeeper, basic mathematical skills are fast becoming unnecessary for the majority of engineers. However, the question remains: how much basic manipulation and computing must the students be able to do themselves in order to appreciate the power and limitations of the computer packages? This argument was exemplified in discussions over the examples in the assessed tutorials. Jim, a tutor from the Engineering Department, held that engineering students only need to know the basic second order differential equations used in solving a simple electrical circuit but do not need to solve implicit differentials analytically; if they met such an equation later they would use a numerical methods package. However, Richard, a mathematician, averred that mathematics was training for the mind and students need to solve inhomogeneous differential equations, even if only a few engineers would meet them later on.

Background to the course

Originally all the electrical engineering students were taught by the Mathematics Department on a conventional course with four lectures a week, one tutorial, two class tests at the beginning of the second and third terms and a three hour degree examination. The students could get exemptions from the degree examination if they achieved a 70 per cent overall mark in the class tests. However, by 1990 the failure rate for this course had become unacceptably high (over 30 per cent) so it was decided to run two courses. The original mathematics course was retained for the more able students, if they wished to take it. A course which concentrated on basic manipulations and contained a high number of examples based on the application of mathematics to engineering and taught by lecturers from the Engineering Department was developed, primarily for the less well qualified students, but available to all. This course was still taught on a conventional model and did not significantly improve the students' understanding or pass rate. Therefore, other approaches were tried, culminating with the version described in this chapter. Because of the success of this model, the inefficiency of running two courses and the problems of a 'two-tier' system, it was decided to amalgamate both mathematics courses and use lecturers and tutors from both departments to teach the course together for the session 1998/9.

Description of current format of course

The class is composed of all the first year electronics and electrical engineering students, most of whom have grades A or B at Highers level in mathematics. Mathematics is at the heart of the first year curriculum. Fifty out of the 120 credits for the first year of study for any of the degrees awarded in electronics and electrical engineering are devoted to mathematics. It is taught by four lecturers, two from the Department of Electronics and Electrical Engineering and two from the Mathematics Department. These, together with eleven other academics, meet for an hour weekly with a tutorial group of six to eight students – there are about 120 students on the course. Each week there is also a short half-hour meeting for the tutors. As convenor of the course, I use this meeting to reflect on the learning environment, improve the material and engender a more critical approach to learning.

We divided the course into four six-week cycles based on different kinds of mathematical techniques the students need to master. In each of the cycles there is a project, an assigned tutorial and a class test. The projects are assessed by an oral exam, followed by a typical degree exam. The first four weeks follow a conventional design, with three lectures, a computer-aided learning session and a tutorial each week. The structure of the contact hours is shown in Figure 8.1.

In the first four weeks the students have skills exercises, designed to give them practice in basic skills, and an assessed tutorial offering deeper problems and applications. The standard textbooks for engineering students (e.g. James, 1996; Croft *et al.*, 1998) provide material for this part of the course and are in agreement with the syllabus and approach given in reports on engineering mathematics (Sutherland and Pozzi, 1995; Barry and Steele, 1998). The work from the first four weeks cumulates in a 'driving test' based on essential manipulative skills in which students have to get 70 per cent or retake it two weeks later. The last two weeks in each block are spent working in groups on the projects as well as studying for the resit test if necessary.

There has been much educational research (e.g. Simpson, 1998) to show that students will work with the assessments in mind, so the design and

Figure 8.1 The structure of contact hours

Weeks	Hours				
	1	2	3	4	5
1–3	Lecture	Lecture	Lecture	CAL	Tutorial
4	Lecture	Lecture	Test	CAL	Tutorial
5	Project	Project	Project	Project	Tutorial
6	Project	Project	Project	Resit/project	Tutorial

implementation of the following four components of these assessments is critically important in fulfilling the aims of the course:

1. Four class tests, each 50 minutes long: 20 per cent.
2. Four assessed tutorials: 10 per cent.
3. Four mini-projects with an oral assessment in term 3: 20 per cent.
4. Degree examination, 3 hours long (resit available): 50 per cent.

Each component measures different skills or understanding and so contributes to a well rounded curriculum, which has elements of routine acquisition of knowledge, applications, abstraction and wider understanding of the use and validity of the techniques. We tried to develop a multiple framework to encourage effective learning. The class tests are 'driving tests', and can be passed with rote learning; for the assessed tutorials we actively encourage students to discuss the work and share their results; the project investigations are assessed by an oral at the end of the year, which encourages the students to review their work and develops their communication skills; the degree examination is the conventional end-of-year assessment. We tried to reduce the amount of material the students need to learn to a manageable foundation that allows them to use mathematics as an engineering tool. At the same time, we work to develop their technical skills so that they can approach a new problem with confidence, concentrating on process. All this, based on encouraging group working, discussion and questioning, constitutes a demanding agenda for a course on mathematics for engineers.

Methods of learning and teaching employed

When we designed the curriculum and the assessments, we tried to interweave all Cockcroft's (1982) different styles of teaching and learning to provide a rich environment. Therefore, I will analyse the course by attributing each of our modes of learning and assessment to one of the styles of teaching described by Cockcroft, and evaluate it in terms of the educational principles that underpin this method. Finally, I will address some of the problems that arise when anti-dialogical banker-educators and dialogical teacher-students are involved in the same course.

Exposition by the teacher

In an ideal situation, where 'The teacher is no longer the-one-who-teaches, but one who is himself taught in dialogue with the students, who in turn while being taught also teach' (Freire, 1970: 61), there is no role for exposition by the teacher. However, mathematics courses are usually taught conventionally and so we encourage the students to read the textbooks and then use the lectures to illuminate the material. Each cycle has eleven lectures given in the first four weeks. Some lecturers give out lecture notes with spaces for the students to work out examples during the lecture, so that a balance is maintained between the students being able to listen and think about the material without needing to copy it down, and actually applying the concepts. Initially we hoped that the students would work from the textbook, so detailed proofs or discussion of special cases would not be needed. We wanted to concentrate on clarifying the basic knowledge the students should acquire and reinforce the learning of fundamental premises rather then presenting all the material they may need later on as engineers. We believed that if the students are helped to become independent learners with a strong mathematical base then they will be able to understand and use any specialized theories or cases they meet in later life. Therefore students were expected to read the relevant sections in the book, try some of the examples and make their own notes before the lecture on the topic.

This turned out to be a fond hope! In 1999 the questionnaire at the end of the course revealed that only 3 per cent regularly, 67 per cent sometimes and 30 per cent never read the relevant section before the lecture. This makes it difficult for the lecturers just to discuss the topic, highlight the important concepts and give some examples, and, as a result, they want more lecture time. Moreover, students still expect all the information to be given in the lecture and many like the banking system of education where 'the teacher teaches and the students are taught' (Freire, 1970: 54).

One problem we have identified is that students may not know what is required when we say 'read the text' – they have never 'read' a mathematics book and cannot see the use of the material. We tried to go some way to setting up a problem-based learning environment (e.g. Woods, 1985; Barrows, 1988) by giving the students applications-based assessed tutorials at the beginning of the block and also skills exercises to do every day. However, the majority seemed to wait until the material was covered in the lecture before attempting the work; they seemed to need the 'scaffolding' provided by the lectures. This raises the question of whether the lectures should provide the basic structure for the course. In a sense Freire was right: we have not created an environment in which the students want to know more about mathematics. We started from the syllabus, not from discussions with them. We stamped our authority on the curriculum and then wondered at the students' passivity and lack of critical thinking. Many lecturers worry because the students may miss basic fundamental concepts but if the mathematical technique or understanding is relevant then the process should start by creating the environment in which that need emerges.

Discussion between teacher/student and student/student

The tutors are the means through which the learning environment is created. In previous years they moved round a large group helping individuals with their difficulties. This is not an efficient way either to help the student or to use the expertise of the tutor. Tutors often had to explain the same problem to different students and some students wasted the whole session waiting for a simple point to be explained. In this course, each tutor has a group of between six and eight students whom he or she meets once a week. The students are expected to have discussed difficulties with each other and if several students have the same problem they work through it on the board or flip chart, under the guidance of the tutor. A good tutorial creates the teacher/student and student/teacher dynamic which is one of the most exciting and rewarding educational experiences.

There is an increasing pressure for large lectures and computer-assessed programmes, especially in mathematics, and small group work is often perceived as being very resource-intensive. However, interactions when individual tutors encourage the students to question the material and try to solve the problems either by their own research or by talking to the other students are an essential part of the learning environment. Tutors get to know their students well and can both help the less able and stimulate those who show evidence of mathematical ability. If such tutorials are used to generate independent learning and critical thinking in the first year of a degree course, then, as one supportive tutor said, 'the tutorials work well and form an excellent basis for going onwards and upwards next year' (Course report, 1999). However there is also disagreement: other tutors said that it is 'not the responsibility of the tutor to get the students to work. In other universities lecturers are approachable, give friendly help but are not much concerned about undergraduate progress, problems etc.'; another remarked that 'too much time is spent on student contact which creates problems in future years' (Course report, 1999).

The tutors also found it difficult to stand back and allow the students to articulate and explore their difficulties because, in mathematics, there is perceived to be a 'right answer'. The one correct approach and the 'right' answer does not encourage the student to deal with uncertainty and conflict. It is perhaps better to start from the premise that we can show a method or answer is wrong but there may be several approaches or ways of presenting and visualizing the problem which give a valid answer.

In this course the format of the tutorial varies according to the work which is covered that week, but we encourage the tutors to ensure that it is always a group exercise with all the students being expected to respond and discuss the material. This happens routinely in arts subjects, but is less usual in the science and engineering disciplines. In discussions with the Barcelona Group, Quintin and I realized how much more active and exciting Alison's and Mike's tutorials were in comparison with our own prosaic approach.

One of the major difficulties with problem-solving in mathematics is that students cannot see where to start a problem. They are used to applying the formula or using a 'recipe' and, if the problem is not identical to one they have met before, many are lost. Therefore, thinking about discussions in the Barcelona Group, I tried to create a dialogue around problems. I asked questions like, 'What are you thinking about when you say that?'; 'Tell us what kind of example you are confident about solving'; 'Why is this different?' A group discussion clarifies the questions and misconceptions. If those who have got a solution are encouraged to explain the basis for their work rather than just write the solution on the board, then very often others realize the misconceptions which have prevented them finding a solution. Statements such as 'you can't do that because . . .' and an analysis of why a particular approach is wrong, rather than 'this is the way to do it', contribute to everyone's understanding. My students began to realize what was blocking their understanding and started to articulate their analysis. Many times the realization of the limitations of their previous experience and the fact that a particular form of analysis only applies to a certain type of problem has clarified a difficulty. In part it is learning to construct a well formed problem. In tutorial groups which work well, there is a dialogue about the problems that is exciting to see.

At the tutors' meetings I found that several tutors encouraged the students to work together and to develop their own solutions, but others believed in demonstrating the answer rather than getting the students to question their assumptions. They did not allow a preliminary brainstorm, based on their previous relevant knowledge, which is a central part of problem-based learning (Barrows, 1988). I tried to convince these tutors that they could help by 're-presenting' the information, while peer discussion dissects the underlying assumptions from which a student is working. However, many lecturers still believe that mathematics is a subject that can only be learnt by an individual. It is true that mathematical understanding cannot be poured into a student on a spoon (although this is what many lecturers believe they can do in their lectures) and that people must struggle with the concepts and do examples for themselves. However, in a problem-posing educational environment, discussions with others illuminate problems and provide some of the triggers on which further learning can be built.

Assessed tutorials are given out at the beginning of each six-week cycle and given in at the end of the third week. The students are expected to consult with each other and check the numerical values of their solutions but they submit an individual assignment. One of the core precepts for this course was that student/student interaction should be fostered during all the activities and that, for many students, this is a crucial factor in their learning. In spite of the fact that engineers need to work together and learn from each other, many academics have expressed reservations about assessed tutorials because 'students will copy from each other'. Persuading some tutors that students are not altruistic, and do not usually allow others to copy out their solutions without some form of return, is difficult. In times of stress students may divide up the tasks so each solves one problem and then they copy the solutions from each other, but even this is unusual and most recognize that they have to understand the work.

For 1999 an analysis of marks for the assessed tutorial shows that 90 per cent of the students got a D or above but the average mark was 57 per cent and only 34 per cent got an A. This suggests that they still don't really believe in cooperating. The pressure to produce an individual piece of work is very strong and we need to do more to get them to question and solve problems together. There is no timetabled space for the students to work together on the assessed tutorial apart from in the tutorials. We hope they will meet outside class but it does seem that the tutors are central to creating a group dynamic. If the tutors believe this is important then, during the year, the groups will form. If the tutors believe learning mathematics is essentially an individual activity, and the bright students will be dragged down by their weaker peers, then the groups tend not to form well. This is difficult to prove because there are outside factors at work, but there is a definite correlation between tutors' positions as revealed in the discussions and observation of the way their groups work in the project laboratory.

The students are expected to work together in their small groups for the projects. These are based on investigations and are timetabled for five contact hours during the two weeks allocated to the project. The students tend to work together during this time and there is evidence of good collaboration and learning. As one student commented, ''Cos we're all working together, it was like, maybe some people were stronger in some areas and you could ask them. It was OK, we got a basic understanding at the end of it, whatever' (Focus group interview, March 1998). However, there are the usual problems when one student does not appear with the work he or she has been delegated to do or a student drives the investigation and does not involve the others. The tutors should recognize and manage this but, again, this requires facilitative rather than mathematical skills, and several tutors are not willing to engage in this exercise.

Appropriate practical work

Appropriate practical work in mathematics can mean either that the students experiment on practical systems which are then modelled mathematically or that they use software packages to solve and graph the equations which model the system. We use both methods. At the beginning of each project the students realize and then describe what is happening physically. The description contains a suggestion for a small experiment or demonstration which makes the students think about the real world that is being described mathematically. Then they use mathematics as a (symbolic) language to describe the patterns or system. Finally, they use a software package (MathCAD) to play with and analyse the equations and graph their results. This structure is shown in Figure 8.2.

The experiment can be very simple: for example, in one project the students constructed an Archimedes spiral. They were left to decide for themselves how best to do this – most used some variation of unwinding

Figure 8.2 The structure of the projects

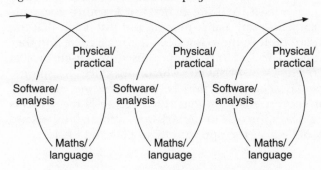

a piece of string wrapped around a cylinder (for example, an Irn Bru cool drink can). Thus they visualized an Archimedes spiral and then thought about how to describe it mathematically. Only then does it make sense for them to use MathCAD to play around with the parameters and graph the functions. Some students 'learn through their fingers' (Wilkinson and Earnshaw, 2000), and for them it is important to link the mathematics to a real situation.

We started from a concrete situation but most engineers need to develop the ability to use their mathematical knowledge in a variety of applications. Lateral thinking involves recognizing the solution or technique that may be useful in analysing a new situation and can be engendered through computer packages and software. As Papert recognized in his work with children, computers can change the way we think about mathematics: 'In my vision the child programs the computer and, in doing so, both acquires a sense of mastery over a piece of the most modern and powerful technology and establishes an intimate contact with some of the deepest ideas from science, from mathematics and from the art of intellectual model building' (Papert, 1980: 5).

In each project the students use a software package to build a holistic environment in which they can interpret the language of mathematics and see the commonality of the patterns of solutions in different applications. It enables students to play with the equations and analyse a system in a variety of ways. They play with the parameters, visualize their results and understand the effect of changing values and initial conditions. These results are often linked to designing a system, and, for engineers, this use of software to show the results of design changes highlights the importance and use of mathematics.

Part of the discussion with the tutors was about the way MathCAD should be taught and this again shows different approaches to teaching. At the beginning I felt that the students should be given minimal instructions but encouraged to 'play' with the package and discover what it could do. MathCAD develops and changes each year and when the students have graduated it is the process of learning how to use a software package that is important, not the package itself. At issue is not just learning a specific package but how to learn. However, many students and tutors felt that too much time was being spent on this; there is a steep learning curve and they wanted formal instruction. The lecturers compromised and each project now contains worked examples in MathCAD which introduce the specific operations the students may need in the project: the 'follow me, imitation' mode of Schon. The project reports show that at least some of the students develop a confident, creative approach to the software, although others are still unsure and do not delight in the opportunity to play and explore.

Consolidation and practice of fundamental skills and routines

Most teachers of mathematics believe that students need to practise fundamental mathematical skills and routines. Engineers need to recognize the form of their equations and have confidence in performing simple techniques, and it is difficult to see how they can achieve this facility without time spent on simple manipulations, if not rote learning. Students must be able to read and understand engineering texts without being held up by the interpretation of the mathematics. Their problems remind me of the children's rhyme: 'The Centipede was happy quite / Until the toad in fun / Said, Pray which leg comes after which? / This wrought her mind to such a pitch / she lay distracted in a ditch / Considering how to run' (Anon.). Students lie, rather like the centipede, in a ditch considering what the mathematical symbols and formulae mean instead of concentrating on the engineering problems. In designing the course we decided that our students must be able to perform simple manipulations automatically, and to do this they should have a 'driving test' at the end of the formal teaching in each block. Because we want them to gain confidence at a simple level we ask them to retake the test if they get below an A (70 per cent). The resit is essentially the same test with different numbers. After the test they have two weeks without any new concepts being taught during which time those who need to can work on understanding the material.

The lecturers design their own class tests and some found it difficult to set a test of fundamental principles on which students should get an A. They wished to test the students by embedding several concepts in one question or concentrating on the exceptions to the rule. However, the driving tests are supposed to be just that – to demonstrate basic competence. It is not an advanced test or a discriminatory device – those are covered in the degree exam. The resit marks have been good and show that the majority of students do reflect on their weaknesses and manage to tackle simple problems they have met before.

The tutors mark them for their own students. We decided not to use the computer-based tests associated with the CAL packages because we found that often the blocks to understanding were different from what we, as lecturers, thought the students would find difficult. For example, students had difficulty with implicit differentiation, but this arose because they had only met explicit forms before and had not thought about what they were actually using. They had absorbed the solutions to simple problems without questioning what they were doing. A discussion about this in my own tutorial showed the assumptions and simplifications the students were making: they found that several of them shared the same misconceptions and this resulted in one saying, 'OK I am happy about that now – I hadn't realized what we were doing.' Emails and discussions at the tutors' meetings about problems such as this which came up in the tutorials enabled tutors to target fundamental understanding more efficiently. A good tutor can get the students to question and think about process, so moving them away from rote learning and dependency on external triggers. As Alison showed, it is the perceptive remark that deepens understanding, not just the instructional approach of either lecturing or CAL.

Associated with the test are simple skills exercises which are supposed to take about half an hour each day to complete and a computer-aided learning lab using CALMAT (written by Glasgow Caledonian University staff) or Mathwise (the package written by staff from a consortium of universities). The CAL sessions were introduced as a resource to help in the consolidation and practice of fundamental skills. The modules follow the material presented in the course. However, we have found that most students do not particularly like the CAL packages – in our questionnaire in 1999 only 7 per cent found the packages helpful, 54 per cent said they were some help and 39 per cent felt they were not helpful. The figures were similar for the 2000 questionnaire. There is an increasing interest in teaching and assessing students through CAL (Croft and Ward, 2000), and it may be that our students did not like the material because we only used it as enrichment, not as an integral part of the course. Many students would not work through the questions using pen and paper but tried to do them on screen and often ended scrolling through the modules. We intend to tackle this problem in future years.

Problem-solving, including the application of mathematics to engineering situations

Problem-solving is incorporated into the assessed tutorials and continued in the project work. The assessed tutorials contain problems based on engineering applications, and the students are expected to hand in a clearly presented, well documented piece of work. I believe there should be a network of activities and problems linking the mathematics to the engineering context in which the techniques are used. These are difficult to find. Although the problems in the assessed tutorial are routine types of question, applying the mathematical techniques to well defined problems, the students do discuss them and can, occasionally, become quite excited about the solutions. We give examples from the students' immediate courses but also from more general engineering situations, so they are encouraged to link the basic mathematical patterns and techniques to a practical situation.

Thus we try to provide pathways and activities that enable the students to appreciate, and move confidently between, the discourses of mathematics and engineering. For example, Bissell (1995: 51) discusses the different perceptions of a linear differential equation with constant coefficients between a control engineer and a mathematician:

> The mathematician will consider particular integrals and complementary functions whereas the engineer talks about standard step response curves, frequency response curves or pole zero plots in the complex plane. They are interested in the initial conditions that will give rise to particular poles in the complex plane that 'explain a particular response of their circuit and will then design an amplifier or control system to shape the frequency response'. Engineers use graphs and plots to explore the mathematical solutions to their models and relate them to the physical system they are describing. They are excited by the control the mathematical results give them to design and interpret their system but they are not, in the main, excited by the mathematical analysis that led to those results – they just want output that they can use and that works.

The tutors can address these approaches and share their understanding either as mathematicians or as engineers, enabling the students to appreciate their own vocation and increase their imagination and intellectual range.

There has been a lot of discussion about the level and expectations from the assessed tutorials. Several tutors worried that they were too difficult. Others wished to direct the students rather than allowing them to explore for themselves. As one tutor remarked in December 1999:

> I feel that the students are being taught too quickly. Material that I covered in the tutorial and essentially solved for the students was done well in the assessed tutorial. Where I left the students to complete the solutions, they rapidly fell apart in their attempts. This suggests to me that they do not really understand what is going on, but instead parrot back what is spoon fed to them.

However, in the focus group evaluation at the end of the 1999/2000 course, the students specifically said they appreciated the challenges in the assessed tutorials and the applications that showed the relevance of the mathematics. Bob Matthew of TLS, who undertook the interview, commented: 'Assessed tutorials – very popular part of the course (honest!) they felt they had sufficient background knowledge to tackle them and that they were challenging enough to be engaging and worth doing' (email report on focus group, May 2000).

Investigational work

The last two weeks of each block are spent on project work. Most engineering mathematics textbooks contain problems based on applications, which can be used for the assessed tutorials. As far as we are aware, no standard textbook has envisaged a need for these broader problems, which aim to encourage a holistic approach to problem-solving and incorporate mathematics into an engineering education. In my experience, many students do not appreciate how fundamental critical reflection is to engineering. Reflective skills are developed by asking them to think about how to describe a system or pattern mathematically, about the forms of the equations or the effects of changing parameters. They learn how to communicate mathematical ideas and begin to understand how useful mathematics is in engineering.

The contents of our projects are not, in themselves, revolutionary. The radical approach in this course lies in embedding application-based learning in a structure which allows students time to acquire a deeper level of understanding from this. For example, in the first block of material, the Fibonacci series was investigated as an example of patterns in mathematics and the relevance of mathematics to the world. Kappraff (1990: 75) writes that 'Fine artists, composers, architects, scientists and engineers have often created their best work by keeping an open dialogue with Nature.' The initial part of the project was simple but encouraged the students to think laterally and reinforced the fundamental dictum that engineering takes knowledge from other disciplines and applies it (for the good of society). Then the students could explore examples ranging from the growth of pine cones to the Fibonacci progression of tones in Bartok's divertimento. One student said that he hadn't previously realized that 'maths isn't just numbers, it's everywhere'. Another was excited when explaining in his oral that the relative size of the bones in our hands is in a Fibonacci sequence and this is approximately true for all humans. His group had discussed how this could be used to design robotic hands. However, the tutors were divided in the relevance of the project. My minutes record that: 'Heidi queried whether Fibonacci numbers is too easy for a university project – she did this in Germany when she was 14. Jim felt we were expecting too much of the students. He feels that we are going faster than in the Maths Department' (Minutes of tutors' meeting, 5 November 1999).

A later student project was concerned with modelling the growth and exploitation of resources using the oil industry as an example. For some groups this enabled a discussion on the wider implications of oil exploration and the global consequences to arise naturally and introduced the relation between engineering and society. Not all students enjoyed it. Again, my minutes record that 'Jim said that some of his students did not like the project – he felt they did not like exploratory work. Susan wondered if an interest in exploring material and questioning came in later years' (Minutes of tutors' meeting, 21 January 2000).

The investigations required joint experimentation between the tutors and the students because the project was new to everyone except the lecturer for that module. This again showed the differences in approach among the tutors. A few really enjoyed the projects and found the discussions stimulating and exciting. A number of tutors were worried about the open-ended nature of the work, one refused to take part because it was not mathematics teaching, another required precise answers and felt very insecure. Several tutors did not spend time on the presentations from the students but instead concentrated on discussing the class test even though the students had been given full answers. At the end of the year the students were asked to reflect on the projects and give in a short assessment with their project files, and these showed that some of them had appreciated the challenges. For example, two students said: 'It helped me to understand the mathematics, saw where it could be used'; and 'You can actually see what is happening with MathCAD' (Student reports, 2000).

The responses to the projects can be analysed in terms of Freire's coded existential situations. Freire (1970: 86) explains thus:

> The coding of an existential situation is the representation of that situation showing some of its constituent elements in interaction, Decoding is the critical analysis of the coded situation. This whole (the coded situation) which previously had only been diffusely apprehended, begins to acquire meaning as thought flows back to it from the different dimensions.

Freire is describing a literacy programme, but it could apply equally well to the role of projects within the mathematics syllabus. For example, models of oil extraction reveal the underlying assumptions made by the oil companies and environmentalists in forecasting when oil will run out. The project description is the coding of the existentialist situation, which is conceived at a different level after the mathematical analysis. Unless the mathematical model is revealed, the validity and robustness of the predictions are taken on trust. By exploring the models, changing both the complexity and the parameters, students begin to see the depth and limitations of the arguments. They can begin to contribute to the discussions themselves, searching out relevant data and processing them to predict outcomes. They are no longer passive receivers of information but can question and challenge.

Freire (1970: 89) goes on to discuss the interaction between group work and individual thinking:

> the investigation of thematics involves the investigation of people's thinking – thinking which occurs only in and among people together seeking out reality. I cannot think *for others* or *without others*, nor can others think *for me*. Even if people's thinking is superstitious or naïve, it is only as they rethink their assumptions in action that they can change, producing and acting upon their own ideas – not consuming those of others.

If the tutors and the students work together to find generative themes and act as co-investigators then we may change the educational process and also their ability and perception of mathematics.

Is the course successful?

In a conventional sense the course has been successful. The degree results are good, with an average 86 per cent pass rate over the past three years. The students seem happier about learning mathematics than previously. This is a fairly typical student comment: 'mathematics is not a problem as it is the other courses' (Focus group interview, 1998 cohort). The software package strand was also liked by a majority of the class. As one student said, 'MathCAD, if you get the syntax right in the programming, was great, as it would give you those lovely graphs you could follow and use' (Focus group interview, 1998 cohort).

Before I joined the Barcelona Group and started reading Barnett and Freire, I would have been happy with the results. I may have recommended minor changes. Most of the tutors and lecturers were in broad agreement with the aims and methods and, on the whole, it was a good course.

However, as an academic I design learning environments and, as an engineer, I believe that there should be a social dimension in all our courses. How we teach reflects our respect for the students, our commitment to the academic community and our responsibility for the world. Respect for the students demands that we acknowledge their previous experiences and work with them to design a course which fulfils their expectations. Our commitment to our community entails inculcating in the students an enjoyment of 'the pursuit of difficulty' (Ryan, 1999) so that they reach the highest intellectual level of which they are capable. Responsibility to the world means developing, with students, critical and reflective tools so that they can discuss and act, with authority, on the dominant political issues which affect their lives. My concerns are now whether all academic courses should satisfy these criteria. Are they relevant in a mathematics course for engineers? Can we design a course which encompasses these wider aspirations as well as teaching students to:

- perform simple manipulative skills;
- understand mathematical texts;
- select and use software to perform calculations;
- to solve and explain the solutions to problems in a clear and logical way both in writing and orally?

References

Backhouse, J., Haggarty, L., Pirie, S. and Stratton, J. (1992) *Improving the Learning of Mathematics*. London: Cassell.

Barnett, R. (1997) *Higher Education: A Critical Business*. Buckingham: SRHE/Open University Press.

Barrows, H. (1988) *The Tutorial Process*. Springfield, IL: Southern Illinois School of Medicine.

Barry, M. D. J. and Steele, N. C. (eds) (1992) *A Core Curriculum in Mathematics for the European Engineer Document 92.1*. Brussels: SEFI.

Barry, M. and Sutherland, R. (1998) Achieving core zero – an investigation into the knowledge of classical algebra among engineering students at the University of Bristol. Unpublished report, University of Bristol.

Berry, J. and Sharp, J. (1999) Developing student-centred learning in mathematics through co-operation, reflection and discussion, *Teaching in Higher Education*, 4, 27–41.

Bissell, C. (1995) Models of technology, in L. Burton and B. Jaworski (eds) *Technology in Mathematics Teaching*. London: Chartwell-Bratt.

Challis, N. (1998) Seeing the positive in engineering mathematics, *Engineering Professors Council Bulletin*, July, 14–15.

Cockcroft, W. H. (1982) *Mathematics Counts*. London: HMSO.

Cowan, J. (1998) *On Becoming an Innovative University Teacher*. Buckingham: SRHE/Open University Press.

Croft, A., Davison, R. and Hargreaves, M. (1998) *Engineering Mathematics*. Reading, MA: Addison-Wesley.

Croft, A. and Ward, J. P. (2000) *Opening learning in engineering mathematics: mathematical education of engineers. Conference proceedings*. London: Institute of Mathematics and its Applications.

Denvir, B., Stolz, C. and Brown, M. (1982) *Low Attainers in Mathematics 5–16*. Schools Council Working Paper, 72. London: Methuen Educational.

Engineering Council (1993) *SARTOR: Standards and Routes to Registration 1997*. London: The Engineering Council.

Entwhistle, N. and Hounsell, D. (1989) *The Performance of Electrical Engineering Students in Scottish Higher Education: Final Report to the Scottish Education Department*. Edinburgh: University of Edinburgh.

Freire, P. (1970) *The Pedagogy of the Oppressed*. London: Penguin Books.

Green, G. and Gerson, P. M. (1999) Open dynamic design: towards a European model for an engineering design curriculum. Paper presented at the Engineering Design Education Conference, Strathclyde University, Glasgow, September.

Green, G. and Kennedy, P. (2001) Redefining enginering education: the reflective practice of product design engineering, *International Journal of Engineering Education*, Vol. 17, 1: 3–9.

James, G. (ed.) (1996) *Modern Engineering Mathematics*. Reading, MA: Addison-Wesley.

Kappraff, J. (1990) *Connections: The Geometric Bridge between Art and Science*. New York: McGraw-Hill.

Molyneux-Hodgson, M. (1999) *Mathematical Experiences and Mathematical Practices in the HE Science Setting*. Final report to ESRC, Grant R00022571.

Papert, S. (1980) *Mindstorms*. Brighton: Harvester Press.

Ryan, A. (1999) *Liberal Anxieties and Liberal Education*. London: Profile Books.

Schon, D. (1987) *Educating the Reflective Practitioner*. San Francisco: Jossey-Bass.

Schon, D. (ed.) (1991) *The Reflective Turn*. New York: Teachers College Press.

Scott, B. and McGregor, R. (1996) Mathematical education of engineers. Unpublished paper, Institute of Mathematics and Its Applications, London.

Simpson, M. (1998) The diagnostic assessment of pupil learning, in S. Brown (ed.) *Assessment a Changing Practice.* Edinburgh: Scottish Academic Press.

Sutherland, R. and Pozzi, S. (1995) *The Changing Mathematical Background of Undergraduate Engineers.* London: The Engineering Council.

Wilkinson, J. (1999) Course report: engineering mathematics EE1. Department of Electronics and Electrical Engineering, University of Glasgow.

Wilkinson, J. and Earnshaw, H. (2000) *Embedding mathematical skills for engineers: mathematical education of engineers. Conference proceedings.* London: Institute of Mathematics and its Applications.

Woods, D. (1985) *The McMaster Problem Solving Program.* Hamilton, Ont: McMaster University.

9

Learning Independently through Project Work

Mike Gonzalez

Caminante no hay camino
se hace camino al andar

Al andar se hace camino
y al volver la vista atrás
se ve la senda que nunca
se ha de volver a pisar
    (Antonio Machado)[1]

The discovery

> They journeyed night and day for more than two centuries . . . Several times they got lost, scattered and joined up again. They were buffeted by the winds and dragged themselves ahead, lashed together, bumping and pushing each other. They fell from hunger and got up and fell again and got up again . . . When they approached the luminous lake under the noonday sun, for the first time the Aztecs wept. Huitzlipochtli welcomed them. 'This is the place of our rest and our greatness', his voice resounded.
>   (Galeano, 1987: 41)

It is always unnerving to be confronted with an open road – the more so when you have been used to the idea that maps would be provided and that the guide would be nearby. It may be little comfort to know that the organizer of your journey will welcome you at its ending. Yet one kind of travelling will teach you little about yourself and much about the idiosyncrasies of your leader. The other will involve some unexpected and undesirable diversions, some unmarked crossroads, a moment or two of anxiety – or even fear – but in the process you will have become your own cartographer.

I should probably begin by saying that, or something like it. But that would be a contradiction in terms – my assumption is that a process of self-discovery must identify its own ending.

This account of one of my Hispanic studies courses will ideally narrate two parallel processes: on the one hand, the development and growth of individual learners for whom each element of understanding should prove another benchmark in their personal transformation; on the other, a recognition of that same impulse in the material they are deploying – in other words, in history itself. If it is my task to create the general conditions in which that can occur, it is also part of my responsibility to deny pre-existing outcomes – to refuse a covert agenda. The 'profit' will be both in the process itself, in a complex, experienced sense of change and growth in the learners themselves, and in the production of a 20-minute video and an accompanying portfolio.

First encounter

The second year Hispanic studies class meets for the first time in the year to consider 'History'. With its forbidding opening capital letter and its institutional status as a 'discipline', it is likely that what the students anticipate is a meeting with authority – hence a slight nervousness, an apprehension at being in the presence of some Great Truth. It might of course turn out to begin like any other university course: with an announcement of what is to be learned, a timetable and a map of the course, plus the hurdles disseminated en route to assess the individual's capacity for assimilation. In that case there will be a syllabus, and the examinations at the end that acknowledge a journey successfully completed in the footsteps of the many that have gone before. It is reassuring to have walked the rutted path where countless others walked before you, and to have entered – albeit as a very junior partner – the august company of the initiates.

This presumption about the nature of learning is embedded in the fabric of the room, in the seats arranged as three sides of a square, the chairs at one side only, and all facing the large table and whiteboard that occupy the fourth axis. The expectations are confirmed in the body language of those who arrive at the encounter, and framed by the institutional definition of what is about to happen here, a one-hour class in familiar surroundings. There is, however, an element of unpredictability, in part because I have taught them some history in the previous year and there is a degree of relaxation and familiarity between us. It is also true that no one is entirely sure what goes on under this rubric of 'Level 2 History Project'. My conduct in the room as they arrive gives no obvious clue, and there are no course booklists or any other material to hand out.

It is that hesitation, that minimum element of uncertainty, that provides a space in which a redefinition of what is understood by both 'learning' and 'knowing' might take place. But it has to be done quickly. The physical place has created presumptions. The rather unhelpful course description says little, but it is typed in the same style on the same paper as the other components of the annual programme, most of them recognizable in style and form, and creating their own predictable responses. Those lists and headings will creep across the sparser 'History Project' page unless it is quickly filled or superseded. And there is another pressure on the moment; there is another choice available to the students in the form of a taught course of conventional shape, and safely embedded in what is largely 'rote' learning. Most students have made their decision, but there are still some who are here to be persuaded that my course is the more worthwhile alternative for them.

Nevertheless, there is, however briefly, a suspension of disbelief, a friendly hesitation. It is my ally. But if history, as they say, abhors a vacuum, how much truer is that of its portentous commentator; History with a capital 'H' will reassert itself unless the silence is broken.

The second year of a Hispanic studies class at Glasgow University attracts well over 60 students; it embraces language, literature and a third element, in which students can elect one of two options, a history of language course, or the nebulously defined history project which I teach. The group usually divides down the middle, with about 30 electing the unpaved road. The grounds for the choice are unclear; they have had no experience of the history of language, but they have met my history classes before. There seems to be some awareness of a difference of style – not the details, simply the people concerned. It seems to be an *ad hominem* choice in part, but it is also a choice that perhaps separates the curious and adventurous from the more conservative. That prior choice shapes the environment on the first meeting – or at least explains the openness. Sometimes – actually with some degree of regularity – students change to history at an early stage. The reasons given are usually that the history of language is 'dull'. The hidden reasons may initially include the feeling that the history project will be less demanding, or more exciting. Presumably the students speak to one another and compare notes.

The spectator observed[2]

Although I have conducted the course in this way for many years, each beginning feels exciting and full of risk. There is an underlying principle on which the whole thing rests. I believe profoundly that everyone, no matter how different their intellectual experience, is able to learn and engage with the questions posed here. I am also convinced that everyone has the desire to know given the space to explore knowledge and its construction without pressure or targets. That raises an immediate dilemma. The prevailing culture in higher education is increasingly tied to measurable outcomes in tandem with an insistence on the interchangeability of those measurements; the pressure therefore is towards clearly defined bodies of knowledge whose categories and laws are globally and unproblematically recognized. Where in such a culture is the unpredictable lodged? Yet what educational value is there in a method that is exclusively instrumental and pre-emptive. Creative engagement with the world, or any stepping across boundary fences into areas of moral uncertainty or explanatory doubt, is therefore inimical to the new ideology of outcomes and targets.

What I am nonetheless proposing to the students is that they should embark on a process without defined objectives. My assumption is that it is the freedom that will tempt them, the risk: 'In the practice of the ethical lecturer there is a kind of alertness, a deep attentiveness to students, a determination to do justice to the tricky business of teaching and learning . . . there are no gains to be made unless a degree of risk is taken' (Blake *et al.*, 1998: 97). Yet the institutional culture is strictly bound to numerical results – albeit for reasons that are managerial and not pedagogic.

In the end, of course, there will be a quantifiable outcome equivalent to the others they might have gained. What is distinct is the process rather than the product. But how do we make it desirable, worthy of pursuit? Somewhere along the line I am asking the students to take a leap of faith which depends entirely on the trust that I can establish with them. It is not all done in an hour, of course: there is an existing goodwill based on a previous year of enjoyable and stimulating classes. Without that, there would be no grounds to ask for their trust; yet, paradoxically, the prior condition for what I hope and believe will be an emancipatory experience is a personal relationship between us. And equally significant is the conviction that there is real choice here, and not a directive masquerading as a referendum. I need the credibility to take them with me, but it has to be disengaged from an institutional authority.

The openness of the choice means that some will turn away from my efforts at persuasion, will resist my passion, and in doing so (it might be argued) refute my belief that the pursuit of understanding for its own sake is common to all. And if, at the other end, we have misjudged each other and the students are unable for any reason to complete the project they have agreed to deliver, they and others will almost certainly attribute any consequential impact to me. And I should acknowledge too that from my own perspective, the additional risk is, or could be, that this would confirm the suspicion of some colleagues who regard this as some kind of 'hippy' throwback to free schools and child-centred indulgences; a charge to which I would happily plead guilty, were it not so palpably absurd.

Sixty minutes

The first meeting is the only time we will meet as a whole class, the only opportunity to establish the ground rules for this particular activity, or rather make clear that (a) there are few rules, (b) the exercise is open but not unstructured (when we meet as separate groups, I will discuss with them the possible shape of their research), (c) the rules are new and different. After that I will only encounter the individual groups.

I had imagined, before exploring the issue with the Barcelona Group, that the situation was inchoate and without regulation – that I was simply providing an opportunity for the students to take wing and that I had voluntarily stepped aside. Minimal interrogation from my Barcelona colleagues in research exposed this as an illusion.

First, the material: what is history after all? Is it a vein of hardened mineral, once fluid and vital but now frozen in a final state, to which we – the investigators – bring chisels and picks (or dynamite for the more obdurate of historical facts)? If the enterprise we are engaged in is mining, then the supervisor/teacher is there to deliver the tools and provide a map of where to drill in reasonable expectation of what to find. The nature of that exercise is to test listening and instrumental skills; the analysis is pre-existent.

My task is to make play on the absence of tools – to refuse the role as given – to place myself, albeit temporarily and problematically, in an unexpected place within the teaching arena. In front of the table not behind, walking not still, with no obvious tools of the trade on display, speaking to people I know. There is no pretence here of hiding within the crowd; I am already known as the lecturer. I am not absent, but I am working to redefine my teaching presence.

The next moment is crucial – to redefine the subject matter, to cast it among the group. What, after all, is the topic here? So far, all that we have agreed is that it is Hispanic history. I ask the assembled students what they are interested in, trying to draw out of them familiar or fascinating elements of the culture of the Spanish-speaking world. But is that still history? Is history not defined as the past, rather than a living process in which they might even be participants? The students are perplexed by the change of balance – they are here to be told, not to tell. They do respond, though not immediately. There is some laughter, someone ventures a thought: 'the World Cup', 'tacos', 'salsa', 'flamenco', 'Joaquín Cortés' (the beautiful young flamenco choreographer who appeared in Almodóvar's very successful film *The Flower of My Secret*). Within minutes my whiteboard is full of scribbled prompts from the students – some 25 or so. There is also a buzz of conversation across the room. I have about 40 minutes left to hone them down. I go rapidly through each topic, what it might entail or where it might lead, and see which areas interest more than one person. The list is progressively reduced until there are five or six groups of students who have expressed a particular interest in a subject. The class ends and I arrange to meet each group separately.

On the concept of exchange

This first encounter defines a number of key aspects of the learning that is to be done.

First, the material is derived from an *exchange*. This to me is crucial; the characteristic of much of the undergraduate learning conducted in higher education cannot in all honesty be described as an exchange. It is most often a relationship of consumption, in which the teacher facilitates access to existing and defined knowledge. The new rhetoric of a marketized educational system, after all, insists on defining students as client groups – recipients rather than producers. Of course, all knowledge acquisition builds on what has already been achieved; but the presumption in undergraduate teaching is that no value can be added in this transmission. The characteristic division between teaching and research, which underlies all discussion about higher education in Britain today, uncritically presumes that the teaching situation will not produce any additions to the sum of knowledge.

What differs in the exchange is that all parties to it will be changed in the encounter and the material exchanged will be enriched and not diminished in the process. It is also a deeply ethical practice: 'If we cannot make sense of teaching relationships in terms of effectiveness . . . then perhaps ethics is a way of thinking that will prove useful . . . Ethics after all is centrally concerned with human relationships and it is ethical language that seems necessary if we are to do justice to what were called earlier the 'internal goods' of education' (Blake *et al.*, 1998: 94).

It is not just individuals who are transformed by active learning – it is knowledge itself. Learning a subject restrains and limits the nature of the knowledge exchange, and reinforces its inequality. The frontiers between disciplines define the organization of the academy, not the actual experience of the world. Where is the line that divides culture from history, music from poetry, the operation of thought from the movement of the body? Thus the key to this earliest encounter between me and the student group is to create a possibility of exchange and to reproblematize the subject boundaries, and all this in a way that will allow the student-learners to establish the pace of recognition.

It is my experience that students will assume that they have nothing to bring, no expertise or accumulated specialist understandings. Their own experience, curiosity and doubts are deemed other and different, and that self-effacement is frequently reinforced within an academy obsessed with the exclusivity of ownership of bodies of information. In this crucial initiation, their experience, their concerns, must be valued in the exchange. And it is not a matter of equivalence: there is no issue for them in a difference of age (between myself and them) or of knowledge; we bring to the meeting whatever gifts we have.[3] The important thing is that the limits or deficiencies in their knowledge can be remedied by study or reading or investigation – *adding to what they already have*, to what they already own.

Exchange to my mind is a key concept. At first sight it contradicts the flow of educational traffic. The teacher vouchsafes, at varying rates of revelation, truths and insights of which he is the possessor. They are acknowledged to be partial truths; the pieces of the jigsaw are acquired through long and obedient apprenticeship ('you can think when you've got a PhD', as one colleague in another department wrote in red ink on the essay of the student who later showed it to me). Its stages are undergraduate, postgraduate, academic experience, patient monopolizing of a corner of the collective *savoir vivre*, the final anointing of the cognoscenti. How then, if that is the process of knowledge acquisition, can there possibly be exchange – when the other party to the contract, the learner, has so little to give?

The answer is not in the possession of those truths but in their assimilation; learning is not the end-point – ownership of measurable quantities of knowledge – but the process. How does the student make sense of these truths, link them to other knowledges, engage with them as an individual, socialize that understanding in an evolving relationship with others, transform behaviour as a result of understanding, interrogate the world for the consequences of that understanding?

The teacher (as opposed to the lecturer, the delivery person) is concerned with that dynamic, unpredictable, inchoate unfolding in its endless multiplicity of permutations. Given the material of knowledge, how is it absorbed into a life lived in a community? The magisterial intervention is there – in responding creatively to the unexpected directions that process may take. Were it not so, then the delivery of graded packages of pre-digested material would be perfectly adequate:

> *Johannes*: I think there's still a gap between lecturers and students.
>   They speak like a totally different language.[4]
> *Eve*: It's not like a chore . . . you go there 'cos you want to.

But is that an exchange? Of course it is, because the material is changed each time it is handled, added to, revisited and reinterpreted.

An example: Latin America for the past twenty or so years has been dominated by oppressive military dictatorships. That fact has been received and reviewed by thousands of people – victims, observers, forensic scientists, ethnic communities, mothers of the disappeared, romanies, squatters, gay movements. It is not that each of them have encountered and absorbed the same phenomenon at different moments; their discovery of it has changed its meaning and its content. Knowledge is taken, but also given.

Possessing

Without a sense of ownership there can be no critical understanding; it comes only with a perception of the learner as a subject, not the object of learning. These are small beginnings – but in that first hour, the initiative for learning, the impetus, had to come from the students. The moment that they inaugurate the process, they become its subjects not its objects.

The first discovery is that their own knowledge has value and can be constitutive of a body of understandings that have intellectual weight. The second key element is the recognition of shared interests among the students, for though they will have met in the first year of the course, only some will know one another already. The 'brainstorming' exercise with which the class began has to return to them, refocusing away from the teacher to the group, leading (forcing) them to seek out others who share their interest in one topic or another:

> *Gheila*: Getting to know the members of one's group can be a daunting prospect and I suppose may rely on the 'luck of the draw' – that we all had a common interest in our subject brought us together even though we found strong individuals in most members of the group.

It is significant that the majority of teaching environments make that inward focus difficult. In fixed rows, students must turn uncomfortably to look behind them, or across the rows. It is imperative that they do that, however much discomfort it may cause. The room we have gathered in has them on three sides of a square, sitting only on one side. I ask them to sit on both sides, looking at one another. In that way the focus moves and shifts and is defined by the students' relationships with one another as well as with me rather than by the conventions of knowledge hierarchies. This has been announced as a moment of definition, in which their reference points are one another; the groups will form out of a mutual recognition of common interest. Dialogue is the absolutely necessary milieu – it should arise out of both physical and intellectual encounters between the people in the room.

While it may not be explicit as yet, there is also an active redefinition of the subject matter itself taking place in this floating dialogue. It is a matter not of debate, but of a practice that allows into the concept of history whatever has made or is *making* history and whatever is constitutive of human actions – be it drugs, football, food or military dictatorship. History in process is more porous and amenable than that which has solidified into 'pastness'.

The project

'Project' is a happy term; it is not confined to constructions in space or time, nor does it presume a necessary end-point. Only the beginning is defined materially.

But that is more than a little naive; the joyous encounter and exchange of gifts does not take place outside a long house or in some Xanadu of our creation. This is not an encounter group. Therefore it does have tasks – purposes. The plural is important here; from the outset it is crucial to express this 'project' as multiple, because the institutional context has quite specific demands to make of me and of them. At year's end the columns of marks must be filled in, the tasks must be assessed and quantified and in some way rendered equivalent to activities of an entirely different kind. The point is to develop the creative and imaginative possibilities of this learning process alongside and within the fulfilment of institutional objectives, but without being entirely shaped or conditioned by those purposes.

The protagonist of this process is now a group, loosely formed, still wary of one another perhaps, barely a week old when we meet – group by group – for a second time.

If the first phase of the learning cycle has been identifying questions, the starting point, the material of foundation, the second step must elaborate and extend the search, define some markers on the way, elaborate the questions to be asked. Point to the road ahead:

> *Johannes*: First you had to define a topic that you wanted to do and then you started finding out information and then you analyse it with other people in your group . . . so there's like three different steps that you can be sure you remember, not just like listening to someone giving a lecture.

Two quite different processes must coincide at this second meeting; the first, as set out, is to deconstruct the initial tentative question, to unpeel its many layers. It is also more than that, because in this independent activity the student group must feel it is worth the discomforts of the journey, that there are worlds worth discovering beyond today. They should be tempted, enthused, inspired perhaps. It is, as it always was, the task of the expedition's leader to motivate; there is no renouncing that responsibility when everything beyond the visible horizon is the merest speculation. And at the same time, something else must also happen – the enthusiasm must cement the group, give it coherence, commonality of purpose, a sense of joint activity to come.

This is a crossroads, and a difficult one. My radical instinct is to withdraw, take to its logical conclusion the concept of empowerment and self-activity which is at the heart of my personal belief. But that would be, I realize, a relinquishing of a professional, teaching responsibility – a duty of guidance – which I cannot renounce. It was an issue I had discussed earlier with Melanie in exploring the contradictions of a libertarian view. Our students do not come equipped with the instruments of understanding, but they do possess the capacity for it that has to grow with time and growing confidence:

> *Melanie*: Why do you need Mike?
> *Kirsty*: In a way it's someone you can go to. You know if you really got stuck, you'd have someone and I think that should never be taken away.

But having devolved ownership of the questions to the students, I cannot now reclaim it in the name of prior knowledge without making a mockery of the claim of this student-centred learning process. It is partly a matter of language – of ensuring that all information is provided clearly and fully, without the characteristic tendency to reserve to oneself, as expert, some key element of the code, as often as not a private language.

When travellers, conquerors or colonizers advanced across new terrain, like Columbus and his inheritors in their invasion of Indian America, they depended on the guides who showed them their way across the mountains. The trailmaker was just that, a facilitator, an opener of the road to travel.

The second meeting, held separately with each project group, will delimit and define to some extent the range of possibilities within what is still little more than a topic title. I talk them through the issues, the possibilities and implications. I cannot claim lack of expertise or ignorance – that would undermine their nascent confidence in the meaningfulness of what they are about to undertake.

The subject matter the 1998/9 cohort of students have identified is widely different. For this group of students it embraces soap operas, military dictatorship, food, Barcelona and Latinos in the USA. I talk through with them what might be done. Within a week or two I assemble as comprehensive a handout as I can; it includes a bibliography, suggestions of web sites and net-based information, of journals and magazines, of films, videos and other broadcast material, and suggestions of people who might help or be available for interview. It is limited by my own knowledge, but past experience reassures me that by the end they will have travelled far beyond my indications and suggestions:

> *Veronica*: I think the subject we chose wasn't really easy so when I said dictatorship when we were brainstorming I just thought 'well, if I get to be in this group it will force myself to get into the subject' . . . so now I think each of us got a really fair insight into it and, yeah, we got to know each other really well.

There is in this encounter a third almost covert process. The groups are rarely preselected (friends will not necessarily find themselves in the same group); in the process of learning the group must forge some kind of collective identity. The work they will do from now on will be their own, an unravelling of issues and an exploration – but it will be done collectively. This opens another area of learning, and not merely as an exercise in social cooperation. Underlying it, unstated but key to the process we are encouraging here, is the notion of learning as a sequence of encounters, debates and understandings in a shared social environment. The students might well be startled at the thought, but the group is a learning community whose dynamic collegiality is precisely what the academy should be like – except that the university's emphasis on the individual appropriation of bodies of pre-existing truths directly subverts such a notion:

> *Desmond*: I think we learned what we could do ourselves and we didn't really read lecture notes and things like that, we could go away and do it ourselves, produce it ourselves. So we learned about you know what we could do basically.
>
> *Chris*: It was different from lectures where it's very ordered and structured and you could go off on a tangent and if it didn't work out there wasn't any pressure on you. You don't have to conform to it, you just go back to where you were and try something else and in that way it was good. You do have moments when you're 'Where's this going, I don't know what I'm doing and I don't know what anybody else is thinking', but because you've got this deadline a long way away you've got enough time to research things, to try things out, and that was the best thing about it for me.

Fiona: I think at the beginning it was hard to motivate yourself to do it, the first term and you haven't got somebody saying 'this is due then and you have to come every week' to kind of get ourselves started . . . But once we did it was a lot better to do something different, taking it wherever you wanted to take it.

Johannes: I think it's better in this case to find your own truth and your own opinion.

In other words – and we come here to the core – the material to be elaborated as history is found in and through the dialogue itself, certainly in the way that history has been implicitly defined through this interaction as the evolving assimilation of the past into the present. The engagement with the past produces a critical engagement with contemporary experience. This result is not specific to history or indeed the social sciences in general; in becoming a thinking subject the student changes his or her relationship with the world from merely reflecting on the world to constructing it. In that transformation understanding moves from a passive to an active posture. What is learned is a sense of oneself in the world:

Kirsty: You've chosen to come to university to do a certain subject because that's what you're interested in but then you sort of get various aspects of it but it's what other people think is going to be interesting for you, not what you yourself would find interesting . . . This was something you really worked for and you had an end-product you could be proud of.

Kirsty and others were adamant that the process was rewarding and life-enhancing; it was also tough for them. Initially, the students experienced their autonomy as a source of pleasure; but it also generated its own anxieties. Access to the past is often preceded by a series of membership tests. Here no IDs were required, but there was a responsibility, which they assumed bravely, to explore, uncover and explain – first and foremost to one another. Access to the present would be gained here by a process of argument, shared or conflicting discoveries:

Stuart: You come to university and you end up getting lost . . . but teamwork brings you together.

Stephanie: Everybody brings ideas forward but it's less a confrontation it's not really 'I really want to do this', it's more 'Well what do you think about this?'

Ideally, historical truth and historical enquiry would then be revealed to be a process of encounters, conflicts, resolutions and negotiations.

> when I am I am another, my acts
> are more mine when they are the acts
> of others, in order to be I must be another,
> leave myself, search for myself,
> in the others, the others that don't exist
> if I don't exist.
>
> (Octavia Paz, 'Sunstone')

Expulsion from the citadel

The next stage is like a parting. Armed with their several pages of bibliography and guidance, the students have an appointment with the university's Audio-Visual Service (whose acceptance of my bizarre rules and cooperation is the sine qua non of the whole thing). The Service introduces them to the techno-logy of editing, gives advice on the kinds of material they might seek out and provides a producer who will see the group through. With a list of names and (usually) an emerging group coordinator, a subject heading and my irreligious benediction, they may now sally forth in search of windmills.

Their task now is to make the group work. It is clear that I am there to return to, but I rely on the hope that other things now supervene to give impetus to a process of self-discovery: some interest and involvement in the topic, an element of curiosity and excitement, and above all pride. Pride in themselves, in the project, in their independence. If that pride does not exist, at this early stage, in some form albeit unstated, the enterprise will come apart. This is the first experience of intellectual autonomy; it may be fearful, exciting, confusing.

Do they feel abandoned, neglected? Do others look in on me and see indolence, an easy route to inactivity?

> *Kirsty*: I think if we'd not actually a lecturer but a tutor sitting in what-
> ever kind of person they are they're always going to try and shape
> your ideas to their point of view . . . in this one, it was good because
> you had that freedom to make your own [opinions] . . . sifting through
> this amazing amount of information and coming up with a balanced
> report on what we found.

Others watch, and, without paranoia, I am reasonably certain that the free-dom and elasticity of it is threatening to many of my colleagues, whose teaching style and method are rooted in the inviolability of the lectern (real or symbolic) and the incontestable authoritative voice. To paraphrase Paulo Freire, the doors to the bank of ideas must be thrown open, the guide and facilitator must renounce his or her institutional authority: 'The world must be approached as an object to be understood and known by the efforts of the learners themselves. Moreover, their acts of knowing are to be stimulated and grounded in their own being, experiences, needs, circumstances and destinies' (Lankshear and McLaren, 1993, quoted in McLaren, 1999: 51).

That is not the same as an intellectual – professional[5] – authority, whose source is the power of the ideas themselves and a willingness to render democratically available all that knowledge. It is a gift – a rendering of self – that marks the most profound of educative acts, which is an act of *exchange*.

Embarkation

The weeks that follow are an anxious time for the groups (and unseen, for me too). I have withdrawn from the process, though I stress over and over again that I am always available. The students have to learn to work

together, to organize their meetings, arrange the distribution of work, meet
with the Audio-Visual Service and develop their new technical and creative
skills, with access to advice but essentially on their own.

The students describe the process – the delays, the interference of other,
more immediate tasks, the perplexity. It seems to be generally the case that
there is a kind of hiatus, when they have their topic and their task, but are
unclear how to work. I am never quite clear how they resolve this moment
of stasis, but they invariably do. Often they describe it as a kind of test of
their commitment and their independence. But they never complain and
very rarely come to me. I hope they have already come to see the project as
their own responsibility.

Perhaps I expect complaint, resentment, a sense of abandonment – that
I will be called upon to explain why I see it as a kind of emancipation. But
despite conversations and interviews, no student has ever expressed a sense
of neglect. I am probably in danger of underestimating the students' own
'seriousness', their sense of commitment.

I do not labour the point with them, but the social experience is key to
the learning process. Learning to collaborate implies a different, and possibly subversive, learning model. Though the term is used liberally and
imprecisely in the university of learning, this is in some sense a genuine
'community of learning'.

There is no sense in which I am in any way qualified to *teach* group
collaboration – even were I not sceptical of the very notion of teaching an
essential social impulse. What I am in a position to do is create conditions
in which such collaboration can flower; I might call it a kind of discovery
zone (had the Millennium Dome not sent the phrase whirling into disrepute
and mockery). Of course, there is an important underlying assumption at
work which I glibly threw out as a truism just above: that it is the natural condition of human beings to operate socially; that we become human in the
degree to which we are social. Defoe was obliged to provide Robinson Crusoe
with a companion (however unequal the relationship) in order to make
him human: 'There is a recognition that no individual exists apart from the
community – or more accurately, communities, since she certainly belongs
to more than one. Thus, the good of a community inevitably has implications for the good of the individual. Likewise, the good of the individual
has implications for the good of her communities' (Griffiths, 1998: 11).

The concept of 'good' here is understood as an intellectual and educational category rather than a moral one – at least in the first instance. It is
what Blake *et al.* (1998: 90) refer to as an 'internal good': 'Learning has a
communal and not purely individual function, that we need constantly to
enquire what its purpose is, and that . . . certain kinds of learning have
internal goods that demand respect and must not be neglected in the quest
for learning outcomes.'

This seems too obvious even to say. Yet the structures of almost all learning in higher education presume something different if not wholly opposed
to that – namely that this business of becoming human (of learning) is conducted in isolation, by individuals, largely in competition with one another.

Knowledge is possessed as private property which may only be delivered to others by a contract of sale closely ring-fenced by patent law and regulations against plagiarism. My truism may have to be fought for, after all, in a world of possessive individualisms and disciplinary boundaries guarded by fences and frontiers both physically and metaphorically defined.

Against that background it should become clear that the business of group work and collaboration by discovery and negotiation (rather than by external regulation) is something more than merely the condition or context for the acquisition of knowledge; it is itself a knowledge which in turn enriches, informs and shapes other modes of knowing:

> *Melanie*: How come you were trusting your own ideas and your own thinking?
> *Kirsty*: Well I think we were always told that it's your own work anyway and that you should believe in what you write.
> *Veronica*: I think you actually gain self-confidence through this . . . just our coming together and exchanging things . . . that was one of the best things really.

Shapes glimpsed through the mist

For a while everything goes very quiet – a noiseless gestation period. I see the students in the corridors, and they are cheerful and don't seem to be crossing the road to avoid me. The introduction at the Audio-Visual Service went ahead and the students comment from time to time on how exciting it is to be playing with editing machines and the like. There are occasional requests for music, pictures, a video or an address. It is a positive silence, of course – or it can be. Either the students have abandoned the whole thing or they are getting on with it, in their own way. I cannot ask; there is a central underlying assumption about these adult learners who have accepted a responsibility; if they own their work then it is their part now. What do I hope is going on? That the students perceive themselves as independent learners, engaging simultaneously with experience, with the corpus of 'established' knowledge, with one another. I know something of their activities, however – but much less of their thoughts.

One group is working on the city of Barcelona – its urban growth, its architecture, its cultural life. They have decided to travel together with a borrowed camera and a set of agreed questions and concerns – four young women in pursuit of a city. Another group is looking at military dictatorships in Latin America. They are arguing a great deal, I hear; they have different views and opinions about recent history and they are looking for a form of cooperation that can recognize the differences. It evoked a more passionately ideological response than some of the other subjects, perhaps, and a powerful sense of injustice and anger that the final video expressed with great effect. The group exploring the issue of food in the Hispanic world have probably moved the furthest in their understanding from what might have been a fairly light and impressionistic piece: 'We thought about culture, we sort of thought about the geography and the agriculture. We thought about the actual foods, the history of food . . . maybe not exploring everything in detail but trying to take a sort of general overview' (Chris). The final product moved from discussing the new enthusiasm for tacos and tapas, to the structure of the global food industry and the changing nature of the family expressed in the rituals of shared eating (or their disappearance). The two young women who worked on Hispanics in the United States met every lunchtime to talk and organize their beautifully crafted and imaginative video on the arts of the Spanish-speaking minorities:

> *Fiona*: To start with it was just Hispanics in the USA and then we changed it to Hispanic culture. We wanted, as I said before, to do something more positive and sort of not forget about all this sort of racism and everything that goes on but to show something positive out of this like negative atmosphere the Hispanic American people lived in.

The last group came ready-formed. They had decided six weeks into the course that they wanted to change to the project from the history of language option. They arrived together, though it was only their desire to join the course that linked them. The brainstorming with them was more intense (and slightly shorter) – but I was impressed by the fact that they come predisposed to accept the method. They had been told how it worked by others. They also had some concerns. But they eventually agreed on soap operas:

> *Hayley*: I think everybody was sort of worried that it wasn't academic enough.
> *Melanie*: What do you mean by not academic enough?
> *Clare*: Well, it's not like a historical study where you can go and look up history books and you get dates and facts and marches and parades and all that kind of thing. It's much more . . . kind of just different people's opinions really.
> *Chris*: It looked like a soft option – it certainly wasn't that . . . if you're interested in something, you know, the time passes quickly. It's not quite such a labour as reading over a subject you're not interested in. You know, there's some use to it.
> *Desmond*: The themes are actually kind of relevant to their lives, like over here it's simply escapism to watch these kind of exotic settings and things. But we were quite surprised by that, that they actually did reflect real life.

Their final video was a soap opera of their own, written and performed in Spanish, with a kind of ironic over-commentary and epilogue.

Making History

People make history, but not in circumstances of their own choosing.
(see Callinicos, 1987: 78–80)

My purposes in this course were extraordinarily ambitious – to create the conditions in which there could occur a multiple transformation. In the many years over which I have organized the course, my aspiration has been to oversee a metamorphosis: of the material and content of the work; of the learners themselves; of my relationship with those learners in a permanent fashion, so that we would meet again a year later having preserved some element of the relationship of exchange I discussed earlier.

How do university students in Britain become what Ron Barnett (1997) describes as 'critical persons', persons with a degree of self-awareness and self-confidence sufficient to ensure that they engage with the corpus of institutional knowledge in a questioning and sceptical way? That engagement in turn produces not only transformations of their individual cognitive universe, but a commitment to unveiling ideology and pursuing the freedom and justice implicit in the concept of a free critical enquiry. There are, of course, powerful countervailing forces.

The first lies in wait as the groups are called in from the cold by their anarchic 'Control'. At the end of the academic year, they bring a video and a portfolio of written and illustrative work, prepared with care and delivered with evident pride:

> *Chris*: It was different from lectures where it's very ordered and structured and you could go off on a tangent and if it didn't work out there wasn't any pressure on you. You don't have to conform to it, you just go back to where you were and try something else and in that way it was good. You do have moments when you're saying, 'Where's this going, I don't know what I'm doing and I don't know what anybody else is thinking.' But because you've got this deadline a long way away you've got enough time to research things, to try things out, and that was the best thing about it for me.
>
> *Kirsty*: You've chosen to come to university to do a certain subject because that's what you're interested in but then you sort of get various aspects of it but it's what other people think is going to be interesting for you, not what you yourself would find interesting ... This was something you really worked for and you had an end-product you could be proud of.

It is the end of the year; on my desk there are rising mounds of essays and classwork for assessment, uniform coloured examination books with flaps concealing the individual identities of the students, dissertations and fat white envelopes full of papers from elsewhere to moderate. The room screams 'assessment', 'marking', 'measurement'. The journey to enlightenment must now be calibrated, not just because the institution requires that the unblinking square space on the appropriate form be filled but because in some way the students seek an acknowledgement of the work they have done. There is no evading this paradox. I can minimize the damage by giving the mark in 8 point, and my elaborate comments and congratulations in 14 point. But that is a pathetic salve to my own conscience.

Yet if I reclaim the work on the university's behalf, if I apply criteria derived from an entirely different system of learning – in which individual tasks are marked against a template which is absolutely uniform for all and assesses against a true/accurate/'fair' version – then I feel I am betraying the philosophy of the course. If I fail to assess in some way then this small space for experiment and alterity will disappear and the students will suffer for their participation in the project. One group member reinforced my discomfort: 'We cheated because we saw each other's work, because we set our own questions and we cheated because we actually quite enjoyed ourselves when we were meant to be doing serious work and I think cheating's very educational' (Jamie).

Over and over again the students affirm their pride in what they have achieved, in what they have *made*, as well as their sense of personal evolution, their delight in their own expertise – or you could describe it as their own authority. We asked them at a final meeting what message I should take back to the university:

> *Louise*: I just hate uni at the moment, because there's nothing that interests me. We just go and sit in lectures and I think we just come out none the wiser at all.
>
> *Veronica*: I think you actually gain self-confidence through this . . . just our coming together and exchanging things . . . that was one of the best things really.
>
> *Desmond*: I would encourage Mike to tell the other lecturers to give the students as much scope as they possibly can . . . giving the students the opportunity to decide for themselves about what they want to do – and obviously the support is important.

The final act in this narrative is an end-of-year gathering in which everyone involved sees all the videos and shares a glass of wine. The characteristic of the bulk of the students' university work is that it is individualistic and competitive; the mark in green ink and the end of their history project is little more than a tally mark, a figure in a credit account in an unnamed currency. What is important is that it is acknowledged as a collective achievement, with a group mark. The disgruntlement that you might anticipate in a context of competitive individualism simply does not arise here. Any non-participant (and there have been two individuals in 15 years) simply does not figure; but there is no attempt to distinguish between different levels of contribution from each group member. I assume that the problems of relative participation have been internally resolved.

But they do have the mark, the token that will usher them through into the subsequent stages of their university education. The learning they have engaged in with the history course does, at the very least, name its currency – though its 'value' can only be qualitatively expressed. You cannot have proportions of self-awareness, degrees of personal development, grades of social skill and cooperation, portions of criticality. Yet the meter may register transformation, self-knowledge, an awareness of others, a sense of a world that changes as a result of human intervention, even the consciousness that the process of learning they have come through is itself a kind of intervention in the world – or, at the very least, leads logically to such involvement.

The things that happen now, or in the past, will hopefully no longer exist 'out there', beyond reach, in some parallel universe whose events we register only in a secondary way – reflections on the wall of the cave, in Plato's analogy. Whatever the starting point, the development of understanding is much more than simply a more sophisticated form of echo-sounding. The relationship between the consciousness and the external world will have become dialectical; history is no longer what is going on out there, but a composite of the event and my understanding of it, my contextualization of it. It is that encounter and that encounter alone that provides the meaning of things – or knowledge.

But so much of what is represented as knowledge in higher education is a given, a corpus of defined extension into which we may be inducted at a differential rate. We consume and observe, but we do not intervene in the process. In this procedure, the learner is in the innate object of knowledge distribution; in the critical learning process, she becomes the subject, the protagonist (since knowing is an active process and not mere recognition).

This is not specific to the subject matter; all knowledges can be owned in the mode of discovery. The problem for a university that is frantically reinventing itself as corporation, however, is that funding and the social existence of the institution depend on utility. The concept of usefulness is deeply embedded in the institutional structures and the awareness of students increasingly crippled by debts incurred as a mortgage on their future. There seems little point in wishing that the university were otherwise; possessive individualism, the division of labour and the subordination of all social relations to the pursuit of profit are the prevailing values in a capitalist society like ours.

What we are seeking to develop, then, is a critical attitude. Let us be clear that this is not merely a questioning of what is, but a questioning *from* the perspective of an alternative which Griffiths (1998) has defined as a perspective of social justice. We know the broad lines of development of this alternative – even though we do not have a blueprint for that alternative future – an end to exploitation, the dominion of justice and equality, the fullest development of the human in us all. The prior step, perhaps the first step, is to acknowledge agency – the willed pursuit of ends that shapes human affairs, past, present and future. That can be learned at the smallest level, and applied at the greatest. But such understanding will not merely question or expose the limitations of what exists, it will contest it. Thus it is not simply empowerment – self-awareness – but the sense of the collective, a feeling for its power and an emancipatory impulse.

After all, as one irascible old German revolutionary memorably put it, 'The philosophers have interpreted the world: the point, however, is to change it' (Marx, 1975).

Notes

1. Traveller there is no road to follow / you open the way as you go / You make the road as you go / and when you look back / you see behind you the path / you will never tread again. Antonio Machado, 'Cantares', from *Proverbios y cantares*. Machado (1875–1939) was one of Spain's most important poets who spoke for the post-imperial generation of 1898. His sympathies lay with the Spanish Republic; facing its imminent defeat by Franco, Machado went into exile in France, where he died in February 1939.
2. 'The first researcher, then, in the classroom, is the teacher who investigates his or her students' (Shor and Freire, 1987: 9).
3. In the tradition of Malinowski, Lévi-Strauss describes exchange not as barter but as an end in itself, for it both establishes and mediates the distinction between self and other (Lévi-Strauss, 1969).
4. This and all the subsequent direct quotes and comments from students arise from a series of recorded conversations between myself, Melanie Walker and each student group during May 1999. These were then fully transcribed. I have also drawn on video-recorded sessions, and written submissions provided by some students at the end of the year.
5. I use the term 'professional', of course, in the sense of the 'critical professionalism' that this volume sets out to explore.

References

Barnett, R. (1997) *Higher Education: A Critical Business.* Buckingham: SRHE/Open University Press.

Blake, N., Smith, R. and Standish, P. (1998) *The Universities We Need.* London: Kogan Page.

Callinicos, A. (1987) *The Revolutionary Ideas of Karl Marx.* London: Bookmarks.

Galeano, E. (1987) *Genesis* (trans. C. Belfrage). London: Methuen Paperbacks.

Griffiths, M. (1998) *Educational Research for Social Justice.* Buckingham: Open University Press.

Lankshear, C. and MacLaren, P. (eds) (1993) *Critical Literacy: Politics, Praxis and the Postmodern.* Albany, NY: SUNY Press.

Lévi-Strauss, C. (1969) *The Elementary Structures of Kinship.* London: Eyre & Spottiswoode.

McLaren, P. (1999) A pedagogy of possibility: reflecting upon Paulo Freire's politics of education, *Educational Researcher,* March, 51.

Marx, K. (1975) Theses on Feuerbach: XI. In K. Marx and F. Engels (eds) *Collected Works, Volume 5.* London: Lawrence and Wishart.

Paz, O. (1991) *Collected Poems 1957–87,* ed. E. Winberger. London/Glasgow: Paladin Books.

Shor, I. and Freire, P. (1987) *A Pedagogy for Liberation.* New York: Bergin and Garvey.

Part 3

Endings and Beginnings

10

Reconstructing Professionalism in University Teaching: Doing Other/wise

Melanie Walker

I felt there were several words that we all had in common at our discussion yesterday: community, alienation, engaging, messy, interaction, never too difficult or too hard, rites of passage, critical thinking.

(Judy Wilkinson, email, June 2000)

Self, knowledge and action

In a conversation I and colleagues had with Ron Barnett (see Nixon *et al.*, 1999), whose work in one way or another influenced all of us in the Barcelona Group, he reiterated the three aspects, or moments, of 'critical being' where critical thinking (whether by students or lecturers) has to be accompanied by a critical self-understanding and hence a critique of self and self-identity. As he explained it, this requires a critique of 'how one relates to others in the world around one on the one hand, and a critique in terms of action, one's actual being in the world on the other' (in Nixon *et al.*, 1999: 564). The three aspects are, then, knowledge, self and action.

In different ways, each of the chapters has offered a reflexive view on our professional work in departments and with each other, in overlapping processes of knowledge about the subject and pedagogy, self-knowledge and our action in classrooms and our courses. Threaded through the book is the story of our own shifting self-identities as we have struggled to practise a professionalism which seeks to develop different forms of agreement-making, through dialogue and action with each other and with students, regarding the ends and purposes of learning in the university. We have sought to act as 'learning professionals' and a 'learning community' who listen to, learn from and develop with the communities with whom they interact and work in higher education (see Nixon *et al.*, 2000). As Judy explained at our final project meeting in June 2000, 'You have to accept being a learner and putting yourself in the position of a learner because you don't understand a lot of the things that are going on and perhaps, I mean for me that's a strength.' Mike then added: 'Having understood then we act upon the world; otherwise our conclusions are merely cerebral.'

Central to our redefinition of professionalism are our educational values and our struggle to live our professional lives in the ways which are most appropriate and consistent with these values and the moral purposes of our professional deliberations and action; our work thus turns on who we are and what we stand for. But our view of 'morality' is not one of personal conversion narratives in which we progress individually from being a 'bad' to being a 'good' person, but a specifically political understanding which involves justice and fairness. This is not to say that our accounts obliterate the personal, far from it. What they try to do is not to collapse the personal and political, with the effect that the personal becomes the political, or substitutes for the political.

Such a 'new professionalism' is at odds with managerialism and a performance culture characterized by aims, objectives and efficiency gains. Some might argue that all we are suggesting is the liberal idea of the collegiate university; at one level this is a valid interpretation. However, at issue here is that under present conditions this now emerges as a much more *radical* proposal. We also hold as problematic older notions of 'collegiality' grounded in 'old boys' clubs' and the exclusions of women and others from higher education, and in the policing of what counts as legitimate knowledge and ways of knowing. As Mike said, 'Our chapters read like attempts to do things otherwise. Of course we do things otherwise because the way things are done in the mainstream are in one way or another unsatisfactory . . . so our action research is a critique from an alternative way of doing.' But our 'action in the world' is necessarily also strategic, in that we act under particular institutional conditions of possibility. As Quintin commented, 'We also need to stay within our departments. I mean how oppositional can you get before you can no longer work with your colleagues.'

What we did not set out to do was to produce checklists of 'effective learning' or 'effective teaching'. Instead we acknowledge and enjoy the contextual complexity of practice. As Alison comments, using her own situation as an example:

> What I was really getting out of teaching my course before I started doing action research was a sense of something that was working, there was a buzz in there, there was something that was connecting, and I wanted to understand what that might be and what the ingredients of that might be. Yet as soon as I find the ingredients I think, OK, this was it, it was this set of questions, or this way of working or this particular set of student groups. And then I put the ideas into practice again this year but it didn't work in the same way. I was constantly having to think again on the spot and work out exactly why the same formula, even with some of the same students, wasn't working a year later.
>
> (Group discussion, June 2000)

Student learning

Nor should we forget the stories of student learning which are at the heart of each case study. Ours are not stories of unambiguous success, constrained as they are by the intersections of subject knowledge, teacher and student interactions, departmental and institutional cultures, and the society within which all this is embedded. As Judy explains in her account of teaching mathematics, for example, what she now takes to be success has shifted and changed. Yet in this case what troubles her is nonetheless experienced by the students as successful learning, within the parameters of what that means in the department. Quintin shares many of her concerns as he wrestles with the dilemmas of how best to teach his first year class. The outcomes are mixed, although there are interesting moments of equity as he struggles to establish a different kind of relationship with his students, one which at least some of them recognize and welcome. Chris, too, points to complex outcomes from his attempt to integrate critical thinking into his class, where his goal was not the limited kind of 'skills' training increasingly prevalent today, but for students to develop a capacity to critique the knowledge they were encountering and become themselves producers of critical knowledge. Not all students welcomed this, while some were confused by how the power worked between lecturer and students in this class. Far less ambiguous in her evaluation of her own teaching is Alison, who is at turns inspired, elated and fascinated by the depth of learning that occurs in her class as students work together to understand difficult texts, to produce academic work and to 'perform' the subtleties of their understanding. Her frustrations turn more on what she sees as the cramped learning experiences many of her students encounter elsewhere, and the drive towards compliance rather than critique. Similarly, Mike's students seem to welcome the opportunities his class offers for independent work; they appear to 'blossom' as they take control of what they wish to learn about, the process of this learning and with whom they want to share the excitement. In the process, many develop their own critical view of the limits of many other aspects of their university education.

Even while acknowledging the limits, then, for the students there have been opportunities to acquire subject knowledge, and to reflect on themselves as learners. The action elements are less easy to pin down for them; they might include taking up positions as active participants in the production of knowledge, critical understanding of the world as a form of action and acting more confidently in and on the world.

Facilitating collaborative action research in higher education

Somewhat paradoxically, perhaps, while my own voice is woven through all the chapters, it is often muted in its direct statements about my own role or learning. I have not offered an action research account of my own facilitation of the professional learning in the group, although this is touched on and implied in the accounts themselves. As the Barcelona Group were at pains to point out to me, it is important to recognize more explicitly, even if briefly, the role an educational facilitator might play: in conceptualizing the project, in raising funds, in accounting for it to university management, above all in constructing the spaces for rigorous educational dialogue and learning about educational action research through the doing of action research in a 'community of practice' (Lave and Wenger, 1999).

My role was seldom the topic of direct discussion; my own reflections turned on how well the action research projects seemed to be unfolding, how they needed to be supported, how group meetings progressed and the generally very positive climate that developed. Nonetheless, from time to time such comments were spontaneously offered. Alison, for example, said at our last meeting in June 2000: 'You've been so pivotal; we've all kind of circulated around you.' Later in the same meeting Mike said: 'It [the project] could so easily have become just an exchange of personal experiences, but your role in this has not just been to create the space in the first place but to give a powerful intellectual dimension. That's directly because of you. We might have met in other circumstances and we might even have got to work together, but it wouldn't have had that dimension.' Much earlier in the project Judy had said: 'Melanie we need your voice, almost as an overarching circle that reflects our experiences with students in your experience with us, how you encourage us to debate, question and learn, and then out of this spins Quintin convincing his colleagues and me enthusing my tutors' (email, November 1998).

In describing my own role, and in our search for how we might describe our 'new professionalism', I have found Angie Titchen's (1998) practice-based research on patient-centred nursing useful. She has developed a conceptual framework called 'critical companionship' to describe the process of facilitating the acquisition of 'craft' professional knowledge, in our case by university teachers. Her explication of a number of concentric circles is useful. At the heart of the framework is the relationship domain and practices of 'mutuality', 'reciprocity', 'particularity' and 'graceful care' which explain much of the collaboration that went on in our project. Mutuality involves a negotiated relationship based on the practitioner's willingness to learn. Reciprocity involves the exchange of feelings, thoughts, knowledge, interpretations and actions. Particularity involves coming to know and understand the unique details and experience of each practitioner. Graceful care is the support given by the educational facilitator through the creation of a caring climate.

Also useful is her explication of the facilitation domain, which involves: processes of conscious-raising about the knowledge embedded in daily practice; problematization of current practice; self-reflection as a cyclical process in which practitioners reflect critically on their own experiences; and critique to uncover personal and professional meanings and the socio-historic factors which shape the situation in order to develop new knowledge about how to change the situation. The learning strategies employed include story-telling about practice, feedback on performance, high challenge/high support and critical dialogue.

In many ways this framework and these strategies mirror practices in our group, and the experiential learning and critical dialogue which were central. Crucially, however, while they included numerous meetings between myself and individual group members, and of group members with each other, all our encounters were constituted as part of our community of practice, rather than as individualized professional learning. Moreover, my own intention had been not to teach about action research or to offer one-off 'workshops' (the favoured tool of academic staff developers) but for lecturers to learn about it through engagement in the project. Thus the circulation of dialogue about this learning, together with the action domain, were the conditions for the effective learning of educational action research. Mastery is then seen not to reside purely in the educational facilitator (myself), 'but in the organisation of the community of practice of which the master is part' (Lave and Wenger, 1999: 23). Expertise in the group was also more complicated than the relationship implied in the Titchen model. For example, I had greater knowledge of action research and educational ideas. Each lecturer knew more about his or her own discipline and teaching within it. Judy shared her expertise in teaching mathematics with Quintin, who was less experienced as a university teacher, and so on. Participation in a community of practice is the way of professional learning. This has clear implications for how academic staff development might or ought to be organized as professional *self*-development, and too seldom is (see Malcolm and Zukas, 2000).

In the same way, no one way of doing or writing about action research was ever suggested or imposed, so that the accounts which are offered in this collection are particular, personal and based in disciplinary cultures and different views of knowledge. However, I did expect the accounts to include some mention of the researcher's story and development as this is central to the educational action research process. This works also to reinsert teaching and the teacher into the learning process, given the potential to obliterate teaching in some versions of student-centred learning, or in the over-enthusiastic rush to substitute facilitation for teaching. Alison explained her point of view:

What we're trying to do is to bring back the personal into these stories, actually saying 'Yes, I am the teacher'. That has implications for these students. These students will have a different experience if they have me as a teacher in this context, at this time, with this subject matter . . . that fact that it's me who is the teacher and they who are the students is going to have an impact, and you can't make it an objective process. You can't just take that out and dislocate it from the body of the teacher.

(Group discussion, June 2000)

My own work has also involved moving the group beyond my own influence, to provide challenge and support, but also to judge the right moment to withdraw from our close connections. In a way the completion of this book represents both a severing of a close on-site working relationship and the evolution of a new kind of collaboration as the project develops new momentum and the opportunities for dialogue multiply.

'Activist professionals'

As a group we were also less satisfied with naming my work or our professional engagement as 'critical companionship' (where I would be the critical companion and the lecturers the practitioners). Critical companionship, in our view, seemed to encourage mostly a one-to-one personal development process. We liked the idea of walking together which it suggested, but felt the concept lacked a kind of political sharpness. We discussed the concept of 'critical companionship', but abandoned this in favour of Judyth Sachs's (2000) work on the concept of 'activist professionalism'. As will become apparent, there is considerable overlap in the processes Sachs and Titchen explicate, but a crucial difference in the political emphasis and meaning that these practices are directed towards. Although Sachs (2000) is locating her ideas primarily in the context of teachers in Australia, in my view her ideas speak powerfully to practices in higher education. Through her idea of a new kind of teacher professionalism, the 'activist professional', she recasts the political and professional roles of teachers. The concept is fundamentally political, recognizing classroom level responsibilities but also wider involvement in schools, the system, other students, the wider community and, importantly, collective professional responsibilities. The focus is thus the group ('communitas', see Chapter 1), not the individual.

Drawing substantially on Giddens (1994), she embeds his notion of 'active trust' in the group's shared work, while Giddens's idea of 'generative politics' then springs from the group. As Sachs (2000: 81) explains this, this active trust is not unconditional but a feature of negotiated professional relationships in which 'a shared set of values, principles and strategies is debated and negotiated'. This involves stronger forms of cooperation in which teachers (lecturers) feel an obligation and responsibility towards colleagues. Thus, writes Sachs, 'Trust, obligation and solidarity work together in complementary ways', based on relations of integrity, positive communication, reciprocity, mutuality and trust in expertise and processes to improve the groups' problem-solving capacities.

In turn this requires new (collaborative) ways of working together. The reciprocal forms of association this requires have, she suggests, three purposes. First, all work towards building joint endeavours that promote collaborative development (for example, this book might be such an endeavour). Through this joint work members begin to understand each other's work, and they begin to exchange expertise (as happened in the

Barcelona Group meetings). Second, the nature of the collaborative development (dialogue, experiential learning, reciprocity and so on) provides opportunities to elaborate our practical theories of teaching and learning, to examine these theories in use and so generate both change ('improvement' in classrooms and context) and the dynamic energy to sustain this change. Finally, she argues, professional dialogue is enhanced, and the analytical insights generated contribute to improving classroom practices. Importantly for academic staff development practices, these new kinds of affiliation and collaboration push beyond technical notions of professional development and 'create spaces for new conversations to emerge' (Sachs, 2000: 84). Such conversations in our case involved a critical dialogue about practice in different disciplines, and at the same time a challenge to conventional disciplinary boundaries by conversations across our disciplinary boundaries, and the learning that this then generated for us. We spoke about how practice could be improved and about how we might share our ideas more widely. We discussed education not just in terms of classrooms, but as part of a wider institutional and policy environment and discourse. As Sachs notes, we too found sustaining active trust demanding and we needed spaces for quiet periods in the spaces between points of contact where active trust was nonetheless sustained, reflected in the easy way conversation was resumed when we all met again.

A second key concept Sachs (2000) adopts from Giddens (1994) in developing her view of the activist professional is that of 'generative politics', which allows and encourages individuals and groups 'to make things happen rather than to let things happen to them' (Sachs, 2000: 85). In the public domain in which we operate as academics, a generative politics enables us, she says, 'to take collective charge of our own destiny and life-political decisions in the wider social order'. Not surprisingly, such a politics must be 'organic', developing out of the needs of those most directly involved in local and global issues, and emerging in response to grassroots-level needs (in our case of lecturers and students) and their preferred outcomes. At issue is that a generative politics and active trust cannot be imposed from outside. Social justice concerns, in Sachs's conceptualization, are crucially important, centring on processes of dialogue, mutuality and reciprocity to generate new knowledge and participatory opportunities for discussion. Such practices stand in direct opposition to managerialist notions of professionalism characterized by 'efficiency', control, fragmentation and the loss of autonomy and morale among many academics.

All this leads Sachs (2000: 87) to ask what her alternative of activist professionalism might look like. To this end she elaborates a number of scaffolding principles:

- inclusiveness rather than exclusiveness;
- collective and collaborative action;
- effective communication of aims, expectations, etc.;
- recognition of the expertise of all parties involved;

- creating an environment of trust and mutual respect;
- being responsive and responsible;
- acting with passion;
- experiencing pleasure and fun.

This constitutes in our view both a retrospective reflexive agenda to consider our work together, and, more importantly at this point, a prospective set of principles to guide the development and expansion of our networks in particular, and our professional work more generally. Such principles take us beyond narrow self-interest, writes Sachs, to implementing a twin strategy of (a) appropriate partnerships (for us with colleagues and students) and (b) practitioner research projects.

Partnerships would adopt an advocacy role (in our case for a new professionalism for university teaching), and support networks which offered members 'a voice in creating and sustaining a group in which their professional identity and interest are valued' (Sachs, 2000: 88). This latter issue surfaced repeatedly in our discussion in and reflections on the Barcelona Group, as earlier chapters demonstrate and captured here too: 'for me it's been like coming in from the cold' (Mike); or 'We've constructed an alternative space for us to get together and talk about issues which were of burning importance to all of us but which we were on our own with' (Alison). What should emerge over time, writes Sachs (2000: 89), are cultures which 'place educational practice at their centre'. She advocates a key role in activist professionalism for inquiry into practice, in other words for educational action research, which enables turning the questioning gaze of research on to our own practice, and advocating that pedagogical research be respected in our universities. Such research seems entirely appropriate when the professional self is so central in understanding one's professional responsibilities, and in examining and negotiating that self, as the earlier chapter on action research elaborated. Sachs's (2000: 93) summing up of what is involved in activist professionalism is worth quoting at some length:

> Activist professionalism is not for the fainthearted. It requires risk taking and working collectively and strategically with others. Like any form of action, it demands conviction and strategy. However, the benefits outweigh the demands. The activist professional creates new spaces for action and debate, and in so doing, improves the learning opportunities for all those who are recipients or providers of education.

This brings us full circle, I think, to Ron Barnett and his notion of 'critical being' incorporating self (development, knowledge), knowledge (about the subject and its pedagogy) and action (to improve practice and its contexts).

'Future work'

We have been aware that our own learning community has operated its own exclusions in the process of building our collaboration; an expansion of the network will be important if the ideas generated are to gain wider support and influence. There are promising signs of pockets of institutional influence developing. Three members of the group now sit on a central university committee addressing teaching and learning issues; group members are being asked to address various working groups on particular teaching and learning issues; another member has been asked to take over his department's Teaching Committee; there are hopeful signs that the Vice-Principal for Learning and Teaching is keen to continue small-scale funding and support for practitioner research projects; and indications that the four members of the group still at Glasgow will now begin to establish their own collaborative networks and research groups under the auspices of a new Centre for Research in Higher Education.

As part of developing a 'future work' strategy, we decided to include a number of questions as part of this final chapter. We wanted to avoid offering any prescriptions for 'good' practice that might read (or be read) like checklists which if implemented would unproblematically 'improve' practice or point to the 'right' way to act. (Although we believe we have useful and important things to say about university teaching.) The questions that emerged from our final group discussion are not necessarily coherent or even well thought out; like our teaching stories they are dynamic, in progress and ragged. They were the questions which at the time we thought might stimulate others to think about their own teaching situation, and help us to continue reflecting on our own teaching. What we want, said Mike, 'is to kind of provoke a narrative':

- What is an ethical practice in higher education? Is it moral, political, critical?
- What happens, what do we learn, when we listen to what students say about their learning in our classes?
- What about the students at the back of the class?
- What is the effect of reflexivity about teaching and learning for us and our students?
- How as university teachers do we work together to construct alternative spaces for professional exchanges?
- What happens when our teaching becomes the focus of our scholarly exchanges?
- What happens when (and what is the importance of) looking at pedagogy within the context of the subject we teach?
- What happens when we deliberately insert ourselves into our teaching and our teaching stories?
- How do we address resistances – from classroom, to department, to university level and beyond?
- What implications does this kind of work have for understanding and 'doing' a fairer higher education?
- What does it mean to be 'true' to ourselves?
- How has this process changed us?

Above all (following Sachs, 2000), as a central question for us and for those with whom we would wish to establish expansive and inclusive educational action research networks in higher education: *What can I do from where I am?*

We subscribe to a kind of cautious optimism in our higher education work. This is not to ignore the current fragmentation and alienation of academic work (see Nixon *et al.*, 2000). As Blackmore and Sachs (2000) point out, the university that many of us entered twenty years ago 'is certainly dead', eroded or killed off by increasing workloads, performativity demands, bureaucratization, shrinking resources and so on. Nor should we ignore the way in which universities perpetuate relations of power and privilege, even while they challenge them. Universities persist in a complicated positioning which does not easily or comfortably map on to a radical agenda for education in late capitalist society. Thus we do not wish to romanticize the possibility of doing things differently, although we believe we might be allowed moments of optimism in our working out of our value-based professional ethic and our commitment to the 'goods' of learning in higher education. Our work has implications for the kind of society in which we would hope to live; it means asking how we want to live our lives in education, why we do what we do and who benefits from it. What kind of world do we create by our actions?

We have always been deeply serious about this work. But as the early chapters pointed out, we have thought it important to emphasize the fun and enjoyment we have also derived from working together. Like our Australian colleagues, Jill Blackmore and Judyth Sachs (2000), we think survival in difficult times demands that we can be 'irreverent and inventive'. We would also want to echo Frank Coffield (1999), who concluded his inaugural lecture on the learning society by saying that in his view the skills needed for success in the new century, as culled from rhetorical statements on the 'learning society' and 'lifelong learning' (information technology skills, teamwork skills, communication skills and so on), 'will not serve you well'. Instead, he recommends 'love, work, music, humour, friends, doubt and good red wine' (Coffield, 1999: 20). To that, we would add courage, the concept of 'exchange' coined by Mike and a 'strictly ballroom' journey of fellow travellers, dancing our own steps and rolling out our maps together as we work to reinvent our professional identities. Demanding though this process has been for us, the benefits have been far greater.

References

Blackmore, J. and Sachs, J. (2000) Paradoxes of leadership and management in higher education in times of change: some Australian reflections, *International Journal of Leadership in Education*, 3 (1), 1–16.

Coffield, F. (1999) *Breaking the Consensus: Lifelong Learning and Social Control*. Newcastle: Department of Education, University of Newcastle upon Tyne.

Giddens, A. (1994) *Beyond Left and Right*. Oxford: Polity Press.

Lave, J. and Wenger, E. (1999) Learning and pedagogy in communities of practice, in J. Leach and B. Moon (eds) *Learners and Pedagogy*. Milton Keynes: Paul Chapman/The Open University.

Malcolm, J. and Zukas, M. (2000) *Becoming an Educator: Communities of Practice in Higher Education*. Leeds: Department of Continuing Education, University of Leeds.

Nixon, J., Marks, A., Rowland, S. and Walker, M. (2000) Towards a new academic professionalism: a manifesto of hope. Paper presented to the British Educational Research Annual Conference, Cardiff, 9 September.

Nixon, J., Rowland, S. and Walker, M. (1999) Imagining the university – a critical dialogue with Ronald Barnett, *Teaching in Higher Education*, 4 (4), 555–73.

Sachs, J. (2000) The activist professional, *Journal of Educational Change*, 1 (1), 77–95.

Titchen, A. (1998) *A Conceptual Framework For Facilitating Learning in Critical Practice*. Occasional Paper no. 2. Lidcombe: Centre for Professional Education Advancement.

Index

The Society for Research into Higher Education

The Society for Research into Higher Education (SRHE) exists to stimulate and coordinate research into all aspects of higher education. It aims to improve the quality of higher education through the encouragement of debate and publication on issues of policy, on the organization and management of higher education institutions, and on the curriculum, teaching and learning methods.

The Society is entirely independent and receives no subsidies, although individual events often receive sponsorship from business or industry. The Society is financed through corporate and individual subscriptions and has members from many parts of the world.

Under the imprint *SRHE & Open University Press*, the Society is a specialist publisher of research, having over 80 titles in print. In addition to *SRHE News*, the Society's newsletter, the Society publishes three journals: *Studies in Higher Education* (three issues a year), *Higher Education Quarterly* and *Research into Higher Education Abstracts* (three issues a year).

The Society runs frequent conferences, consultations, seminars and other events. The annual conference in December is organized at and with a higher education institution. There are a growing number of networks which focus on particular areas of interest, including:

Access
Assessment
Consultants
Curriculum Development
Eastern European
Educational Development Research
FE/HE
Funding
Graduate Employment

Learning Environment
Legal Education
Managing Innovation
New Technology for Learning
Postgraduate Issues
Quantitative Studies
Student Development
Vocational Qualifications

Benefits to members

Individual

- The opportunity to participate in the Society's networks

- Reduced rates for the annual conferences
- Free copies of *Research into Higher Education Abstracts*
- Reduced rates for *Studies in Higher Education*
- Reduced rates for *Higher Education Quarterly*
- Free copy of *Register of Members' Research Interests* – includes valuable reference material on research being pursued by the Society's members
- Free copy of occasional in-house publications, e.g. *The Thirtieth Anniversary Seminars Presented by the Vice-Presidents*
- Free copies of *SRHE News* which informs members of the Society's activities and provides a calendar of events, with additional material provided in regular mailings
- A 35 per cent discount on all SRHE/Open University Press books
- Access to HESA statistics for student members
- The opportunity for you to apply for the annual research grants
- Inclusion of your research in the *Register of Members' Research Interests*

Corporate

- Reduced rates for the annual conferences
- The opportunity for members of the Institution to attend SRHE's network events at reduced rates
- Free copies of *Research into Higher Education Abstracts*
- Free copies of *Studies in Higher Education*
- Free copies of *Register of Members' Research Interests* – includes valuable reference material on research being pursued by the Society's members
- Free copy of occasional in-house publications
- Free copies of *SRHE News*
- A 35 per cent discount on all SRHE/Open University Press books
- Access to HESA statistics for research for students of the Institution
- The opportunity for members of the Institution to submit applications for the Society's research grants
- The opportunity to work with the Society and co-host conferences
- The opportunity to include in the *Register of Members' Research Interests* your Institution's research into aspects of higher education

Membership details: SRHE, 3 Devonshire Street, London W1N 2BA, UK. Tel: 020 7637 2766. Fax: 020 7637 2781. email: srhe@mailbox.ulcc.ac.uk
word wide web: http://www.srhe.ac.uk./srhe/
Catalogue: SRHE & Open University Press, Celtic Court, 22 Ballmoor, Buckingham MK18 1XW. Tel: 01280 823388. Fax: 01280 823233. email: enquiries@openup.co.uk